Strategic Management

Theory and practice

2nd Edition

G.A. Cole BA MA MIPD MIMgt

Research Associate, Institute of Continuing & Professional Education,
University of Sussex

Gerald Cole has worked in a wide range of organisations – large and small, public sector and private industry. He has been a lecturer and researcher in management and business subjects for many years. His other books for Letts Educational include *Personnel Management: Theory and Practice*, *Organisational Behaviour* and the hugely popular *Management: Theory and Practice*. He is a non-executive director of two medium-sized companies, an executive director of two small companies, and is an external examiner in Management Studies for the Middlesex University Business School. His research work has covered education and training practices in leading UK professions, covering such aspects as professional competence, ethical behaviour and workplace learning. He is an active member of the Society of Authors.

Thomson Learning
High Holborn House
50-51 Bedford Row
London WC1R 4LR

Strategic Management: Theory and Practice 2ed

For more information, contact Thomson Learning, High Holborn House; 50-51 Bedford Row, London WC1R 4LR or visit us on the World Wide Web at:
http://www.thomsonlearning.co.uk

British Library Cataloguing-in-Publication Data
A catalogue record for this book is available from the British Library

ISBN 1-84480-0087-3

First edition 1994 by Continuum
Second edition 1997 by Continuum
Reprinted 199 by Continuum
Reprinted 2003 by Thomson Learning

Typeset by Kai, Nottingham

Printed in UK by Ashford Colour Press, Hants

Acknowledgements

I am very grateful to Genesys Editorial td, who helped to bring this edition to publication. I wish to record my thanks for the Information Officers of the following organisations for sending relevant information about their enterprises, and where necessary for giving permission for extracts to be quoted:

Abbey National plc; Anglian Water plc; BAA plc; British Aerospace plc; British Airways plc; British Biotech plc; British Petroleum plc; British Telecommunications plc; GEC plc; Hanson Industries plc; John Lewis Partnership plc; Laporte plc; Legal and General Assurance plc; London Transport; Marks and Spencer plc; Nuclear Electric plc; Railtrack plc; Rover Group; J. Sainsbury plc; WH Smith Group plc; Toyota Manufacturing UK Ltd; Unilever plc; Universities Superannuation Scheme Ltd; Virgin Group plc; Catholic Children's Society; The Church Commissioners; Institute of Personnel Management (now Institute of Personnel and Development); The Leonard Cheshire Foundation; The National Trust; Oxfam; Royal Opera House, Covent Garden; Water Industries Association and York Minster Fund.

Preface to Second Edition

Aim of the book

1. The aim of the book is to provide students and lecturers with a clear, concise and comprehensive introduction to the theory and practice of strategic management. To achieve this aim the book is set out in three parts. The knowledge base of the subject is mapped out in the sixteen chapters which form Part 1 of the book. This essentially theoretical part is followed by a workbook section (Part 2), which is designed to provide opportunities, on a chapter-by-chapter basis, for reflecting on the reading of the text, and wrestling with problems of a strategic nature, in order to find appropriate answers to important questions about formulating and implementing strategic decisions. Finally, there are eighteen case-studies illustrating how a range of differing organisations have dealt with strategic issues (Part 3). This part helps to reinforce Part 1 by marrying theory with practice in the context of real enterprises.

2. The text is aimed at the requirements of those students looking for a concise introduction to Strategic Management, such as in BA (Business Studies) courses in Strategic Management, Business Planning and Policy-making, or postgraduate courses in Management, or Business Studies, including the Diploma in Management Studies and other post-qualification courses. It is also aimed at those taking the relevant examinations of accountancy and other professional courses, such as the ACCA Management and Strategy paper (Module F) and CIMA Paper 14 (Strategic Management Accountancy and Marketing).

The need

3. Students faced with a course on Strategic Management require a textbook that not only gives adequate coverage of the subject, but also maps out the subject-matter in an easily-understandable manner. Achieving such a map means reducing the natural geography of the subject into a simpler representation on paper, so that readers can see both the overall landscape (in simplified form) and the relationship between the different features. This book outlines the concept of strategic management and sets out some of the principal ideas that have been put forward for dealing with strategic issues in organisations. Problems and conflicts arising from attempting to adopt these ideas are noted, and commented on, throughout the text. Small and medium-sized enterprises, and not-for-profit organisations are considered, as well as large commercial organisations. The idea throughout is to enable students to gear their reading to their lecture topics, and to provide lecturers with reference and exercise material to support classroom activity.

4. The book covers a wide range of strategic management issues, and attempts to introduce the subject in a comprehensive way. It avoids the narrow focus and considerable complexity of many other books in this area. Where in-depth treatment is required, students are recommended to read relevant texts by leading contributors to ideas about strategic management thinking and practice. Ample references to these are provided on a chapter-by-chapter basis.

Approach and layout

5. The subject-matter has been set out in easily-digestible portions, which should enable the reader to identify, and make connections between, the principal features, issues and options of strategic management. Part 1 analyses the concept of strategic management by breaking it down into its essential elements. The sequence of chapters is based on a gradual unfolding of the concept in terms of developing goals, assessing the environment, developing strategic choices, implementing them and reviewing results.

6. The underlying assumption in the book is that strategic decision-making serves the interests of a wide range of stakeholders (i.e. interested parties). It thus affects not only individual organisations, their customers, suppliers and employees, but also the community at large. The organisations themselves are affected at every level from the boardroom to the point of delivery of their goods or services. Issues such as the nature of organisational culture, attitudes towards excellence, quality and the management of change are therefore included as part of the organisation's response to its stakeholders. At the end of chapters are questions for reflection/discussion.

7. Part 2 of the book is a workbook devoted to scenarios and exercise questions on important issues of strategic management. The order in which the cases and questions are presented follows the development of the material in the knowledge-based part of the book, thus enabling the students to apply their reading of the text to tackle issues and respond to them thoughtfully. A lecturers' supplement will be provided to supply ideas and comments as an aid to assessing the exercises (see paragraph 13.).

8. Part 3 extends the knowledge base of Part 1 by recognising that students need to see how strategic management is applied in practice. To meet this need, eighteen real-life case-studies have been described. These cover a range of organisations, each providing a different context for thinking about strategic issues. They include a high street retailer, an airline, a motor vehicle manufacturer, an electricity generating company, an oil company, an industrial conglomerate, a railway company, an insurance company, an airports business, a racing car business, and a pharmaceutical company, as well as an international charity organisation.

Use of the book

9. Ideally, the opening chapter should be read and digested first. This should give the reader an opportunity to get the 'feel' of the subject matter. Thereafter, it is suggested that chapters should be read in the order which is appropriate to the topics being covered in lectures. This is not likely to be too far removed from the sequencing of the book, which is similar to the approach adopted by other books on this subject. Apart from the opening chapter, which is an introduction to the subject as a whole, and the final chapter, which is essentially a summary of an eclectic model of the strategic management process, the logic that underlies the whole of Part 1 is as follows:

- Organisation purposes, goals and objects are defined.
- Internal and external environments are evaluated.
- Future prospects are assessed.

- Strategic plans are developed.
- Strategic plans are implemented, taking account of international dimensions, organisation culture, change and issues of quality and excellence.
- The key roles of Marketing and Personnel are noted.
- Performance is measured and decisions reviewed.
- A refined model of strategic management emerges.

10. Since different courses have different proportions of time allocated between formal lectures and self-study, students should use their own judgement as to how they can best tackle their reading. The fact that the knowledge base is set out in relatively short chapters should make it easy to 'pick and mix', as appropriate.

11. The exercises in Part 2 can mostly be tackled on an individual basis, but some lend themselves to group work. All should provide the basis for individual reflection, class discussion and the sharpening of insight into strategic management issues. The case-studies in Part 3 are referred to, when appropriate, in the relevant chapters in Part 1, and a few are the focus of Part 2 questions. They may, of course, be read quite separately. The idea is to achieve a partnership between all three parts of the book, enabling students to follow up their reading and lecture-notes by examining relevant case-studies and working on significant questions and problems.

12. For students who wish to go deeper into a topic, or explore ideas further, there are ample references at chapter-ends to important theorists and practitioners who have contributed to ideas about strategic management.

Lecturers' supplement

13. A lecturers' supplement is provided free of charge to lecturers adopting the book as a course text. Application should be made, on departmental headed notepaper, to the publishers.

Readers' suggestions and comments

14. Every textbook represents a compromise between sufficient coverage, adequate depth, and overall clarity of presentation, and this one is no exception. If readers have any suggestions or comments to make, they will always be welcome.

Gerald Cole,
Sussex, England
August 1997

Contents

This comprises a chapter-by-chapter range of questions and scenarios on aspects of
strategic management. Questions are based primarily on information obtainable from
each chapter, but may also arise from case-studies, press reports and discussion points.
Some answers and discussion points will be the subject of a separate lecturers'
supplement.

This part of the book is devoted to an examination of strategic management in practice
by illustrating the behaviour of real-life organisations in tackling strategic issues. The
following enterprises are represented:

Part I The knowledge base of strategic management

Introduction

This part of the book contains sixteen chapters covering, essentially, the theoretical aspects of strategic management. The sequence of chapters is based on a gradual unfolding of the concept in terms of developing goals, assessing the environment, developing strategic choices, implementing them and reviewing results. Whilst this sequence provides a logical progression, the chapters can be read in any sequence to suit individual course requirements. However, it is advisable to read Chapter 1 first of all as it provides an overview of the subject.

Once the student has read a chapter, he/she is in a position to tackle the reflective questions at the end of the chapter and the application exercises in the Workbook (Part II). The student will also be ready to look at appropriate case-studies in Part III. The topics of the Workbook are in the same sequence as the chapters of Part I and the table on page 188 indicates cases that can be considered at each point of study.

1 Strategic management: the concept

Introduction

1. The purpose of this opening chapter is to introduce the concept of strategic management and to consider why it is important to every kind of organisation. The activities that are encompassed by strategic management have in the past been referred to variously as strategic planning, long-range planning, corporate planning and business policy. Perhaps because of its association with neatness, detail and structures, the term 'planning' has been put aside in recent years in favour of 'management', which suggests a broader approach to the activities involved. Thus, strategic management is seen to be as much about vision and direction as about mechanisms and structures.

2. Strategic management is fundamentally about setting the underpinning aims of an organisation, choosing the most appropriate goals towards those aims, and fulfilling both over time. Steiner (1979), writing some years ago, saw it as 'designing a desired future and identifying ways to bring it about.' Strategic management is usually contrasted with operational management, or tactical planning – which is basically short-term and detailed – both in content and processes. Planning at an operational level usually takes place in the context of immediate or near-future events, which have a fair degree of predictability about them and are generally related to the affairs of a business unit. Strategic management, by comparison, involves thinking and actions that are focused on the long-term future of the whole organisation, and which are conducted in conditions of considerable unpredictability. Nevertheless, the act of implementing a strategy automatically leads into the operational domain, so the two forms of management activity are closely linked (see Figure 1.3).

Comparative definitions of strategy

3. It is always useful to set down some markers for the term 'strategy' so that it is possible to make some early connections between the various issues of strategic management referred to in the following paragraphs, and subsequently throughout the book. We can do this by highlighting some of the definitions which have enjoyed wide currency among students and practitioners of strategic management.

4. One early definition of strategy was provided by the American business historian, Alfred D. Chandler (1962), as follows:

> '(strategy) is the determination of the basic long-term goals and objectives of an enterprise, and the adoption of courses of action and the allocation of resources necessary for carrying out those goals.'

Chandler subscribes to the view that strategy is as much about defining goals and objectives as it is about providing the means for achieving them.

Another contributor, Kenneth Andrews (1987), also combines goal-setting with the policies and plans needed to achieve goals. In his definition of strategy he distinguishes between *corporate* strategy, which is the lead strategy, and *business* strategy, a secondary, though vital, aspect of corporate strategy. Andrews' definition is as follows:

> '... a pattern of decisions ... (which represent) ... the unity, coherence and internal consistency of a company's strategic decisions that position a company in its

environment and give the firm its identity, its power to mobilise its strengths, and its likelihood of success in the marketplace.'

Ansoff and McDonnell (1990), by comparison, separate goal-setting (concerned with ends) from strategy (concerned with means). On the subject of strategic management they provide the following definition:

'... strategic management is a systematic approach for managing strategic change which consists of the following:

1. positioning of the firm through strategy and capability planning;

2. real-time strategic response through issue management;

3. systematic management of resistance during strategic implementation.'

This definition favours an adaptive approach to strategic management, where it is important to watch the process in operation and make appropriate changes as soon as possible. Thus, initiating short-term responses is seen as part of strategic management as well as preparing for the future. They are also aware of the potential for conflict between interested parties and the need to have a conflict-management plan.

5. Two further contributions to the analysis of the term 'strategy', including the various ways in which it is approached by organisations, are given in paragraphs 9–14 below.

In the meantime, for the purposes of this chapter, the following working definition of strategy is proposed:

Strategic management is a process, directed by top management, to determine the fundamental aims or goals of the organisation, and ensure a range of decisions which will allow for the achievement of those aims or goals in the long-term, whilst providing for adaptive responses in the shorter term.

As noted above, there are theorists of strategic management who separate out the setting of aims and goals from the mechanisms and decisions designed to ensure their achievement. However, for our purposes it is easier to consider strategic management as a whole process, incorporating decisions about *ends* (aims and goals) as well as about *means* (strategic decisions). A fuller definition of strategic management, in the light of the major issues set out in subsequent chapters, will be given at the end of Part 1 (see Chapter 16 page 168).

Strategic management: a working model

6. It makes sense to consider strategy as a *cycle of decisions* where each set of decisions has a 'knock on' effect on subsequent decisions, as well, of course, as having consequences for all those affected by them (customers, suppliers, employees, and so forth). The cycle incorporates a review element which enables decisions to be questioned, and changed if need be. The model illustrated in Figure 1.1 below simplifies the actual strategic management process for the purposes of highlighting the key elements, and it should be understood that strategic decisions are not always made in the step-by-step approach implied in the model. There is a good deal more to-ing and fro-ing between the elements in actual practice. The basic model can be set out as follows:

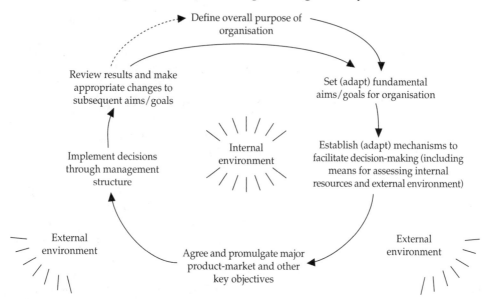

Figure 1.1 A basic strategic management cycle

7. The logic of this model of strategic management is as follows:

❶ The overall purpose, or mission, of the organisation is defined; such a task will be undertaken only infrequently.

❷ The fundamental long-term aims and goals of the organisation are agreed (i.e. the 'core business'); these aims/goals may be changed, or added to, from time to time.

❸ Mechanisms are established to ensure that the strategic thinking process does take place; these will include data collection mechanisms and consultation arrangements as well as decision-making meetings; the key investigations at this stage will relate to the organisation's position in its market and especially to its competitive situation.

❹ The key product-market, resourcing, quality and other major decisions are agreed by the senior management.

❺ Appropriate organisational structures are put in place to ensure that strategic decisions are promulgated throughout the organisation and implemented in accordance with agreed policies.

❻ Results are reviewed and appropriate changes made as necessary to aims/goals and objectives, which completes the cycle.

8. As mentioned above, the model simplifies the strategic management process, which is considerably more complex in its activity than is shown here. However, it does set out the basic principles on which strategic thinking takes place, and is implemented. The structure of Part 1 of this book is based on the cycle. Before proceeding further, it will be helpful by way of comparison to summarise the views of two different groups of researchers on the subject of the strategy process. Firstly, we look at the views of Mintzberg and colleagues (1991) and secondly at Johnson and Scholes (1993).

Two comparative sets of views on strategy

9. Mintzberg (1991) sees strategy as 5 Ps – plans, ploys, patterns, position and perspective. He describes a *plan* as 'some sort of consciously intended course of action.' Basically this amounts to deciding what you want to do and how you intend to achieve it. This is a definition that appeals to those who take a rational-logical view of strategic management rather than an intuitive-opportunistic view. A *ploy* is a sub-set of a plan, and is a strategy in the sense of a stratagem (i.e. a ruse or trick designed to put a rival company off the scent by disguising the real intention of the company). A *pattern*, according to Mintzberg, is the consistent behaviour and processes which emerge from strategic thinking, whether as a result of intended or unintended actions. Mintzberg sees plans and ploys as deliberate strategies, while patterns are seen as emergent strategies.

10. The remaining two Ps are *position* and *perspective*. Position refers to what the previous three are all aiming at, i.e. an acceptable location for the organisation in the environment. As Mintzberg puts it, 'Strategy becomes the mediating force … between organisation and environment, that is, between the internal and external context.' For a commercial enterprise 'position' boils down to its product-market position in its chosen market. This refers in particular to (a) its standing in relation to its competitors, and (b) its market share. Position can also take the form of a market niche, i.e.. by offering a marketing mix to a specialised market where there is no real competition. Position is strongly related to power in the marketplace, and thus has political overtones.

11. *Perspective* is an approach to strategy that is both conceptual and cultural. Mintzberg describes it as 'looking inside the organisation, indeed inside the heads of the collective strategist … its content consisting not just of a chosen position but of an ingrained way of perceiving the world.' An organisation with a strongly perspective approach will be one where the senior management have a shared view, or vision, of the special, or even unique, contribution that the organisation can make to society. Companies which have developed out of small businesses originated by charismatic owner-managers often demonstrate perspective features. As we shall see later (Chapter 10), perspective in the sense of organisation culture is an important ingredient in success. However, an ingrained culture could suggest an inability to challenge existing ways of looking at the environment, and firms need to question their basic culture from time to time to ensure that it does still meet their needs.

12. Mintzberg's analysis suggests that the five Ps are interrelated. Strategic management, therefore, is unlikely to work successfully if it is just founded on logical and mechanistic approaches. Allowance has to be made for pattern and perspective approaches too if an organisation is to optimise its strategy. As in many other areas of life, good planning comes down to a question of balance. Some structure, some mechanisms are needed, but to be fully effective they have to be combined with 'softer' intuitive and visionary approaches.

13. Johnson and Scholes (1993), in their thoughtful text *Exploring Corporate Strategy*, categorise a number of different approaches to strategy as follows:

    ❶ A 'natural selection' view, i.e., where organisations are under great environmental pressure and have constantly to adapt to changes in their environment.

    ❷ A planning view, i.e., where strategy comes about through highly systematised forms of planning; this is the rational approach to strategy.

❸ A logical incremental view, i.e., an evolutionary step-by-step approach to strategy; it is an adaptive approach but one which is more controlled than the natural selection example mentioned above.

❹ A cultural view, i.e., an approach to strategy based on the experiences, assumptions and beliefs of management over time and which may eventually permeate the whole organisation.

❺ A political view, i.e., where strategy emerges after a variety of internal battles, in which managers, individuals and other groups bargain and trade their interests and information.

❻ A visionary view, i.e., where the strategy is dominated by one individual, or sometimes a small group, who have a particular vision of where the organisation can and should be; this is a particularly intuitive approach.

14. It is possible to see several common features between the above list and the one generated by the Mintzberg analysis. The basic strategic management cycle selected as the working model for this chapter clearly tends towards a planning view of strategy. This is because it makes sense to have a rational model to start with so that readers can see the basic elements clearly. As Johnson and Scholes themselves put it (following a fairly lengthy list of the *disadvantages* of the planning view):

> 'However, the discipline and components of planning approaches can be useful because they provide a framework for strategic thinking; and if managers also address the problems of managing strategy within the social, cultural and political world of organisations, then such thinking can be very helpful.'

15. The examples in Figure 1.2 illustrate some of the different approaches to strategy in UK organisations.

The responsibility for strategy

16. Initiating and driving the strategic management process is primarily the responsibility of the top management of the organisation, for it concerns the future direction and survival of the organisation. It is this major responsibility that separates the top management from the rest of the management hierarchy. Every organisation has to make some preparation for the future as well as for today. Someone in the organisation has to be looking beyond the present, at least to the short-term (3–5 years) and preferably on a much longer timescale. This need applies as much to small businesses and charity organisations, as it does to central and local government departments, hospital trusts, retail groups, manufacturing concerns and multi-national conglomerates. Thus, every board member, or equivalent senior manager in the organisation, has to accept prime responsibility for securing the organisation's future direction, survival and growth.

17. The discipline of thinking about, and planning for, the future does not come easily to many senior managers. There are always plenty of current problems ready to take up their time and energy and to distract them from future concerns. But, if the top management of an organisation pay insufficient attention to the future, no-one else can make up the shortfall. Senior managers below board-level tend to be involved in aspects of their annual budget cycle, especially in reviewing monthly performance, and are rarely looking much further ahead than the next two to three years. Middle and junior managers are primarily concerned with getting on with the day-to-day running of the organisation's affairs, and their concerns are rightly with meeting short-term targets and

working to budgets. Whilst all levels of management may be encouraged, in the light of their experience, to suggest ideas and plans for the future, and should be consulted appropriately about how operations could be extended or improved, it is not their principal role to create strategy. Senior managers below board-level will probably have a shared accountability for strategy and middle managers will have a contributory accountability, but the prime accountability rests with the top management.

Figure 1.2 Different approaches to strategy – examples

Strategic emphasis	Organisation	Example of current strategy
Cultural/perspective	Hanson Industries	'Our philosophy is to develop, promote and delegate real authority to managers of the highest quality. They are trained in our proven system of financial controls, which concentrate on profit and return on capital employed ... The success of that philosophy rests on channelling capital investment where it will be most profitable ... Over the next decade Hanson aims to enhance shareholder value by increasing earnings per share and dividends generated through profitable internal growth and selective acquisitions.' *(Source: Hanson Industries, Annual Report, 1993)*
Planning	York Minster Fund	1. Establish priorities for a 10-year repair and renewal programme (1991–2001) 2. Maintain band of 'dedicated and skilled craftsmen' 3. Train apprentices 4. Provide adequately equipped stoneyard 5. Obtain 'necessary good materials' for repairs 6. Fund the programme. *(Source: York Minster Fund brochure)*
Natural selection/ patterns	British Telecommunications plc	'...the growing threat from competition in the UK market, and recognition that telecommunications is increasingly becoming a global industry, have underlined the importance of the company's pursuit of a global strategy ... focused on providing networks and network-based services to multinational and other major business customers in Europe, North America and the Asia-Pacific region.' *(Source: BT Review 94, May 1994)*

18. Outsiders, such as management consultants or academics, certainly cannot act as surrogate strategists, ready to produce new offspring in the form of fresh goals, values and structures. As external advisers or consultants, their role is to provide information, alternatives and suggestions, but not to make the fundamental decisions that will determine the future direction, size, strength and, hopefully, success of the organisation. These fundamental decisions can only be taken by the top management.

Strategic and operational planning

19. Before going on to examine the key strategic issues that senior managers have to deal with, it will be useful to look briefly at the relationship between strategic and operational planning in an organisation. At its simplest, strategic management planning produces both the primary goals for operational plans, and the framework within which they can be realised (including feedback channels), as indicated in Figure 1.3.

Figure 1.3 Relationship between strategic and operational planning

20. A more detailed representation of the relationship is shown in Figure 1.4, which takes account of the overlapping of strategic and operational activities. It also indicates primacy of responsibility, main outcomes and major concerns. As mentioned earlier, strategic management is the primary role of top management, whereas operational management is primarily the responsibility of senior and middle management. The main intended outcome of strategy (at least for all commercial enterprises) is the successful positioning of the company in the marketplace (including satisfactory market share, possible market leadership, adequate profitability and so forth). The main intended outcome of operational planning is efficient attainment of budgeted sales and/or revenue targets. The concerns of strategy are *effectiveness* (i.e., ensuring that the organisation is doing the right thing); the concerns of operations are *efficiency* (i.e., doing things right). Within each general area of concern are more specific concerns, and, where the two aspects of management overlap, there are concerns which are shared, as illustrated in Figure 1.4.

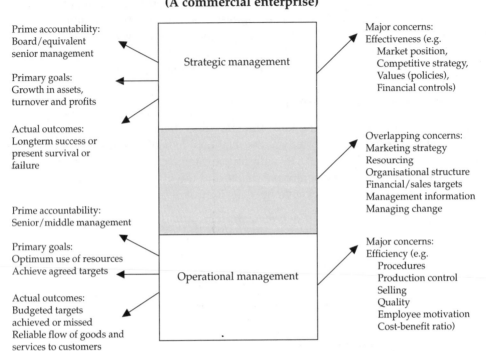

Figure 1.4 Interrelationship between strategy and operations (A commercial enterprise)

Prime accountability:
Board/equivalent
senior management

Primary goals:
Growth in assets,
turnover and profits

Actual outcomes:
Longterm success or
present survival or
failure

Prime accountability:
Senior/middle management

Primary goals:
Optimum use of resources
Achieve agreed targets

Actual outcomes:
Budgeted targets
achieved or missed
Reliable flow of goods and
services to customers

Strategic management

Operational management

Major concerns:
Effectiveness (e.g.
  Market position,
  Competitive strategy,
  Values (policies),
  Financial controls)

Overlapping concerns:
Marketing strategy
Resourcing
Organisational structure
Financial/sales targets
Management information
Managing change

Major concerns:
Efficiency (e.g.
  Procedures
  Production control
  Selling
  Quality
  Employee motivation
  Cost-benefit ratio)

21. Figure 1.4 shows that the primary goal of strategy in a commercial enterprise is growth in assets, turnover (total sales) and profits. Overall aims and goals of organisations will be examined at greater length in the following chapter (Chapter 2). The Figure also shows that the major concerns include market position, competitive strategy, values (policies) and financial controls, which will be looked at in subsequent chapters. The actual outcomes, which may or may not be the same as the intended outcomes, are likely to be broadly between (a) success in the long-term (see Chapter 15), (b) survival for the present, or (c) at the worst, failure of the business (leading to bankruptcy, liquidation or takeover by another firm). These goals, concerns and outcomes can be contrasted with those at the operational level, which focus on the implementation of strategic decisions in order to meet customers' needs and achieve financial and sales targets.

22. The overlapping area between strategy and operations is an important aspect of the relationship between the two dimensions of management activity. This overlap acts as a sort of bridging stage between the key decisions about strategy and their actual implementation throughout the operational units of the business. This bridging stage enables senior line and functional managers to discuss and plan their priorities with their middle management colleagues, whilst clarifying issues and eventually gaining approval for operational plans to be put into effect. Some organisations have a formal round of planning meetings designed to ensure that strategy and operations are articulated; others have a small number of key meetings between top management and their senior line and functional managers, but any number of less formal meetings designed to facilitate the process of moving from strategy formulation to strategy implementation. Given the effect that the strategic management process has on an organisation, it is not surprising that one of the shared concerns is the management of change (see Chapter 11).

Strategic issues

23. There are references throughout the book to strategic concerns and strategic issues. The difference between the two is based on the fact that a concern is an area of attention that is supported by agreement between those persons involved, whereas by comparison, an issue is a matter about which there may be divergent opinion. Basically, strategic issues arise from major strategic concerns. These are the matters which are so important that they require the considered, and concerted, attention of the top management of the organisation, such as the following:

① the major purpose of the organisation (its raison d'être)

② the principal aims and goals of the organisation

③ the fundamental values, or culture, of the organisation

④ the organisation's interaction with its external environment (i.e. its community, customers, competitors and so forth)

⑤ the future profile of the organisation in the longer term

⑥ the structuring of the organisation's internal resources (especially people)

⑦ the decision-making mechanisms of the organisation

⑧ the renewal and replenishment of the organisation's key resources (such as people, materials, plant etc.)

⑨ the *effectiveness* of resources (rather than just their efficiency)

24. At a general level the questions raised when considering strategic issues tend to be expressed as follows:

① How satisfied are we with our present purpose or mission?

② How relevant are our existing aims and goals?

③ What other/new/different aims should we be considering?

④ What changes do we see or anticipate in our external environment, and what impact are they likely to have on our organisation?

⑤ What new or different markets should we be operating in?

⑥ How should we behave towards the competition?

⑦ When should we consider making any changes brought about by numbers 1–6?

⑧ How effective are our present organisation structures, and will they suffice for the future?

⑨ What kinds of people should we be employing to meet future demands on the organisation? What personnel and training development might be required? Where do we stand in terms of senior management succession?

⑩ How do we propose to fund developments/changes deemed necessary?

⑪ Should we be re-considering our underlying values as an organisation? What additional or alternative values should we adopt?

How real-life organisations have dealt with some of the above questions may be seen in the Part 3 case-studies (Nos. 1–18).

25. The questions raised in practice by individual organisations are usually prompted by the demands on their operations and have their basis in pragmatism. A study of strategic

management as a subject of value in its own right, however, must be firmly rooted in theory, as well as grounded in practice. The remainder of Part 1 of this book describes and explores many of the leading ideas that have been put forward by academics, consultants and practitioners. The headings under which these ideas are described and discussed are as follows:

- Defining the organisation's mission, key aims/goals, ethical stance and overall values (culture)
- Assessing the internal and external environments in which the organisation operates, including evaluating internal strengths and weaknesses and external opportunities and threats (economic, political, social and technological)
- Gaining competitive advantage using a variety of approaches
- Formulating strategy – making strategic choices
- Implementing strategy by developing appropriate organisation structures, decision-making mechanisms and leadership styles
- Developing business plans in the light of (a) strategic decisions, and (b) business forecasts, including assessing their international dimensions
- Implementing plans with attention to key areas such as organisation culture, managing change, achieving excellence, managing innovation and quality
- Reviewing strategy in the light of results of business plans, using a range of key assessment measures.

The changing external environment

26. In recent years several factors have contributed to the importance of the strategic dimension of management. These mostly arise from the changing external environment in which organisations operate and include the following:

- increased customer expectations especially in terms of the quality and range of consumer goods and personal services
- the rapid advance of microelectronic technology, which has revolutionised many of the processes by which goods and services are made available
- increased competition in domestic and world markets
- greater concern worldwide for the protection of the environment, leading to government and international action against certain industries (e.g. timber, coal-mining, heavy chemicals, oil production, fishing)
- greater emphasis on consumers' rights (e.g. in terms of safety, reliability, better information)
- vast improvements in worldwide communication systems, enabling faster flow of information between customers, suppliers, agents and so forth
- increased supra-national laws and regulations affecting business as result of decisions made by groups such as the European Union, GATT (the General Agreement on Trade and Tariffs) and OPEC (Oil Producing & Exporting Countries)
- changing political situations in major markets (especially the opening up of the former Soviet Union).

27. The scenario presented by all these changes is a complex one which requires organisations to look well beyond their domestic boundaries, and to do so with a perspective that addresses the longer-term prospects for their activities. For example, in considering whether or not to invest in Russia, the Ukraine or other former Soviet Union states, a large industrial firm will want to see an acceptable long-term return. It will want the reassurance of reasonable political stability and an acceptable level of demand for their products. It will also want labour relations to be satisfactory. Of course, there are rarely any guarantees in such situations, and any new business venture entertains some element of risk. What strategic management tries to ensure is that opportunities are grasped, risks are acceptable (that is, failure can be contained) and success can be built upon.

Stakeholders in strategic management

28. All organisations exist to serve one or more interests outside themselves. Most, in fact, have relationships with a range of interested parties, or 'stakeholders'. The most obvious example of an interested party is the customer, who may be a private buyer, a work colleague, or another organisation. Customers have concerns such as the quality, price and timeliness of the product or service they are buying. Supplying organisations are thus under pressure to meet these concerns, and to do so in a profitable manner, if they are a commercial enterprise, or within their spending limits, if they are a public sector organisation. Customers' preferences enable goods and services to be differentiated, and this encourages competition amongst suppliers, at least in the private sector. Competitors are another example of interested parties, for they are affected by the activities of other organisations supplying common, or similar, groups of customers (markets). The expression 'stakeholder' for competitors does not seem quite so apt since their stake in another organisation's affairs is not direct. However, it is quite possible to describe interested parties in terms of their being *direct* or *indirect* stakeholders.

29. A typical list of interested parties would comprise the following groups:

Direct stakeholders (i.e., those engaged directly in transactions with the organisation)

- customers (i.e. clients, members, patients or other users of the organisation's goods or services)
- shareholders (companies) or taxpayers (public sector organisations)
- creditors (especially banks and similar financial institutions)
- employees (who could be considered as dependent stakeholders)
- suppliers (of a range of goods and services, some of which may be tailored to the organisation's requirements and thus where the stakeholding is critical).

Indirect stakeholders (i.e., those not necessarily engaged in direct transactions, but nevertheless significantly affected by the organisation's activities)

- the community (local, regional, national, or international)
- competitors (i.e. all those other organisations providing similar goods and services to the same market)
- stock markets (e.g., London Stock Exchange, Wall Street)
- the government (i.e., those charged with the management of the economy as a whole on behalf of the community)

- supra-national bodies (such as the European Union).

30. There are two particular points of interest that can be made about the above list. Firstly, it is often the case that individual stakeholders have an interest in more than one category. Thus, some people may be employees, shareholders and customers of the same organisation (for example, an electricity supply company) as well, of course, as being members of the local community. Secondly, it is likely that conflicts of interest will occur between the different stakeholders, both within and between the two categories just identified. This possibility is particularly important when substantial numbers of stakeholders come into conflict (for example, if shareholders and/or creditors want to close or sell-off part of the business due to losses, but where employees, suppliers of parts and so on and even customers want the operation to continue). Such conflicts necessarily bring pressures to bear on top management when considering how to prioritise the organisation's actions in relation to the differing interests and priorities of stakeholders. In such situations the balance of power is tilted towards those who have directly invested their money in the organisation. The other groups are usually less powerful and invariably have to accept unpleasant consequences.

References

1. Steiner, G.S. (1979) *Strategic Management*, The Free Press
2. Chandler, A.D. (1962) *Strategy and Structure*, MIT Press
3. Andrews, K. (1987) *The Concept of Corporate Strategy* (3rd edn.) Richard D. Irwin
4. Ansoff, H.I. & McDonnell, E. (1990) *Implanting Strategic Management* (2nd edn.), Prentice Hall
5. Mintzberg, H. & Quinn, J.B. (1991) *The Strategy Process: Concepts, Contexts, Cases* (2nd edn.) Prentice Hall International
6. Johnson, G. & Scholes, K. (1993) *Exploring Corporate Strategy* (3rd edn.) Prentice Hall

Questions for reflection/discussion

1. To what extent is it either feasible or desirable to design a 'desired future'?
2. What are the key features of a strategy? How would you distinguish a strategic plan from an operational plan?
3. What do you see as the main advantages and drawbacks of (a) a planning approach to strategy, and (b) a visionary approach?
4. How would you describe the differences between effectiveness and efficiency? Give examples from your own organisation.
5. How far should strategies be influenced by the organisation's **direct** stakeholders?
6. In what ways might community interests be either threatened or enhanced by the activities of a large business organisation in a non-capital city?

2 Defining purpose, goals and objectives

Introduction

1. In the final analysis strategic management is about achieving success for the organisation. How can this success be judged? One immediate yardstick is success in achieving the stated purpose, goals and objectives promulgated by the top management. This is not the only measure of success, but it is a fundamental one. This chapter examines the various purposes, goals and objectives that typify different types of organisation, and outlines how such intentions are developed and adapted over time. Many texts on strategic management set aside a discussion of goals until after they have examined the issue of the organisation's environment and the strategic choices that are affected by it. In this text, however, the assumption is that, whatever stage the organisation is at, there is always some underlying purpose at work, and always some goals and objectives that are being followed, however implicitly. In most cases the purpose, goals and objectives are made explicit and are used to motivate staff as well as to provide standards of performance.

2. The process of defining an organisation's purpose, goals and objectives is not always a neat and tidy exercise, conducted logically and progressively in conditions of fair predictability. The setting (or reviewing) of the overall purpose, or mission, of the organisation raises fundamental issues and challenging questions such as 'Why are we here? What's our purpose in life? What do we want from being in business/offering this public service/running this charity?' It is often considered by the directors of an organisation that this exercise should be conducted in a considered and reflective way preferably by means of a weekend retreat away from the usual pressures of the business. The whole purpose of a mission statement is that it should not only set out the key parameters of the organisation's business and conduct, but also stand the test of time. A working definition, together with some examples from current practice, is given later.

3. The key goals or aims of the organisation usually embrace all the major units and functions of the organisation (thus covering specialist functions as well as the front-line units). These goals or aims are usually intended to provide for the medium term, and thus will not be adapted unless conditions warrant change. However they will be subject to regular review probably on a three-year rolling basis. As with purpose-setting, any substantial review of goals or aims is likely to take place formally outside the normal business environment. A working definition and some examples are given later.

4. Objectives are the organisation's operational targets, usually for periods of one year or less, and closely tied to annual budgets. They represent the intended outcomes·of the organisation's efforts to meet the day-to-day needs of its customers and other direct stakeholders. Unlike purpose and goals or aims, objectives are subject to frequent (that is at least annual) amendment as the organisation responds to changes in its stakeholder relationships and in its income and expenditure. A working definition and some examples of objectives, taken from a range of different organisations, are given later.

Working definitions

5. The terms 'purpose (or mission)', 'goals (or aims)' and 'objectives' are given brief working definitions for the purpose of this chapter, and examples from a number of real-life organisations are provided to illustrate them. The examples are taken from different categories of organisation, so that readers can make comparisons between them.

Mission statements

6. Purpose/Mission: a public statement on behalf of an organisation which sets out its raison d'être in terms of the customer needs it intends to satisfy, the markets within which it will meet those needs, and the manner in which it will meet them. The statement also sets out the organisation's intentions towards other stakeholders and/or interested parties (usually shareholders, employees and the community at large). The mission statement is intended to provide a rallying point for everyone working in the organisation, but the prime responsibility for ensuring that its broad purpose is achieved is that of the top management.

    A feature of mission statements is that they are very broad, and this sometimes causes them to be stated with such generality that they may not make their point clearly enough. These statements are intended to provide a vision of why the organisation exists, where it intends to operate and how it intends to achieve its goals. This vision is intended to motivate managers, other employees and customers as well as other interested parties. However, it is important for a statement to be sufficiently focused in its message for it to be understood, and believed in, by those affected by it.

7. The following extracts from published mission statements provide some contrasting examples of the way such statements are expressed in practice.

Example 2.1 British Airways

'Our mission

To be the best and most successful company in the airline industry'

(Source: The World's Most Successful Airline – A Special Review 1992/3)

Example 2.2 W H Smith plc

'Group Vision

We will have a range of products and a quality of service which meets our customers' needs more effectively than any of our competitors.

We will develop a climate which emphasises directness, openness to new ideas, personal accountability and the recognition of individual and team achievement. We want all who work for the Group to contribute as much as they can to its success.

We will achieve a consistent and competitive growth in profits and earnings for our shareholders, our staff and the community.'

(Source: W H Smith Group plc, Annual Report 1993)

Example 2.3 Royal Opera House, Covent Garden

Mission Statement

The three Companies of the Royal Opera House, Covent Garden, are the Royal Opera, the Royal Ballet and the Birmingham Royal Ballet. They are supported out of public funds provided by the Government through the Arts Council of Great Britain.

'They aspire to be at the heart of the nation's artistic and cultural life.'

... (they) seek to serve the following purposes:

- To provide the widest possible access to British audiences for opera and ballet;
- To extend as widely as possible public understanding and enjoyment of opera and ballet;
- Through tours by the three Companies overseas, to act as cultural ambassadors for the nation;
- To preserve and develop the art forms of opera and ballet for the audiences of today and tomorrow.'

(Source: The Royal Opera House, Covent Garden – 'Putting our House in Order', Progress Report, April 1993)

8. The above mission statements, though varying in the way they choose to express their mission, do share the purpose of announcing to the public their key intentions in regard to their major stakeholders. They are also very upbeat in their messages to stakeholders, and there is little doubting the high ambitions behind them. How far these ambitions will be realised can only be judged over time, but each year the directors of these organisations will be called to account for their stewardship in their Annual Report to the shareholders. One major industrial company, the General Electric Company plc, expresses its mission in the form of a substantial commitment, and this is given as a further example:

Example 2.4 GEC plc

The GEC Commitment

'GEC recognises that continued success can only be assured through commitment to its customers, employees and shareholders.

For customers, the commitment is to provide value for money and high standards of service whilst ensuring technological leadership through excellence in research and development. In short, a service that not only meets customers' needs but also exceeds their expectations.

For employees, the commitment is to encourage ingenuity and productivity through competent management and reward. The Company also plays a constructive role in the local community where it operates, not least by safeguarding and enhancing the quality of the environment.

For shareholders, the commitment is to maximise the value of their investment by consistently increasing earnings and by encouraging growth through acquisition, partnerships, joint ventures and technical collaboration.

Above all, the Company believes in its products and is dedicated to sustaining its leading position.'

(Source: GEC brochure, 1994)

9. Charitable organisations, whose purely commercial operations are usually just a small proportion of their total income, also have their mission statements. Two well-known British charities are the National Trust and Oxfam. Extracts from their published statements are given as further examples to complete this section of the chapter.

Example 2.5 The National Trust

'The National Trust shall be established for the purposes of promoting the permanent preservation for the benefit of the nation of lands and tenements (including buildings) of beauty or historic interest and as regards lands for the preservation (so far as practicable) of their natural aspect, features and animal and plant life.'

(Act of Parliament, 1907)

Example 2.6 Oxfam

1. 'Oxfam believes in the essential dignity of people and their capacity to overcome the problems and pressures which can crush or exploit them ...

2. We believe that, if shared equitably, there are sufficient material resources in the world to meet basic human needs on a sustained basis for all people ...

4. We are committed, therefore, to a process of development by peaceful means which aims to help people, especially the poor and underprivileged, regardless of the politics or style of the regime under which they live ...

6. ... Development should be sustainable in the sense that it involves preservation or improvement of the environment ...

11. Fundraising, trading activities, the stewardship of our resources and our personnel policies (including those relating to salaries and equal opportunities) should reflect the same values we work towards in our development programme. Simplicity, frugality and avoidance of waste will be elements in our corporate lifestyle ...

(Source: Oxfam – An Interpretation, OXFAM 1989)

10. The above mission statements, which are representative of leading organisations in widely differing sectors of the economy, supply many clues to the goals, aims and objectives of the organisations involved. We will return to some of them later when analysing *how* businesses achieve excellence, efficiency, value-for-money, care for people and the environment, and all the other purposes they exist to meet. It can be seen that some of the above statements have a degree of timelessness about them, and the National Trust example has survived for over eighty years already. It is also obvious that mission statements frequently contain explicit policy statements, in which the public are made aware of the *manner* in which the organisations involved will attempt to fulfil their purposes (see paragraphs 18–20 below).

Strategic goals and aims

11. **Goals/Aims**: these are the more finely focused statements of intent directed at those aspects of the organisation's operations which are critical to success – often described as 'the core business'. Such statements usually encompass product-market (or service) intentions, resourcing (people, plant, materials, funding, etc.), the use of technology, quality standards, and financial parameters. Such statements are usually intended to have a life which extends beyond the immediate future, and at the very least will be

reviewed thoroughly every 3–5 years. They are likely to be described as strategic aims in most organisations. The primary responsibility for fulfilling these intentions lies with senior line and functional management.

Some examples of the organisational goals promulgated publicly by five leading organisations in varying industries are given below:

Example 2.7 W H Smith Group plc

'Our Strategy:

How we will achieve our vision

Our goal is to be recognised as the leading company in each of our markets and to maintain standards of excellence in everything we do which will distinguish us from our competitors.

Our strategy is to focus on businesses in which our core skills and experience in retailing and distribution can be brought to bear. Each business will aim to be a leader in its own area, enjoying a sufficient market share to achieve the scale benefits available to market leaders.

The Group at the centre will add value to its businesses by fostering and guiding their strategies, by facilitating the development and sharing of skills between businesses, and by coordinating the strategies of different businesses which are addressing overlapping markets.

The Group will concentrate on the retailing and distribution of books, news, stationery, recorded music, video and related products: these are businesses which can draw on the Group's knowledge and skills, particularly in the management and control of multiple line item retailing and distribution. The Group will build on the strong positions it already enjoys in these businesses in the UK, and will seek to develop similar strengths in the USA and Europe.'

(Source: W H Smith Group plc, Annual Report 1993)

12. The above statement of strategic aims applies as much to the corporate business of the Group as it does to the individual businesses (referred to henceforth in this text as strategic business units). It is made quite clear that the W H Smith Group aims for market leadership in all of its chosen businesses, but stresses that it will only operate in areas in which its present core skills and experience can be brought to bear. This is a statement that can only be made by a powerfully positioned firm that knows what it is good at, and is determined to stick with it. Interestingly, the role of the Group in shaping the strategies of the business units is stated quite definitely. This is probably because of the nature of the retail trade which is all about distribution and merchandising. The Group is its own wholesaler for much of the distribution chain for business units.

13. A further example is taken from an organisation which has major commercial operations (i.e., in concert promotion and ticket sales) as well as educational and cultural functions, which are subsidised by public funding, patronage and voluntary support.

Example 2.8 Royal Opera House, Covent Garden

'... their (the three Companies) strategic aims are:

- To present opera and ballet of high quality at the highest possible standard of performance;

- To offer a wide range of repertory, including new and lesser known works as well as established classics;

- To encourage and promote creativity in composition, production, choreography and design;

- To provide performance opportunities for and promote the development of British orchestral musicians, singers and dancers;

- To secure financial viability and to eliminate income and expenditure deficits;

- To realise equally at the Royal Opera House the full potential of both the Royal Opera and the Royal Ballet and to provide a regular London venue for the Birmingham Royal Ballet.'

(Source: The Royal Opera House, Covent Garden, Progress Report, April 1993)

14. In this example, the generality of the Royal Opera House mission statement (paragraph 7 above) is made a little more explicit. Here, goals are qualified in terms of high standards of performance, range of repertoire, the encouragement of creativity and the securing of financial viability, etc. Achievement of most of these goals can be measured in some degree from year to year, and within a season. Much will depend on what further targets the management aims for in implementing its strategy. In some respects the aims of the Royal Opera House are the same as for other business enterprises in that features such as 'product' quality and variety are emphasised. In other respects there are aims which have a less 'hard-nosed' feel about them for instance, offering a wide range of repertory (which may attract fewer patrons) and providing performance opportunities for musicians (which may lead to overmanning or bad feelings between staff). The realising of the full potential of three different companies with only one main theatre in London seems problematic. Thus, the overall impression of these aims is of an organisation which is being pulled in several directions at once. Business, educational, innovatory and community expectations are placed on an organisation which is not able to generate enough of its own income to subsidise the last three sets of expectations, and has to rely partly on public funding to narrow the gap between outgoings and revenue.

15. The three further examples of strategic goals which follow are taken from widely differing commercial operations. The first example embraces the corporate goals of a world-class airline, while the other two represent goals in particular aspects of company operations, one from a powerful and old-established manufacturing company and the other from a newcomer to the pharmaceutical industry.

Example 2.9 British Airways

'Our Goals

To be a safe and secure airline

To deliver a strong and consistent financial performance

To secure a leading share of air travel business worldwide, with a significant presence in all major geographical markets

To provide overall superior service and good value for money in every market segment in which we compete

To excel in anticipating and quickly responding to customer needs and competitor activity

To sustain a working environment that attracts, retains and develops committed employees who share in the success of the company

To be a good neighbour, concerned for the community and the environment'

(Source: The World's Most Successful Airline – A Special Review 1992/3)

Example 2.10 GEC plc

'Environmental Protection Strategy

GEC recognises the importance of global environmental protection ... and continues to work towards the implementation of sound environmental standards and practices ...

Every GEC business shall:

- fully comply with the required legal standards
- use all resources as efficiently as possible
- introduce and maintain appropriate monitoring to ensure compliance with environmental legislation
- increase employee awareness and active involvement in environmental matters
- require good environmental practice by all employees as an integral part of health, safety and welfare and quality management practices
- minimise waste by the re-use and recycling of materials whenever possible
- prepare contingency plans to deal with foreseeable environmental incidents
- encourage suppliers to make a commitment to environmental standards.'

(Source: GEC, 1994)

16. The GEC example relates to one particular aspect of strategy, that is to meet the mission statement intention to 'safeguarding and enhancing the quality of the environment.' The company's intention to comply fully with the law is made explicit. Some companies state that they will go further than the legal minima. In actual practice, GEC gives top priority to pollution control, water pollution, CFC elimination, and waste minimisation and recycling under its various environmental management programmes (based on British Standard BS7750). It should be noted that several of the points made in the above 'strategy' are, in fact, policy statements (rules of conduct) rather than strategy statements. A definition of 'policy' as understood in this text is given in paragraph 18 below.

17. The final example in this section is taken from the *commercial* goals (that is, as opposed to the *research* goals) of a young company engaged in developing new drugs to combat cancer, vascular disease, AIDS and inflammatory conditions. In the year 1992/3, the company made an operating loss in excess of £17m, but confidence in the long-term future of the company can be gauged by the successful Stock Exchange listing gained during the year, when a net amount in excess of £30m was added to the company's assets. Pharmaceutical companies typically have to invest millions of pounds/dollars in discovery research, pre-clinical development, clinical trialling and product registration before obtaining any revenue from new drugs. Such development in well-established companies can be paid for out of the profits generated by the sales of earlier and existing drugs, but in this case the new company had to seek funding from external sources.

Example 2.11 British Biotech Plc formally British Bio-technology Group plc
(see also Case-study CS8)

'Commercial Planning:

... [our focus will be] on five target markets – the UK, France, Germany, Italy and the USA ... more than 50% of the world's pharmaceutical market ...

... In other territories we will seek partners to bring our drugs to market under licence.

In target markets our sales team will be compact and technically expert, focusing on hospital-based specialists.

We intend to concentrate on building businesses in cancer and critical care products

...

For chronic disease drugs [including treatment for asthma, arthritis and AIDS], we have adopted a strategy of seeking development and marketing partners.

As each of these new drugs reaches the market, we expect to have commercial arrangements in place to ensure effective international distribution and rapid growth in sales and revenues.'

(Source: British Biotech plc, Annual Report and Accounts 1993)

Policies

18. **Policies**: these are statements, or ground rules, concerning the *manner* in which an organisation will conduct its business or operations. In effect they represent a code of conduct and/or statement of key values that the organisation intends to pursue. The term 'policy' is sometimes used to describe a strategic, or planning, choice, but this is not the sense used here. A policy in this book is a statement, or practice, which guides managers and employees in the execution of the organisation's affairs. A policy is as much about what the organisation will not do as it is about what it will do. Policies often encompass such areas as personal integrity, bona fide behaviour towards potential customers/suppliers and so on, safety of employees/members of the public, and equal opportunities.

19. Typical concerns covered by policy statements include the following examples, which are taken from recent annual reports of the organisations concerned:

- Minimisation of environmental impact of production emissions
  (Pharmaceutical manufacturer)
- Energy conservation
  (Retailer/Manufacturer/Airline)
- Reduction in use of CFCs
  (Retailer/Industrial goods manufacturer)
- Reduction in noise levels/air pollution
  (Airline)
- Replace unsatisfactory goods without question
  (Mail order firm)
- Health and safety in the workplace
  (All)

- Equal opportunities for staff and potential staff
  (All)
- Design and build (capital projects) so as to fit into the local environment and community interests
  (Water Company)

Less typical issues include:

- Banning nudists from beaches/continuing to permit hunting on Trust property
  (Heritage Organisation)
- Offering special (low) prices to selected customers.
  (Opera House)

20. Two examples of policy statements, indicating the kinds of concerns dealt with, are supplied below. The first extract applies to personnel practice (Marks and Spencer plc), and the second applies to business practice (British Telecommunications plc):

Example 2.12 Marks and Spencer plc

'The Chairman and Board of Directors believe that the Company's Personnel Principles play a fundamental part in the growth and success of the Business. They are corporate principles which apply both in the United Kingdom and Overseas. This document has been prepared to summarise these principles.

Marks and Spencer is committed to the following personnel principles:

1. Good Human Relations

   People should be treated as individuals with respect and honesty

2. Good Communications

   Communication should be open and honest at all levels

3. Equal Opportunities

   Everyone should have full and fair consideration of all job vacancies for which they offer themselves as suitable applicants. We do not discriminate against anyone on any grounds. The sole criterion for selection for promotion in the Company is the suitability of any applicant for the job ...

4. Good Conditions of Employment

   People contribute to the success of the Company, and should therefore be rewarded accordingly ...

5. Ethnic Minorities

   ... Marks and Spencer recognises that Britain's society is multi-racial and we are concerned that the ethnic population should be fairly reflected at all levels within the Company. We also wish the staff employed to reflect the community they serve ...

6. People with Disabilities

   ... We wish to help people with disabilities to realise their full ability within the working structure of the Company; to provide them with the same facilities, career prospects and promotional opportunities that are available to all our staff ...

   We ensure that these principles remain at the core of the Company's operations via the coordinated activities of the Personnel Group.'

(Source: Marks and Spencer plc, Staff Handbook 1993)

Example 2.13 British Telecommunications plc

'BT will conduct its affairs as follows:

Customers – BT is committed to providing its customers with:

- excellent telecommunications services and products
- value for money; and
- choice and flexibility.

Our main services are backed by guarantee, and we give our customers compensation if we fail to meet our published standards ...

We will compete vigorously but fairly in the marketplace; we will not seek to use our market position in a way that unfairly disadvantages our competitors.

We will respect our customers' confidentiality, and be helpful and honest in all our dealings with them ...

We will be truthful and accurate in all our communications with customers ...'

(Source: BT Report to Shareholders, February 1994)

Objectives

21. **Objectives**: these are the short-term and specific intentions of the various operational units of the organisation. They are often called 'targets' and are a key element in tactical plans. They are usually incorporated into an annual plan or budget. The responsibility for achieving them is usually shared between middle and senior management.

    The area of short-term objectives is one which is familiar to most practising managers. The use of target-setting and allocation of budgets to unit managers is a practice which in recent years has extended gradually from the commercial world into the public sector as part of the moves towards greater enterprise in bureaucratic environments. Compared with longer-term aims, which are related to the potential and *effectiveness* of the organisation, objectives are easier to identify, linked as they are to the day-to-day issues of *output and efficiency*. The key distinction here is that whereas effectiveness is about doing the right thing in the first place, efficiency is concerned with *productivity*, that is, the relationship (preferably positive) between outputs and inputs. In the first situation the organisation's actions are considered (even challenged) in terms of their relevance and appropriateness to stated purposes or goals; in the second these factors are taken for granted and what is important is the *use of resources*.

22. In setting objectives a number of important criteria need to be considered, if the objectives are to be viable. These criteria can be summarised as follows:

    ❶ Objectives should further the purpose and strategic aims of the organisation.

    ❷ They should also conform to the organisation's values and policies.

    ❸ Objectives should be realistic in the circumstances.

    ❹ Their achievement (or otherwise) should also be measurable (in terms of *time, quantity, quality, cost or a relevant ratio*).

    ❺ Objectives should preferably be set by agreement, so that those responsible for carrying them out have some 'ownership' of them.

    ❻ Objectives should set clear and challenging targets for individuals.

7 Objectives should be open to adaptation in the light of changing circumstances, especially where these are unforeseen.

8 Groups of objectives set for individuals, or groups, should not be in conflict with each other, but should serve a common purpose and direction.

23. Some examples of short-term objectives that might be set by different organisations are given below:

1 Increase sales turnover in the division by 10% over the next year

2 New production line to be operating at full capacity within 6 months

3 Reduce unit labour costs by 5% in every operating department over the next year

4 Double the present output of the new model from the middle of next year

5 Reduce number of staff from 10,000 to 6,000 over the next two years

6 Launch advertising campaign for new male cosmetic range within three months

7 Increase proportion of money raised from sponsorship from 15% to 25% over the next year

8 Reduce reliance on income from legacies by raising more donations from street collections

9 Reduce waiting time for patients in casualty from 1 hour to half-an-hour or less

10 Reduce coal output from state-owned pits by 30% over the next two years.

It is likely that the expansionist objectives in the above list of examples will be greeted with some enthusiasm by those involved. However, those seeking reductions in capacity, especially where this leads to a loss of jobs, are likely to incur considerable conflict within the organisation. For some stakeholders not all changes are for the better!

Hierarchy of goal-setting activities

24. Although, as stated earlier, defining purpose, goals and objectives is rarely a tidy affair, it is useful for the purpose of analysis to see these key activities in diagrammatic form. Such a representation helps to identify the links between the different priorities expressed in purpose, goals and objectives. So long as the reader accepts that, in practice, there will be frequent visits by the management between and within each level, then the hierarchy will not be taken too literally, but will serve as a guide.

25. At the top of the hierarchy (Figure 2.1) is the corporate mission statement, which sets the broad boundaries for, and the tone of, the other goals and objectives. Supporting the mission statement are the principal policies of the organisation – the rules of conduct that both reflect, and contribute to, its culture or values-system. The next level is that of the strategic business unit – the semi-autonomous profit centre, or other key organisational unit. Here the key product-market, competitive and resourcing goals are set, within the overall mission and culture of the organisation. The base level is the operational level, where strategic business unit goals are put into effect. At this level specific targets, usually prescribed in budget form, are agreed by strategic business unit managers, and implemented by line and functional managers at operating unit level. The time horizons at each level vary considerably, and much will depend on the nature of the business, especially in terms of the lead time required to launch new products or services. Time horizons for pharmaceutical manufacturers and electricity generating companies, for example, have to be lengthy (e.g. 5, 10, or even 20 years) due to the time

taken to develop the product to the point of sale. Other producers may manage with a horizon of just 3–4 years. The one time horizon that most organisations have in common is the 1–2 year rolling budget cycle, where operational targets are set and achieved over approximately an 18 months period.

Figure 2.1 A hierarchy of goal-setting activities

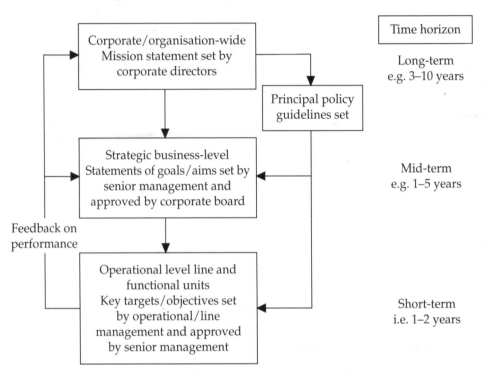

26. The whole hierarchy is affected by the interplay of goals and policies coming down the organisation, and the feedback of results coming back up the organisation. Thus the whole strategic goal-setting process is theoretically open to change in response to internal pressures as well as the influence of the external environment, which is the subject of the next chapter.

Questions for reflection/discussion

1. To what extent could you anticipate common perspectives in the mission statements of a large manufacturing company and a well-known charitable organisation? What conclusions do you draw about mission statements in the light of your answer?

2. What circumstances might force an organisation (of any kind) to reconsider its basic mission?

3. What issues would you expect to be addressed in the corporate strategic goals of the following:

   ❶ a large retailing organisation?
   ❷ a manufacturer of personal computers?
   ❸ a national charity for the elderly?

4. Why do organisations publish their rules of behaviour (policies)? What benefits might they receive as a result of these public statements?

5. Describe some situations where you could foresee a conflict of intentions between short-term objectives and strategic aims? How do you think the directors of an organisation should deal with conflicts that arise?

3 Assessing the environment

Introduction

1. The processes of strategic management take place in a complex environment of business, economic, technological, social and political influences. Understanding this external environment, or background, is crucial to strategic decision-makers, and has to be taken into account alongside any assessment of an organisation's own internal environment. This chapter looks at some of the leading ideas and techniques that have been put forward to help strategy planners to (a) identify key opportunities, threats and other issues in the external environment, and (b) analyse internal strengths and weaknesses. The combined analysis of the external and internal conditions in which an organisation operates is often referred to as a SWOT analysis, or, in some American texts, as TOWS. The SWOT acronym refers to Strengths, Weaknesses, Opportunities and Threats, and TOWS refers to the same factors but in a different order. This text will use the term SWOT when referring to the combined analysis, even though our examination of the environment in this chapter commences with what are effectively the Threats and Opportunities!

2. Another acronym which is often found in texts on strategic management is PEST. This refers to the following key headings under which the *external* influences on the organisation can be analysed – Political, Economic, Social and Technological. A PEST analysis, which can be considered as a sub-set of a SWOT analysis, can usefully be extended by adding a specifically *Business* dimension, since that ensures that suppliers, competitors and shareholders are included, as well as matters which are more properly covered by Economics. It may thus be easier to remember the full coverage as a BPEST analysis.

3. The lay-out of the rest of this chapter is as follows:
    ❶ the key *external* influences on the organisation are described
    ❷ a generic model of a BPEST analysis is discussed
    ❸ the key *internal* influences on organisational strategy are outlined
    ❹ a typical SWOT analysis is discussed
    ❺ the life-cycle concept of industries and businesses is introduced.

Key external influences on organisations

4. The principal external forces that bear on an organisation are depicted in Figure 3.1. They are composed of the major stakeholder groups together with other factors, such as technological developments, the state of the industry, and the nature of the labour market. The dominant groups in the external environment are usually the organisation's customers, shareholders, suppliers and the representatives of the community at large. The activities of these groups have the greatest repercussions on the organisation. The two most important other factors are technology (especially technological advances), and the state of the industry (i.e. in terms of its life-cycle). All of these external influences are described below, and the issues they give rise to are considered later in the chapter.

5. If the main external influences on an organisation are mapped out, the following picture emerges (Figure 3.1):

Figure 3.1 Key external influences on an organisation

Each of these sources of influence is summarised in the following paragraphs.

6. **Customers (existing)** – These are the individuals (in the case of consumer goods/services), or the organisations (in the case of capital goods and services), who purchase the goods or services of the organisation. These stakeholders are always important to firms, and may be considered the most important. Existing customers are particularly important to firms that supply goods or services on a continuing basis (such as a high street retailer or a parts manufacturer in the motor industry), where repeat orders are looked for. Such customers are crucial to those firms whose customers absorb the major part of their production. Witness the dismay expressed by a number of Midlands car component manufacturers at the take-over of Rover cars by BMW. These firms have geared their production standards and output requirements on the basis of their current contracts with a Rover-Honda consortium. Any change of supplier and/or production standards by the new Rover-BMW* company could cause major problems for existing suppliers. It may be convenient, but it is rarely wise for any company to rely on just one or two major customers for its products or services. Such a situation breeds dependence and reduces strategic options. The power of existing customers is much weaker for firms who supply goods or services on a one-off basis. Here, in theory, it is quite possible to lose interest in the customer once the deal has been made. However, firms who set out to be market leaders are likely to take as much care of their one-off customers as their regulars, on the assumption that reputation in the marketplace is a key factor in winning orders from potential customers.

* See Case-study CS3

7. **Customers (potential)** – These are the individuals and organisations who are either newcomers to the marketplace, or who already make purchases but from a competitor. Where products are still at the growing stage of their life-cycle (see paragraph 32 below), much of the marketing effort of a firm will be directed at potential customers. Thus, British building societies advertise heavily for the 'first-time buyer' of a property, while motor car manufacturers try to persuade drivers to desert competitors' models in favour of theirs. Attracting potential customers may carry high costs (and also risks) but is likely to be very profitable if successful.

8. **Competitors** – These are the organisations which are supplying similar products to a similar range of existing and potential buyers in the marketplace. As world economies move away from large-scale state ownership in favour of private enterprise, competition in domestic markets is increasing. There is also increasing competition from overseas firms as international trade barriers are gradually lowered and worldwide communications improve. The whole issue of competitive advantage is considered in the next chapter (Chapter 4).

9. **The Industry** – This refers to the collective situation of all the firms or organisations providing identifiable groups of goods or services to their public. In the UK a system of standard industrial classification (SIC) enables statisticians to sort out the dividing lines between one industrial classification and another. What is more important for our purposes now is where the industry is placed in its life-cycle (see paragraph 32 below). Some industries are at a new-born stage (for example, as in bio-technology, silicon chip manufacture, and satellite communications services); others are at stage of rapid growth (such as lap-top computer manufacture, compact disc manufacture); others are well into maturity (e.g. high street banking services, production of beers, wines and spirits); and others are in decline (e.g. coal-mining, village stores and typewriter manufacture). The position of the industry in its life-cycle has major repercussions for the strategic future of its individual constituents, especially in terms of their competitiveness and their prospects for diversification into other industry groups. Another important aspect of the industry from the strategic point of view is its attractiveness. This is mainly a question of size and growth and whether it serves a profitable market, where costs and prices are advantageous.

10. **Suppliers** – These are the external organisations that are supplying goods and services to the organisation. They are important in that they are providing essential resourcing elements for the organisation's own productive effort. They need to be reliable and quality-conscious as well as value-for-money. How much power they exert depends on the nature of their product (e.g. commonplace or highly-specialised), the extent to which it is available (especially a raw material, such as paper pulp, precious metals, etc.), its importance to the customer's final product (e.g. routine service or critical component), and the extent to which the customer can turn elsewhere (i.e. to the competition, or to substitutes). Leading firms tend to exert strong quality controls over their suppliers, but treat them fairly and pay them regularly.

11. **Shareholders and creditors** – These are the individuals and organisations who have invested or loaned their cash to the organisation in order to receive an adequate return in the form of increased share values and regular dividends (shareholders), or interest on their loans and repayment of their capital in due course (the creditors, such as banks). If such groups withdraw their support from a firm, it will be unable to sustain adequate growth and is more likely to go bankrupt.

12. **Labour market** – This market is made up of *potential* employees, who either possess knowledge and skills of use to the organisation, or who are part of the pool of talent leaving the schools, colleges and universities. The state of the labour market is extremely important to organisations who need specialist knowledge and skills; it is less important to those requiring less talented individuals. The labour market is becoming increasingly international, especially so within the European Union.

13. **Technology** – Rapid developments in technology can exert a powerful influence on all organisations, and not just on those operating in a high-tech environment (e.g. micro-processor manufacture, pharmaceuticals, fibre-optic technology). The combined impact of the computer, digital technology and telecommunications affects most business and public sector organisations. Organisations which want to maintain a competitive advantage have to be ready to adopt and adapt technological developments to their production and administrative procedures in order to stay ahead. However, such a strategy costs money and many firms cannot afford to invest quickly in machines and systems which are likely to be out-of-date in a year or two. Thus many firms carry a permanent level of obsolescence in their factory and office processes.

14. **Government and the Law** – The activities of the state through its legislature and law enforcement agencies impinge considerably on organisations – businesses, public bodies and charities are all affected by government fiscal and economic policies, and all have to operate within the law of the land. Business enterprises, for example, are affected by changes in direct and indirect taxation and interest rates; they have to abide by numerous laws relating to labour relations, health and safety and environmental factors to name but a few constraints. Organisations usually get a good period of notice before legal changes are enacted, but fiscal and economic changes can be brought about literally overnight (e.g. fuel tax increases implemented immediately following a budget announcement in Parliament).

15. **Supra-national bodies** – These are organisations which exert their influence outside that of national governments and sometimes overrule the latter. Examples include the European Union, which can issue laws binding on the member states, and bodies such as OPEC (Oil and Petroleum Exporting Countries), which have a major influence over the production levels, and hence price, of crude oil.

16. **Pressure groups** – These are unofficial bodies which are usually concerned about the impact of an organisation's activities on the community. They tend to have a narrow focus of interest and pursue it with varying degrees of intellectual and emotional vigour. Typical examples in Britain include Greenpeace (conservation issues), the National Trust (heritage and conservation), the Royal Automobile Club and the Automobile Association (road safety and drivers' interests), the British Safety Council (safety at home and in the workplace), trade unions (labour relations) and various animal welfare groups. Organisations operating in controversial activities or products are likely to maintain policies to deal with both the rational and violent reactions that they might meet in the course of their operations.

17. **Private individuals** – The influence of private individuals may not generally be very great – hence the formation of pressure groups – but occasionally an individual member of the public may successfully sue a company or public body and win substantial damages and even bring about a change in the law.

18. The influence that any one of the above sources exerts over an organisation at a particular point in time depends on a number of factors. In general terms, it is clear that certain elements in the environment have a direct impact on the organisation's activities, whilst others have only an indirect impact. Stoner and Freeman (1989) illustrate these two scales of impact in their model of direct and indirect-action environments (Figure 3.2). This shows the organisation's (direct) stakeholders as having a direct impact on organisational decisions and activities. However, they in turn are influenced by sociocultural,

technological, political and economic variables, which themselves may be influenced by international factors. The basic model provides a useful tool for analysing the environment of an organisation.

**Figure 3.2 Direct/indirect action environment model
(Stoner and Freeman, 1989)**

19. The sources of influence that are generally more powerful than others will probably conform to the 80–20 rule of Pareto's Law (e.g. 80% of the significant influences are likely to arise from only 20% of the sources involved). Who are the more powerful stakeholders? What are the most powerful factors? In a rough order of priority, and assuming that the organisation is a commercial enterprise operating in a competitive situation, they are likely to be as follows:

- *potential customers* (i.e. those who have yet to make up their mind whether to purchase the firm's goods or services, and who are thus in a position either to refrain from buying or to buy from a competitor)

- *existing customers* (i.e. those whose recommendation of the firm's goods or services may lead to repeat orders, new orders from other firm's customers, new orders from entirely new customers, or, if the recommendation is negative, to a loss of future sales).

20. It is possible to end the list here, on the basis that for any commercial organisation 'the customer is King (or Queen!)'. However, it would certainly make sense to include one other major group of stakeholders, whose influence on the organisation is important, regardless of the type of business and its relative dependence on, or *independence* from, suppliers, creditors or other stakeholders. This other group is the competition:

- *Competitors* (i.e. those other enterprises whose products are competing for customers in the same or similar marketplace, and whose relative success could lead to a reduced market share for the company; the options available to competitors are, it should be noted, greatly affected by their industry life-cycle).

The influence of competitors need not be negative. Their activities can be a spur to the company's marketing and sales staff as well as senior management. It is no coincidence that where one company leads others will tend to follow. So, if Ford and Vauxhall introduce driver's airbags into their standard fleet cars, other manufacturers will quickly follow suit so as not to lose any competitive advantage they might have enjoyed as a result of earlier benefits of a safety type, such as Volvo's 'safety cage' approach to passenger zone construction. More will be said of competitive advantage in Chapter 4.

21. In addition to the three stakeholder groups just described is technology, which is a most important factor. Few organisations can escape the consequences of not making the fullest use of computer technology and other office-related technology (fax machines, colour copiers, digital telephone exchanges, scanning devices, etc.). The introduction and use of office technology alone requires expenditure on equipment and training, and time to devise new work systems. For firms operating in manufacturing, the size of the challenge is greatly increased by the application of microprocessor technology to the very processes of production as well as to office, warehouse and delivery systems. The judicious application of technology can serve to extend the life-cycle both of industries and their products, a point which will be taken up later. In contrast to the impact of technology, the effect of the labour market is now much less than it was a decade or so ago, when job vacancies far outnumbered available applicants. Today few firms suffer a dire shortage of key staff.

22. The importance of stakeholders depends considerably on the enterprise's reliance on them. For example, a slaughterhouse business, being subject to various health and safety laws, must pay considerable attention to public health inspectors. The laws are aimed at ensuring (a) that the firm's products are free from disease and fit for human consumption, and (b) that working conditions are safe and healthy for the employees. Failure to conform to legal requirements can lead to major sanctions such as fines and even closure of the business. In another situation a firm might be reliant on just one or two sources of supply for its major components. In such a case, it is important to ensure that the suppliers are happy, especially if they have plenty of other outlets for their goods. Of course, a strategic decision on this problem could well lead to a number of alternative solutions including (a) a search for new suppliers, (b) a possible takeover of one of the suppliers, or (c) the components being manufactured in-house. In a different scenario, it is possible to visualise creditors exerting a powerful influence on company actions. If a firm has had to borrow heavily in order to invest in new plant and machinery, it is likely to be deeply concerned either to get an early return from the investment (which could be over-optimistic) or to increase profits in another part of the company in order to satisfy the banks that the business is viable. The firm might consider selling-off a subsidiary operation to improve its cash position and rely less heavily on outside financial support, as well as to reduce the threat of an unwanted take-over bid from a competitor.

23. A public sector organisation, receiving its funding from taxation (whether from local taxes or from State taxes), will be faced with a different league table of stakeholders. The most influential in this situation is likely to be the funding agency (the Local Authority or the Treasury). This is the group that the administrators or managers will be aiming to influence in order to win bigger budgets for their departments or to stave off reductions in funding if that looks likely. Although the funding agencies themselves are under the direct control of politicians, those who are responsible for delivering services to the general public are not, so their lobbying has to be with the funding bodies. At one time

public sector organisations took little notice of their 'customers', who had to seek redress in a roundabout way through local or national politicians. Today in many countries this has changed for the better, and public sector organisations have made big improvements in their care of customers. Citizens' Charters and similar statements of policy towards users of the services are aimed at greater efficiency and humanity in their delivery. Organisations such as British Rail are now prepared to refund travellers' fares if they have been subject to intolerable delays (specified in certain ways). Such improvements would have been unthinkable a few years ago, and are due to government efforts to introduce greater enterprise into public bodies.

24. Having briefly described the key external influences on organisations and having considered their relative importance, it is now time to consider the issues which arise from them. For this purpose, a short BPEST analysis is provided to illustrate the generic issues that are likely to affect a wide range of organisations, both business and public sector.

BPEST analysis

25. Figure 3.3 sets outs a range of generic issues that might arise in the external environment under each of the five headings – Business, Political, Economic, Social and Technological. An organisation can compare its current domestic (i.e. internal) situation against each of these issues and analyse the results. Much of this analysis will already be conducted in parts of the organisation, for example by carrying out marketing audits in the marketing department, and labour market analyses in the personnel department. The key point about a BPEST analysis, however, is that it enables the senior management planners to bring together a comprehensive review of the external environment, which embraces the interests of separate functions and departments across the organisation. If an inter-disciplinary team of managers can be involved, this is likely to enhance the value of the exercise, because managers from one discipline can question the assumptions made by colleagues commenting on their own function or department. Another important consideration in conducting a BPEST analysis is to ensure that the exercise concentrates on *leading* issues and not on secondary ones. Thus, the generic framework aims to focus on key issues only.

26. The key issues are set out in Figure 3.3 under the five separate BPEST headings. Information obtained under one heading is often likely to be relevant to another heading (for example, Market demand information under Business, and Spending patterns under Social are clearly likely to overlap), but this does not adversely affect the usefulness of the exercise.

27. An analysis along the lines of Figure 3.3 is likely to spotlight both negative and positive consequences for the future. Such consequences are usually categorised as Threats and Opportunities, and form part of a SWOT analysis. Laws, for example, sometimes act to restrict a company's actions (such as in labour relations or waste management), and this could be interpreted as a threat by causing the company to raise its costs in order to meet legal requirements. On the other hand, a law permitting public transport licensing can provide a real opportunity for a newly-formed bus company. Taking another example, the arrival of a newcomer to the marketplace might be seen as a threat to market share, but equally could be seen as a spur to the development of further competitive advantages. On the international economic front, an economic crisis in a major customer nation is likely to cause great anxiety in a company's Board. However, each apparent threat also

carries within it the seeds of an opportunity. Thus, to take the earlier example of a legal threat, a firm may decide that full adoption, or more, of the new legal requirements may give them an edge over the competition.

Figure 3.3 Generic issues in the external environment

Business	Political	Economic	Social	Technological
• State of the industry – known – projected	• Legislation – Company law – Labour laws – Environment, etc.	• Interest rates • Employment levels	• Skill levels • Population changes	• Developments in: – IT – Industrial applications (electronics)
• The market: – current demand – projected demand – buyer behaviour – market segments	• Support for enterprise • Taxation	• Inflation • Exchange rate	• Consumer confidence • Consumerism • Spending patterns • Attitudes to work/ leisure, etc.	– new energy sources – raw materials (plastics, metals)
• Competitors: – market share? – newcomers? – mergers? – failures? – alternative products? – international? • Suppliers: – reliability? – alternative?	• Developments in EU • Political changes in major markets	• Public expenditure (infrastructure) • State of US economy • Third World economies • Shareholder confidence • Terms of trade		

28. Some consequences of change in the external environment are entirely beneficial. For example, when demand in an overseas economy causes a substantial increase in orders for the company's products. However, most opportunities also carry potential threats within them. Where demand for a product is so great that it becomes impossible to supply customers in the short term, this provides a competitor with an opportunity to supply some of the customers instead. Once that competitor has a foot in the door, it may be difficult to dislodge him! The important point for strategic management is to recognise that both threats and opportunities feed off each other. You cannot have one without the other!

29. A further point to consider in conducting the above analysis is that the overall rate, or tempo, of change usually varies for each of the main headings. For example, political and social change may be relatively stable, but business, economic and technological changes may be taking place with bewildering speed. Clearly, a firm engaged in the production of microprocessors is going to experience a much higher rate of technological change than one manufacturing chain-link fences. Firms operating in highly-competitive mass-markets, such as supermarket chains and newspaper publishers, may find themselves in a constant whirl of marketing activity aimed at staying in contention, or gaining competitive advantage. By comparison, firms engaged in relatively stable and specialist markets (e.g. piano makers, jewellers) need not be so concerned to react to competitors in

the short-term. Few business organisations, however, can afford to ignore them in the long-term.

Analysis of internal strengths and weaknesses

30. An important element in assessing an organisation's overall situation is the identification of the strengths and weaknesses in its *internal* environment. The assessment of internal performance, and the nature of internal conditions can be tackled from a number of different perspectives. These include organisational, cultural, financial, research and development, production, marketing and resourcing perspectives. Several of the factors referred to in this paragraph will be dealt with in some detail later in the book, but it is important at this stage to get an overview of the sort of factors and issues that might be encompassed in an organisational review of internal strengths and weaknesses. These factors, together with examples of issues they may give rise to, are summarised in Figure 3.4.

Figure 3.4 analysing the internal environment – factors and issues

Factors	Issues
Organisational:	
• **Structure**	Coping with the business? Facilitating change? Achieving co-ordination? Meeting customer needs? Channels of communication?
• **Decision-making**	Quality and acceptability of decisions? Facilitating relevant and timely action? Adequate for strategic purposes? Adequate for operational purposes?
• **Management chain**	Encouraging initiative yet maintaining control? Optimum levels of hierarchy? Adequate management development and succession? Encouraging effectiveness as well as efficiency?
Cultural:	
• **Mission statement**	Reflects what we truly believe and/or want?
• **Organisation ethos**	Properly understood by management and staff? Sufficiently communicated down the chain? Responsive to change? Acceptability to staff, customers, suppliers? Conforms to, or betters, any legal requirements?
• **Management style**	Facilitating achievement of aims/goals? Motivating to staff? Encouraging younger managers? Awareness of equal opportunities?
Financial:	
• **Profitability**	Present targets and performance satisfactory, or better? Balance of retained versus distributed profits?
• **Growth in assets**	Overall situation? Source of growth acceptable?
• **Key ratios**	Satisfactory relationship between operating income and net assets? Return on capital employed? Return on sales? Liquidity position? Earnings per share?
• **Cash flow**	Negative or positive? Sources of cash? Investment policy (short-term)?

- **Gearing (Leverage)**   Satisfactory balance between sources of funds – share capital, long-term/short-term loans, reserves (retained profits)?

- **Management information**   Budget system informative and efficient? Invoicing/cash collection procedures etc efficient?

Research & Development:

- **Products**   Satisfactory rate of new products/designs? Product development?

- **Funding**   Long-term research funding versus short-term development funding? R&D share of total budget?

- **Technology**   Return on investment in new technology?

Production:

- **Output**   Meeting/bettering targets? Productivity level?

- **Quality**   Quality standards achieved? Customer complaints? Supplier quality standards?

- **Development**   Innovative systems employed? Application of new technology?

- **Stock/Inventory**   Satisfactory levels? Lead-times/quality, etc. satisfactory?

Marketing:

- **Product range**   Meeting customer needs? Comparison with competitors? New products/brands available?

- **Market share**   Growing/stable/declining?

- **Market development**   New markets being targeted? New segments identified?

- **Profitability**   Product/brand profitability? Pricing structure?

- **Cost of sales**   Meeting/bettering targets? Apportionment of costs between promotion, distribution and direct sales?

- **Turnover**   Sales revenue at target level/better/worse?

Resourcing:

- **Purchasing**   Purchasing costs within budget? Suppliers satisfactory? Operation of just-in-time/other cost-effective purchasing measures? Quality control?

- **Personnel**   Recruitment satisfactory? Retention rates? Departmental needs met for relevant skills? Wage and salary costs within budget? Staff development satisfactory? Promote from within or recruit? Management development procedures satisfactory?

- **Funding**   Adequate sources of funding for existing resource requirements? Funding for new developments? Long–term/short-term loans? Share issue? Reserves available?

31. The list in Figure 3.4 is a lengthy one, and most of the issues it raises are dealt with in other chapters (see especially Chapters 10, 12 and 15). However, it is useful at this point to see how real organisations deal with a sample of the factors and issues just referred to. Strategic analysis is not primarily about generating lists, but about identifying the few key issues that are critical for the organisation, and asking the right questions about them. The illustrative examples are taken from recent annual reports and reviews of a range of different organisations:

① Abbey National plc – focusing the corporate business

The former high street building society, Abbey National, took the major step, about five years ago, to convert to a public limited company offering a range of banking services in addition to its traditional mortgage lending business. Thus it greatly extended its product range at one fell swoop. Since its transformation it has added life assurance and treasury operations (wholesale money markets) to its core activities. For a short time, it also went into the estate agency business, but withdrew fairly quickly after the housing market collapsed. Following the sale of its estate agency subsidiary, the company underlined its intention to focus its corporate business on financial services, based on retail banking, life assurance and treasury operations. (Annual Report 1993).

② British Biotech plc – employee motivation through share ownership

British Biotech (formerly British Bio-teccnology Group) is a new and growing pharmaceutical company. Following a successful Stock Exchange listing in 1992, the directors gained shareholders' support to open up employee access to its shares in two schemes – one for executives, and another for all staff with at least one year's service and working at least 16 hours a week. The response to the offer was such that one year later about two-thirds of all staff had taken out share options, and thus gained an additional stake in the company's future, as shareholders as well as employees. (See also Case-study CS8.)

③ Catholic Children's Society Ltd – maintaining sources of funds

The Catholic Children's Society provides a range of family support services to disadvantaged children and families in London and the South East of England. Like most other charity organisations, it relies for much of its income on the generosity of voluntary donors. However, it also relies on several other sources of income – legacies, bequests, Trust funds, central/local government grants, and fee/other revenue-earning activities. Most of the income arises from the operation of children's homes and related projects, which receive fees from local and central government for the residential care of children. Other sources of income are rather unpredictable. Thus, maintaining the various sources of funds, and strengthening the underlying operating revenue represents a major strategic issue. (Report and Accounts, March 1993)

④ Laporte plc – R & D in the chemicals industry

Laporte plc is one of the UK's premier chemical companies, developing and marketing a range of industrial chemical products through five divisions – Organics, Absorbents, Metals and Electronic Chemicals, Hygiene and Process Chemicals, and Construction Chemicals. For such a company, R & D (Research and Development) programmes are essential to maintain the flow of new products and processes as well as enabling existing products and processes to be refined and improved. In a divisionalised structure, there is always a balance to be maintained between the central corporate functions (including R & D) and the divisions. It was decided in 1991 to decentralise much of the R & D effort to the divisions by transferring control of product and process development to the latter, whilst providing them with the technical centres needed to carry out the work. The early results of this restructuring showed a significant enhancement of new products in the course of 1992. (Annual Report, 1993)

Industry and business life-cycles

32. Ultimately, the object of assessing the internal and external environments is to identify where the business is currently positioned in its market(s) in order to be able to make strategic decisions about where it ought to be in the future. Such decisions can be improved if the management planners are aware of where the industry lies in relation to its life-cycle. A life-cycle model attempts to map out a projected life-story either for a *person* (e.g. for use by an insurance company), or for a *product* (e.g. for a market planner) or for an *industry* (e.g. for a strategic planning manager). The concept, which was first applied to *products* by marketing planners, suggests that the subject of the life-cycle moves from initial start-up, or entry to the market, (Birth) through growth and maturity stages (Prime periods) to eventual decline (Old Age). Porter (1980) suggests that there is some argument as to whether the life-cycle concept ought to be applied to industries. He then proceeds to do so. This seems to make sense, even though it has to be acknowledged that any life-cycle analysis can do no more than provide a broad picture of where its subject lies at any point in time. Like other models used in strategic management, the industry life-cycle has to be seen for what it is, that is an *aid* to thinking, not a substitute for it!

33. Whilst the strategic choices that are made as a result of life-cycle analysis are the subject of Chapter 6, the concept itself is a useful one to consider at this point, as we come towards the end of this chapter on the subject of the organisation's environment. Figure 3.5 shows a basic life-cycle for a mature industry (such as motor-car manufacturing):

Figure 3.5 Basic industry life-cycle – motor manufacturing

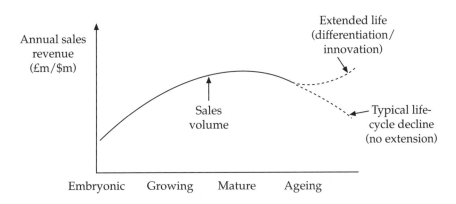

34. The usefulness of the basic model is that it can be used as a platform for analysing the conditions that might be expected at each stage of the cycle. In the case of a mature industry, such as motor-car manufacturing, it can be expected that competition will be intense, prices will be very competitive, margins and profits will be lower than at the growth stage, and sales will show little or no increase. The strategic emphasis is likely to be on product differentiation and market segmentation to gain a competitive edge. Thus a new model, or some new benefit, will be introduced ahead of the competition, and sales will be targeted at specific markets (for example, young women drivers, existing owners of the make). Another key strategy at this time is likely to be to reduce costs at all stages and to improve productivity. Industries, like individual products, can receive an extended life by differentiation. Thus, by finding additional market segments, main-

taining innovations and widening the application of new technologies, industries can halt their decline and even return to growth. Life-cycle analysis can make a constructive contribution to the overall study of the internal and external environments. It can be especially useful when sizing up the organisation's competitive position, when the basic model shown above can be adapted to highlight strengths and weaknesses in the market position (see Chapter 4).

SWOT analysis

35. The *combined* analysis of external and internal issues affecting organisational performance, known as a SWOT analysis, was referred to in paragraph 1 above. The concept of assessing organisational conditions in terms of strengths, weaknesses, opportunities and threats can be applied at various levels – corporate level, business unit level and even department or section level. Exactly how the concept is applied will vary from one organisation to another, and will depend partly on where the organisation lies in its life-cycle. Most organisations are likely to select just a few key factors and issues relevant to them, and will then analyse them systematically in terms of strengths, weaknesses, opportunities and threats. An example of the points that might arise in such an analysis is given in Figure 3.6, which highlights a number of the issues faced by a well-known high street retail chain in a mature market in 1993.

Figure 3.6 SWOT Analysis – high street retail business

Factor/Issue	Strengths	Weaknesses	Opportunities	Threats
1. **Customer base**	• Regular customers • Slow, steady growth	–	• Sustain growth via 2-4 below	• Competitor activity
2. **Product range/ attractiveness**	• Wide range • Seen as good value • Availability good • Quality established • Own brands selling well	–	• Improve bulk purchasing • Maintain high quality	• Failure to recognise what product the customer wants • Imposition of VAT on books/newspapers • Price-cutting by main competitors
3. **Store Layout**	• New design being implemented to re-enforce brand image • Well-lit, air-conditioned • User-friendly check-outs linked to stock control system	• Many stores yet to be modernised	• Attain standard beyond reach of competitors	• Increasing costs of the improvements
4. **Staff efficiency**	• High recruitment standards • Thorough staff training • Regular manager training and briefing	–	–	• Less than satisfactory performance by some individuals • Low turnover leading to slow career development

Figure continues

Factor/Issue	Strengths	Weaknesses	Opportunities	Threats
5. **Market share**	• Number One in most markets	• Less secure in some markets • Acquisitions and joint ventures have ground to make up	• Strengthen position in all markets	• Weaker operations could take 2 years to reach profit • Some market shrinkage at home due to recession
6. **Financial position**	• Slow but steady growth in sales • Profitability of Group steady • Excellent cashflow • Stable earnings per share	• First half of year usually weak	• Focus on improving reductions in costs while maintaining quality	• Restructuring costs from acquisitions/joint ventures • Losses on property sales • Possible dip in consumer spending due to recession

36. An analysis such as the above shows a very healthy situation, and many similar businesses could not match it. Nevertheless, even when a bright picture emerges from a SWOT analysis, it can be very useful. It is, after all, extremely important for a firm to recognise why it is succeeding, as well as where it needs to attend to problems. There is nothing particularly exact or scientific about a SWOT analysis, but it can help to focus senior managers' attention on major strategic issues, enable possible problems to be identified before they occur, and provide an opportunity to identify organisational strengths.

References
1. Stoner, J. & Freeman, R. (1989), *Management* (4th edn), Prentice Hall.
2. Porter, M.E. (1980), *Competitive Strategy – Techniques for Analyzing Industries and Competitors*, The Free Press.

Questions for reflection/discussion
1. Which three external groups are likely to exercise the greatest influence on the affairs of each of the following:
   ❶ an industrial chemicals manufacturer?
   ❷ a children's charity?
   ❸ a retail banking organisation?
2. How far can the 'customers' of a public service exercise consumer influence over the services they receive?
3. Discuss the proposition for a motor-car manufacturer that 'In the 1990s technology exerts a greater force over business success than government economic policy '.
4. Discuss where you think the following organisations might be in their life-cycle, and give reasons to substantiate your answer:
   ❶ cellular telephone network service
   ❷ manufacturer of breakfast cereals
   ❸ distributor of personal computers
   ❹ a manufacturer of pain-relieving drugs.

4 Competitive advantage

Introduction

1. This chapter looks especially at a business organisation's relationships with its competitors. One of the cardinal principles of enterprise economies is that healthy competition should be encouraged and extended. The extent to which competition can be regarded as 'healthy', as opposed to 'damaging' or 'non-existent', is often a product of government legislation or intervention. In practice, any firm that does not have a monopoly (i.e. where the competition is non-existent) has to enter its marketplace with one eye firmly on the competition. As multiple and mass markets have appeared in many of the world's nations, so the competition amongst those supplying goods and services to those markets has increased markedly. Nowadays, it is only the monopoly supplier, or the feckless, who will market their goods or services to their end-users on a take-it-or-leave-it basis. Most suppliers, on the contrary, adopt a marketing approach to their consumers, i.e. they look to see what customers need and want before all else. Their second consideration, therefore, is to provide goods and services to meet these needs and wants, and to do so at a profit. At this point, however, they come up against their rivals – the competition – who also want to provide such benefits profitably. In the last decade or so, there has been much greater attention paid to competitor behaviour, and no-one has made a more significant contribution to the debate about competition than Michael Porter, the American academic from Harvard. Much of what follows in this chapter derives from his analyses of competitive strategy and competitive advantage.

2. Although the emphasis in this chapter is on commercial enterprises, all organisations, commercial and non-commercial, are in competition in one form or another. Government departments are in competition for Treasury funds, local authorities have to compete for central government funds, and charities are competing with others for people's voluntary donations. So, for all who are engaged in the provision of goods or services, the issue of competition is central to their strategic planning.

The nature of competition

3. In relation to the content of the previous chapter, Porter (1980), writing about competitive strategy, is clear that ' ... the key aspect of the firm's environment is the industry or industries in which it competes.' He argues that the intensity of competition in an industry is neither a matter of coincidence or bad luck, but more a question of how that industry is structured. He then proceeds to analyse the structure of an industry in terms of five basic forces, of which only one is the existing competition. The others are buyers, suppliers, potential competitors and substitutes. The collective strength of these five forces not only determines the intensity of the competition for any one firm, but also determines the potential profitability of the industry as a whole. Just as some firms are either strongly or weakly placed in their industry, so too whole industries can be either relatively very profitable or barely profitable. The pharmaceutical and financial services industries, for example, can be extremely profitable, whereas the road transport and steel-making industries can only generate modest profits. Nevertheless, within each industry, whether a profitable one or not, there is competition between those supplying the goods and services to the customers. This competition, and its relationship to the

other four factors can be shown diagrammatically as in Figure 4.1, which is based on Porter's original model.

**Figure 4.1 Competitive forces
(adapted from Porter, 1980)**

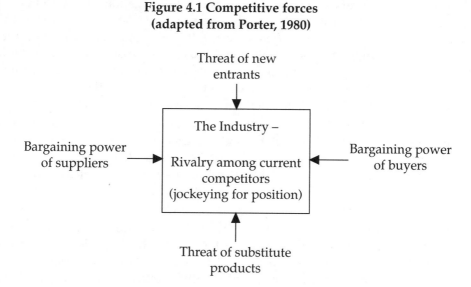

4. Porter's model is now used by many organisations as an important element in their strategy formulation, and especially in their assessment of strengths and weaknesses (see SWOT analysis, previous chapter). Any analysis of the nature of the competition is considerably improved by weighing up the relative strength of the other four forces. As was noted in the previous chapter, when industries and their leading products are at the maturity stage, there is intense competition between them. At a time of such rivalry as, for example, in the wake of an economic recession in the motor car industry, competitors can adopt one or more of the following tactics:

❶ advertise strongly, even to the extent of making public comparisons with other makes

❷ offer incentives to buyers (interest-free credit, free membership of breakdown services, free car alarms, etc.)

❸ devise ways of differentiating their products ('lean-burn' engines, safety air-bags, engine immobilisers, etc.).

Individual manufacturers have to consider how to respond to, or counter, these immediate threats to their sales from rivals. If such manufacturers focused their attention just on the competition they would be overlooking other key factors which could work to their advantage. For example, when competition among principals is high, those who are serving them in a subsidiary capacity (i.e. suppliers) are in a relatively weak bargaining position in relation to them. The reason is that the suppliers' sales are dependent on the end products (i.e. new motor cars) being sold, and suppliers stand to lose or gain depending on the relative success of their principals. If a car manufacturer is stockpiling vehicles this is bad news for its suppliers. Thus, they have more than a vested interest in seeing that their principal customers not only survive, but also shift their stocks. In these circumstances, principals would be foolish not to look for savings on their components' bills, and put pressure on suppliers to ease their prices, thus allowing themselves scope for introducing judicious price-cuts against the competition. Trimming costs is always worth considering as a way of obtaining a competitive advantage.

5. Of course, *buyers* of cars are in a strong position in this situation – what is often called a 'buyers' market'. They can drive a hard bargain with dealers (e.g. by seeking a good trade-in price, extra accessories, free delivery). It is also open to the manufacturers to squeeze price margins for their dealers and thus reduce distribution costs. However, such a step has to be weighed up against the possibility of causing the distributor to go out of business. It can be seen that under severe competition there is a tendency for prices to come down right through the chain, which ultimately benefits the end-user.

6. Substitute products are hardly likely to be an issue in the above situation, given the remote possibility of potential customers giving up motoring in favour of a motor bike or a pedal cycle. Neither are new entrants to the industry likely. Given the intensity of the competition, the low profit margins and the high costs of entering, the industry would be unattractive to newcomers. In considering the issue of new entrants, Porter lists seven major barriers to market entry, which can be summarised as follows:

❶ **Economies of scale**, i.e. newcomers have to come in on a large scale or accept inevitable cost disadvantages. This factor alone is likely to deter most would-be entrants, unless they can buy their way into the market by purchasing a firm already active in it, which accounts for the collaborative agreements and mergers that many airline firms have been pursuing recently.

❷ **Product differentiation**, i.e. newcomers have to find ways of overcoming existing brand loyalties in order to get their own product/brand accepted. In the UK the arrival on the national radio scene of a station totally dedicated to popularising classical music raised some sceptical eyebrows. The new station – Classic FM – had to overcome both the established reputation of BBC Radio Three, and the perceived wisdom that the majority of listeners preferred pop music anyway. On both counts the new radio station has confounded the sceptics, attracting a following well in excess of its BBC rival, and providing advertisers with a useful extension to their existing outlets.

❸ **Capital requirements**, i.e. the need to invest considerable sums of money in a new venture, much of which will be unrecoverable (e.g. start-up losses, advertising, research & development). This is another huge disincentive to newcomers, unless they have cash surpluses or some other possibility of raising the initial capital resources, as in the case of British Biotech (see Chapter 2 paragraph 17).

❹ **Switching costs**, i.e. the initial costs of machinery, equipment and other first-time resources required by users to enable them to switch to the new product. A well-known example is when Apple computer users decide to change to an MS-DOS system, or vice versa. Fortunately, in this example, the problems of incompatibility are being overcome by action on the part of Apple Computers to make all their new machines able to read DOS as well as Apple's own operating system.

❺ **Lack of access to distribution channels**, i.e. newcomers must work their way into existing distribution channels (e.g. dealer networks, wholesalers, etc.) or establish brand-new ones.

❻ **Cost disadvantages regardless of size**, i.e. newcomers will always tend to have certain cost disadvantages compared with established firms, who will have gained experience in the market, may have access to proprietary technology, readily available supplies of raw materials, and favourable locations; existing firms may also have benefited from government subsidies. New entrants may have none of these advantages, and are likely to have to pay a premium price to share in them.

❼ Government policy, i.e. through licensing and legal regulation, governments can limit or even prevent newcomers from operating in the industry. Typical licensed industries in the UK include road transport, oil exploration and retail alcohol sales. Other industries affected by regulation include camping site development, house building and golf course development, all of which are subject to planning requirements capable of stifling their projects at birth.

7. Porter's work on competitive strategy has been very influential. His ideas are not without their critics, however, and other commentators have pointed to the lack of reference to issues of the legality and ethics of the barriers described in Porter's list. Also in the schema of the five forces, there are no explicit references to other stakeholders in the firm's environment, especially the community at large, and employees. When Porter talks of buyers and suppliers he does so in terms of their power (or, by implication, lack of it) and avoids any issues concerning the *obligations* that firms might have when determining their market strategy.

8. Before moving on to consider how to analyse competitors, it will be helpful to reflect on the broad aspects of competition by asking 'In what way are competitors competing?'. One of the most obvious ways is through price, where for goods or services *of a comparable quality* the competitor is offering a lower price. The proviso of comparable quality is important. Cheap prices can often mean cheap, shoddy goods – the 'You get what you pay for' approach. If, however, the goods are of a comparable quality to others', then lower prices will be attractive. One major high street retailer (Marks & Spencer) started life with the slogan *'Don't ask the price, everything is a penny!'* For many years that particular company built its reputation on cheaply-priced but good value products. Today its emphasis has shifted away from relatively cheaper prices to product quality, although still within the price range of its customers. In the final analysis, what counts with private buyers, in particular, is value-for-money, or what Porter in another context (1980) calls simply *'value'* or *'the amount buyers are willing to pay'*.

9. Another way in which firms compete is by means of lower costs, where comparable goods or services are produced with lower unit costs, thus offering the competitor the prospect of higher margins on competitive prices, and putting them in the position of being able to lower prices, or some other inducements to customers, if and when it suits them. Where competitors are able to offer lower prices or other benefits for the same quality of product, this will represent superior value to the customer. Many firms do in fact compete very successfully by providing some unique benefit for their customers which more than offsets a relatively higher price for their product. The art is in discovering what customers truly value in the product or service – speed? convenience? reliability? variety of function? flexibility? – for that is what they will pay extra for. For example, what is it that business-people like about portable computers or telephones that their firms will pay considerably more for these products compared with their office versions? Clearly, portability is a key factor, but this is only a benefit because it enables a wider use of the equipment, both in the office and on the move. The principal underlying factor is probably convenience, i.e. the use of portable equipment facilitates communica-

tion in a wide variety of situations and is of undoubted benefit to the employing organisation.

10. Other platforms for competitive behaviour are quality and reliability, for these again are aspects of a product or service for which users are usually prepared to pay a premium price. Some firms build their reputations on such aspects of competition, including Rolls Royce motor-cars, the Hilton Hotel group and Harrods store. Customers may pay well for the privilege of driving a Rolls Royce, or shopping at Harrods. They obtain not only the highest quality of goods, but a status symbol as well.

11. In high street retailing, the range of products available to shoppers is an important factor, and all the top retailers aim to achieve the widest possible range of goods in their stores. However, for every general rule there are exceptions, and the retailing industry also has numbers of very successful firms who supply only a specialist range of goods. In most industries extending the product range is a frequent strategic aim, but equally there are firms whose role in life is to provide goods and services for highly specialised markets, often called niche markets.

Analysing the competition

12. The analysis of the competition can be conducted along similar lines to the internal analysis of strengths and weaknesses referred to in the previous chapter. Whilst the emphasis in analysing competitors is likely to be on *marketing and financial indicators*, there are important implications in such items as *mission* (i.e. key values) statements, research and development direction and *production* developments. All will provide clues as to where competitors are focusing their priorities and placing their emphasis. On the *marketing* front it is important to find out how, and how well, competitors are meeting customers' needs in the following areas:

❶ the range of goods or services on offer
❷ the reputation of those goods or services in the marketplace
❸ attractive pricing
❹ typical product or service features (e.g. quality, reliability, accessibility, etc.)
❺ unique features and/or benefits on offer.

13. Other aspects of marketing that are important in competitor analysis include obtaining information (intelligence) about the following:

❶ overall market share (growing, declining, stable?)
❷ share of specific markets (segments)
❸ launch of new products or brands
❹ changes in sales force organisation
❺ changes in distribution channels
❻ operations in new market segments (including joint ventures with other competitors)
❼ changes in promotional tactics (including advertising, point-of-sale promotions, etc.)
❽ addition of new production/service facilities (e.g. factories, shops, offices).

14. On the *financial* front it is important to know how well competitors are performing in terms of their overall financial health (profitability, growth in assets, cash flow and so on), and where they are investing their capital (R & D? Production facilities? Purchase of

other companies? Staff training and development? etc.). It is also useful to know where competitors are obtaining their funds in order to finance new developments (undistributed profits/reserves? sale of assets? bank loans? other loans? share flotations? collaboration with other, bigger, competitors?).

15. The sources of information available to aid intelligence-gathering include both public domain information (for example, as in published Annual Reports & Accounts, other information made available by competitors in press releases, and in official government publications), and more restricted information arising from trade meetings, specialist advertising, market research analysts and word-of-mouth information from sales staff, suppliers and end-users. Other information can only be gained by underhand methods, such as employing undercover personnel or using methods of electronic surveillance.

    Reputable firms, however, will only make use of open-handed sources of information. Successful companies, according to Goldsmith & Clutterbuck (1984) in their survey of 38 leading British companies, develop a positive 'hunger for market information':

    'For our successful companies a close understanding of their markets is a prerequisite for an aggressive marketing thrust. Action is rooted in confidence that they know what they are doing and have the resources to accomplish their objectives, and this confidence in turn is rooted in the detailed information they gather about their customers and their competitors.'

16. The analysis of the competition can be assisted by using Porter's model of the intensity of the competition. The basic model is a matrix that takes the five competitive forces (rivalry, entrants, etc.) and compares them against three levels of impact, or intensity – Low, Medium and High. The model can be applied in a wide variety of settings, and is as relevant to a charity seeking to understand its competitive position in the voluntary sector, as it is to a business in the marketplace. The illustration supplied in Figure 4.2 is based on the experience of a well-known retail group in the United Kingdom. The picture it draws is one of intense competition from rivals and a high need to maintain its customer base against them. It also indicates the extent of the power that major high street chains can exert over their suppliers. In this situation, new entrants are unlikely (except as a result of a takeover in the industry) since the costs of entry are so high. As the principal product lines of the company are clothes, there are no substitutes of any importance. The major threat, of course, is that existing customers will go to the competition.

Competitive position

17. As noted above, the collective forces of current and potential competitors, buyers, suppliers and the threat of substitutes determine both the intensity of the competition for individual firms, and the profitability of the industry. In making an assessment of their own and competitors' relative position in the market, firms should not just concentrate on market *share*, but on the *profit* that comes from it. In Porter's further ideas on competitive strategy (1985), which coined the phrase 'competitive advantage', he insists that:

    'Satisfying buyer needs may be a prerequisite for industry profitability, but in itself it is insufficient. The crucial question in determining profitability is whether firms can capture the value they create for buyers, or whether this value is competed away to others.'

Figure 4.2 Analysing the impact/intensity of competition in a retail business

Competitive forces	Strength of impact/intensity		
	Low	Medium	High
Rivalry			Extremely intense competition from high street rivals. Additional threats from niche chains.
Entrants	Few new entrants due to huge market shares held by main competitors.		
Substitutes	Unlikely, since company aims at basic styles rather than fashion items.		
Customers			Vital to retain own customer loyalty and prevent defection to main rivals.
Suppliers	Power of the company as the major customer of the key suppliers enables competitive pricing with good quality to be insisted on.		

Value, in Porter's meaning, is defined as follows:

'Value is the amount buyers are willing to pay for what a firm provides them. Value is measured by the total revenue, a reflection of the price a firm's product commands and the units it can sell. A firm is profitable if the value it commands exceeds the costs involved in creating the product.'

18. Porter argues that, in analysing competitive position, it is much more important to focus on *value* rather than *cost*, because some firms may deliberately raise their costs in order to command a premium price. Focusing on value leads Porter to develop a model of a 'value chain', which consists of 'value activities' and 'margin' which produce a total value. Value activities are 'the physically and technologically distinct activities that a firm performs', and are preferred over a *functional* analysis as a key measure. These

value activities can be separated into five generic forms, which have a strongly systems identity, summarised briefly as follows:

'**Inbound Logistics** – activities associated with receiving, storing and disseminating inputs to the product ...

Operations – activities associated with transforming inputs into the final product form ...

Outbound Logistics – activities associated with collecting, storing and physically distributing the product to buyers ...

Marketing and Sales – activities associated with providing a means by which buyers can purchase the product and inducing them to do so ...

Service – activities associated with providing service to enhance or maintain the value of the product ...'

19. Each of the above five categories will be a factor in the business life of most firms, and some categories will be critical. For example, a manufacturing organisation based on the assembly of components and parts supplied by a number of different sources will pay considerable attention to its purchasing costs and arrangements (inbound logistics). A manufacturer of silicon chips will focus especially on production facilities (operations), whilst a supplier of photocopying machines will need to ensure that servicing, maintenance and repair facilities are second to none (service). In addition to these core (primary) activities, Porter includes in his model four support activities, which are focused around the following: Firm infrastructure (including general management, planning, accounting and quality management); Human Resource Management; Technology Development (intended to have a broader meaning than Research & Development); and Procurement (the Purchasing function). Most of the support activities contribute to the entire value chain as well as to particular activities.

The basic model is shown in Figure 4.3.

Figure 4.3 Porter's generic value chain

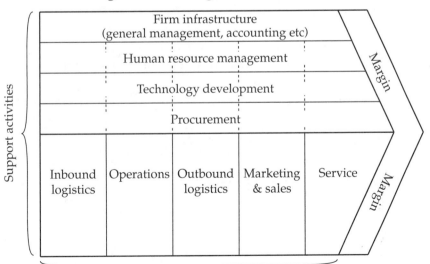

20. The term 'margin' is used by Porter to signify the difference between the total value (revenue) and the total cost of the value activities (primary and support), and makes up the final element in the value chain. The model assumes that firms' goals are directed towards the achievement of a satisfactory margin. He argues that the concept of *'the value chain'* is more useful than that of *'value-added'*, which is made up of selling price less the cost of purchased raw materials, and is therefore a narrower concept than the chain. In analysing competitors' performance, the value chain concept can be very useful as a basis for analysing the elements of the chain and estimating how well the competitor is performing in each of them. The model can also be used as a framework for assessing competitors in terms of the issues referred to in paragraphs 12-14 above (such as range of goods/services, product features, distribution channels, etc.).

The value chain is referred to again in the discussion of 'value' in Chapter 12 (Managing Quality).

References

1. Porter, M.E (1980), *Competitive Strategy – Techniques for Analyzing Industries and Competitors*, The Free Press.
2. Goldsmith, W. & Clutterbuck, D. (1984), *The Winning Streak*, Penguin Books.
3. Porter, M.E. (1985), *Competitive Advantage*, The Free Press.

Questions for reflection/discussion

1. Discuss the proposition that 'to succeed in business it is more important to know what *competition* you are up against than to know what your *customers* want.'

2. In relation to either (a) a house building firm, or (b) a builder of luxury yachts, what is likely to be the relative strength of the following competitive forces on the firm, *in a period of modest recession*:

   ❶ existing competitors?
   ❷ potential competitors?
   ❸ bargaining power of suppliers?
   ❹ bargaining power of buyers?

3. Taking a high street retailing chain (but not a foodstore) as an example, identify what questions the senior management need to ask about their competitors in order to achieve a competitive advantage over them.

4. To what extent are *service* activities likely to be seen as more critical than other value chain activities to the following:

   ❶ a supplier of personal computers for businesses?
   ❷ a manufacturer of chocolates?
   ❸ an overnight parcels delivery service?

5 Forecasting the future

Introduction

1. The previous two chapters have concentrated on the key aspects of an organisation's internal and external environments. A major portion of the assessment of those environments has to be focused on present and past performance of both the organisation and its competitors. This in itself is no small task. However, from the point of view of strategic management, it is even more critical to look to the future and predict *potential* performance and trends. This has to be attempted internally for the organisation's own performance, and externally for the competition in terms of the political, economic, social and technological environment. This chapter outlines the key issues that organisations have to address in looking to the future, and describes some of the leading methods and techniques adopted by organisations to forecast the future.

2. One of the distinguishing features of strategic management, compared with operational management, is its element of unpredictability, and hence risk. Strategic management involves making major organisation-wide decisions in conditions of considerable uncertainty. The price of such decisions can be failure of the business, especially during periods of economic recession. For example, in 1992 there were a record 24,425 business failures in England and Wales compared with 12,067 ten years earlier. Thus, even during less recessionary times, more than 200 firms a week were going to the wall in England and Wales alone.

3. Understandably, senior managers do not want their business enterprises either to collapse or to be so weakened that they are ripe for take-over by one of their competitors. Thus, they want to reduce the uncertainties and risks attached to decisions about the future, and this entails not only gathering as much relevant information and data about the organisation itself, its main competitors and the rest of its external world, but also using tried and tested techniques for improving predictions of future performance, based on the information collected. Not many of them would be bold enough to share Peters' (1987) view, in *Thriving on Chaos*, that 'Nothing is predictable'. In defence of his statement Peters points, among other things, to the volatility of currency markets and energy prices, to the ever-growing numbers of new competitors, to the *'unsettling impact – on everything'* of technology and to changing tastes among consumers. The outcomes of these pressures, according to Peters, include uncertainty, more choices, market fragmentation, product/service explosion, demand for quality, more complexity and mid-size firms. His advice for managers seeking strategic solutions to such problems will be examined in the next chapter, but suffice to say here that one of his proposals is that 'winning' firms should be responsive and adaptive. This of course, raises the question 'responsive to what?', which brings us neatly onto the subject-matter of forecasting.

The focus of forecasting

4. Forecasting is about making the seemingly unpredictable predictable! The following working definition of forecasting is suggested for the purposes of this chapter:

    > Forecasting, in a strategic context, refers to any attempt, whether qualitative or quantitative, and usually based on past performance, to predict future outcomes and trends in the internal and external environments of an organisation in order to limit the risks involved in devising and implementing a strategy.

This definition is given against the broad, corporate-wide background of strategic planning and not as it might be applied to tactical or short-term planning at operational levels. It suggests that potential outcomes as well as trends need to be faced, and implies that both qualitative and quantitative approaches may be used. It does not assume that future predictions depend upon past performance even though most forecasts are based on such evidence. Finally, it emphasises that the raison d'être of forecasting is to reduce the risks involved in making strategic choices (see next chapter).

5. What strategic issues will benefit from forecasting? They will be similar to the issues referred to in Chapters 3–4, which can be broadly categorised under the following main headings:

    ❶ Organisational performance (past, current and future)
    ❷ Trends in the external political, economic, social and technological environment
    ❸ Trends in the external business environment, especially those affecting competitors
    ❹ Gap analysis of shortfalls between predicted trends and desired organisational performance.

    It is not too difficult to see in these categories the BPEST and SWOT analyses mentioned earlier (Chapter 3), and indeed they generally provide the framework within which many organisations will make use of forecasting techniques in assessing where they are, and what prospects they have of moving onwards from there.

6. If we take the above four categories in turn, we can build up a picture of where the forecasting focus should rest. Essentially, there are three questions that organisations need to ask themselves in this context, and these are:

    ❶ What factors are so crucial to the organisation that they need to be estimated several years ahead?
    ❷ How much data and information is available, and what is completely unknown?
    ❸ What forecasting methods are going to be the most helpful?

7. Any assessment of organisational performance is likely to focus on the following:

    • Markets and market segments (including niche markets)
    • Product (or service) range
    • Sales (by product (service), brand, market, etc.)
    • Production levels/service activity
    • Costs (of production, sales and overheads)
    • R & D effort
    • Investment programme
    • Organisation structure
    • Management style (including delegation and control)
    • Personnel (numbers, skills, training, effectiveness)
    • Management accounting system
    • Financial management

8. The above list provides organisations with a checklist for possible attention. Each organisation must choose its priorities for analysis. Some observers (for instance Porter, 1985) suggest that only two really crucial items require attention, and these boil down to (a)

product differentiation, and (b) *cost reduction*. However, most organisations are likely to scrutinise a wider set of factors, even whilst recognising the underlying wisdom of Porter's suggestion. A considerable amount of information about these performance factors can be found in the organisation's management information and accounting system. Forecasting methods will draw on key accounting mechanisms, such as the Balance Sheet and the Profit and Loss Account, as well as the organisation's master budget and capital investment plan. The usual approach is to take comparative figures over a period (e.g. five years) so as to highlight trends in performance and identify any special reasons for particular results (such as one-off costs involved in installing a new computerised accounting system or 'windfall' capital gains on the international money markets). Once the appropriate data has been collected, realistic projections of future performance over the period can be discussed by the senior management in terms of a range of possible scenarios (worst, best and middling cases) produced by specialist staff on the basis of the information obtained.

9. When forecasting trends in the external political, economic, social and technological environment, organisations are likely to focus on the following:

- **Political/legal changes** – here the key emphasis will be on *changes* (e.g. change of government, changes in support for businesses, fiscal actions, privatisation, new laws). Few organisations are immune from the effects of political and legal changes, and some are highly sensitive to them. Since laws have to pass through Parliament, there is always a certain amount of notice before *legal* changes have to be implemented, but government *fiscal* action can occur with very little notice (for instance fuel taxes increased at midnight on the day of announcement) and government attitudes to particular issues (e.g. towards the privatisation of state-owned enterprises) can be rather unpredictable.

- **Economic trends** – trends in national performance (Gross National Product, inflation rates, etc.) are given a wide public airing both by government and by forecasting agencies ranging from Treasury officials to specialist forecasting groups, such as Henley/Cambridge, etc. Industry trends are additionally supplied by trade associations, the CBI, City analysts and other major bodies representing key economic groups. The problem for strategists is not so much a lack of information about the future, but too much information, and too many different interpretations about what it all means!

- **Social trends** – these can be sub-divided into three separate groupings:
  demographic (population changes, i.e. numbers, age-groups, gender balance, racial groups); **life-styles** (women at work, single-parent families, divorce rate, 'nuclear' families replacing extended groups, etc.); **social values** (attitudes towards authority, respect for others, attitudes to work and leisure, etc.). In Britain, there is a massive survey of lifestyles conducted under the aegis of the National Household Survey. This provides a welter of reliable data about population trends and profiles, family situations, expenditure patterns and leisure activities. Information about occupational matters is contained in Employment Department publications, and in a variety of other regular bulletins published by trade associations, recruitment agencies and management bodies. The likelihood is that most social changes will take place over a period of years, as changing values gain ground throughout the population. However, expenditure patterns tend to change much more quickly, depending on the

economic climate (for example when employment is buoyant and people feel secure in their jobs, they are likely to spend more on immediate wants; if employment is difficult to find/retain, people feel insecure about the future, will tend to spend less and, if possible, put spare cash into short-term savings.) When the economy is in recession, the enterprises that suffer least are those whose products (or services) are regarded as well-nigh essential (such as foodstores, water services, basic footwear). Those that suffer most are the purveyors of luxury goods (and services), such as luxury cars and health farms.

10. The area of strategy where forecasting is the most difficult is undoubtedly in the external business environment, where competitors, suppliers, employee groups, shareholders and governments are all jostling for position in their efforts to optimise economic benefits for their constituents, who, in one way or another, are the buyers of those benefits. As if Porter's five forces did not present enough challenge in themselves, here we have a further three forces at least (employee groups, shareholders and governments).

11. Although, in recent times, the influence of trade unions and other employee groups in the UK has diminished, due partly to a shift in economic power from employees to employers, and partly to the removal of protective legislation from trade unions, there are still important pressure on organisations from their employees. It is significant that even in the present recessionary times, the best UK firms are maintaining their staff development and welfare policies. They may well be employing fewer staff than in the previous decade, but they intend to look after those who remain, and clearly want to be seen as 'good employers' by school and university leavers, and other potential employees. Forecasting employee requirements is an activity engaged in by many organisations. Those adopting *systematic* approaches, such as manpower/human resource planning, will employ a range of tried and trusted methods. A typical model of human resource planning (Cole, 1997) can be seen in Figure 5.1.

Figure 5.1 Human resource planning

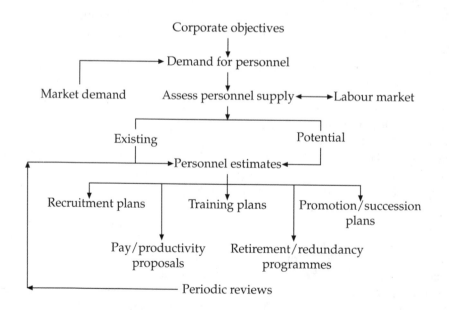

12. Forecasting human resource requirements can only be carried out within the framework of a strategic plan. Otherwise it is impossible to answer such vital questions as 'What new skills do we need to employ?', 'Have we sufficient personnel to carry through the changes planned for production?', 'Who should we recruit for our (e.g.) European operation – French/German-speaking managers from Britain or local managers?', 'How best can we prepare our own managers to move from specialist roles to general management roles?'. Thus, like any other major function in the organisation, the personnel function has to be planned against the background of the overall plan for the company, or strategic business unit.

13. The impact of *shareholders* on the future of a company is most likely to be felt in terms of:

    ❶ their continuing support for the company's shares (for example by retaining their shares rather than selling them to a hostile bidder; by subscribing to new issues)

    ❷ their support at the Annual General Meetings for changes proposed by the directors

    ❸ their willingness at AGMs to question or criticise the directors (for example by questioning pay-offs to directors who have been sacked; criticising directors' handling of the pension fund).

    The forecasting issues involved here include projections about growth in the value of shares, likely earnings per share, need for new rights issues, proportion of equity to be allocated to debentures rather than shares. Forecasts are likely to rest heavily on the advice of City analysts, advisers and the firm's accountants, and will reflect predicted conditions in the *industry* as well as the firm's individual performance.

14. Industry conditions, especially the activities of competitors, can precipitate marketing decisions that may have an adverse effect on shareholders' opinion, as the recent example of *The Daily Telegraph* illustrates. In this case, as a result of price-cutting by one of its main competitors (*The Times*), the *Telegraph* management saw its daily sales drop gradually over a six month period, until in April/May 1994 they fell below one million copies for the first time in 40 years. When the *Telegraph* responded by matching *The Times'* cover price, the effect on the stock market was devastating – the *Telegraph's* shares fell by 191 pence over the next 24 hours, wiping more than £250 million from the company's market value – a heavy price to pay for engaging in a price war with a competitor. As a result many investors lost heavily, and the company's ability to regain its share price is extremely doubtful. Also, it is likely to be difficult for the company to raise funds from a rights issue in the future. This is a clear example of shareholders making their views felt about a major strategic decision.

15. The equivalent of shareholders for many charitable and not-for-profit organisations (e.g. National Trust, Institute of Management, etc.) is the membership. In a recent proposal to merge two professional management bodies (the Institute of Personnel Management and the Institute of Training and Development) the members of both bodies were not only consulted by the leadership but were asked to vote on the proposal. In this situation the members (shareholders) had the power to reject the directors' proposal, which on this occasion they did not, although they had done so in previous years when the conditions of the merger were not thought satisfactory to the membership.

16. Government policy towards business and enterprise can be very unpredictable for commercial organisations. In the UK, Conservative governments generally encourage private enterprise and the free market economy, whilst discouraging public ownership

and restrictions on trade. Nevertheless, they cannot escape entirely the demands of the voters for public health, education and certain local services, nor can they ignore the need to sustain certain infrastructure developments, such as road-building programmes and energy provision. Thus, there are always some interventions in the public dimension of the economy under a Conservative government, but no guarantee of support for the business sector. In contrast to this approach, Labour (Socialist) governments tend to favour a greater share of public ownership and investment in the economy, and are more likely to intervene in matters such as labour relations, economic development grants, transport provision and consumer protection as well as in health and education. Increasingly, however, all member governments of the EU are accepting a greater intervention of the European body in national government. Many large business corporations now employ Members of Parliament as 'advisers', and some offer directorships to former members of the Cabinet, in order to ensure that they are kept informed about, or can influence, government policy. Such a practice is even more widespread amongst charities, where the presence of MPs and Members of the House of Lords on the governing bodies has been almost obligatory. In these cases the politicians concerned are usually serving in a voluntary capacity, but they can bring useful experience of top-level negotiating to bear on the affairs of charitable organisations.

Strategic forecasting techniques

17. In contrast to forecasting at an operational level, where the focus is on the next few months to a year, and a considerable degree of exactness is expected, the need at a strategic level is for reasonable prediction of trends in the medium and long term, often on the basis of a rolling three or five year plan. What are the principal means of forecasting for strategic purposes? As in other contexts, forecasting techniques can be considered under two main headings:

   • **Quantitative** (i.e. where projections are based on numerical data, such as statistics and accounting data, often analysed by computer-based models); this approach uses so-called 'hard' data.

   • **Qualitative** (i.e. basing projections on explicit assumptions and individual judgments about them); this is a so-called 'soft' approach to forecasting.

18. Examples of the two types of techniques are shown in Figure 5.2. Some of the techniques mentioned in Figure 5.2 have already been described in earlier chapters (e.g. BPEST and SWOT analysis). The others will be briefly outlined below, and assessed in relation to strategic management purposes.

19. **Budget forecasts,** as such, are well-known to middle and senior managers. They are used to the yearly round of budget planning, in which they attempt to quantify their targets for the coming year, qualify their costs and justify the resources they want. Since the annual budgeting process devotes more attention to costs than to other aspects of operations, it is not the best mechanism for dealing with longer-range predictions across the whole of the organisation's business activities. It is only useful if several years of such forecasts are reviewed so that trends in key items can be identified (e.g. sales volume, turnover, and profit as well as various costs such as labour, raw materials, overheads, etc.). Any trends that are identified can then be considered *in conjunction with other evidence* collected by senior management and their strategic advisers. This is an important qualification, because budget trends on their own can be misleading, since

much depends on the assumptions on which they were established in the first place. Since strategic management is essentially about *challenging* existing assumptions, the results of earlier budgets have to be seen in context. There is no automatic reason why a budget trend should be projected into the planning future merely on the basis of past history – so much will depend on what senior management want to achieve over the next 3, 5 or even 10 years, and how they evaluate the impact of *external* forces, in particular.

Figure 5.2 Forecasting for strategic management

Quantitative techniques	Qualitative approaches
1 Budget forecasts 2 Simple projections 3 Key ratio analysis 4 PIMS analysis 5 Computer modelling (incl. econometrics)	1 BPEST analysis 2 SWOT analysis 3 Scenario development 4 Delphi technique 5 Brainstorming
Outcomes: demonstrates **what, and how much,** can be achieved given certain data	**Outcomes**: scenarios and other background information leading to judgements about possible alternatives
Overall approach: deterministic/rational	**Overall approach**: intuitive/judgemental

20. **Simple projections,** in this context, are straightforward projections of anticipated performance of specific aspects of company operations, such as sales turnover and trading profit. Such projections are made on the basis of past performance and assume that no major changes will occur in the external environment and no changes in company strategy. The use of such projections for strategic planning can be enhanced by incorporating best and worst case projections for future years based on certain assumptions. For example, (i) if there is a steady growth in key export markets, then a best case figure can be aimed for; (ii) if there is a downturn in the domestic economy, then the worst case figure can be targeted. Each of the two assumptions themselves have to be tested against evidence from elsewhere. The task of management in pursuit of *strategic* intentions has to be to question and challenge every assumption. Nothing ought to be taken for granted at this stage.

21. **Key ratio analysis** refers to the analysis of selected management and financial ratios for the purposes of identifying trends in key performance areas. In essence a ratio signifies a quantifiable relationship, often expressed as a percentage, between key aspects of an company's activities. Walsh (1993), refers to ratios as '*the guiding stars*' of management, and makes the important observation that 'the financial numbers are only a reflection of what is actually happening and that it is the reality not the ratios that must be managed.' The most important ratios, from the point of view of strategic management, are those highlighting the relationship between certain *financial* outcomes, which have a major impact on assets, profits and growth. Such ratios are also used by analysts to make inter-firm comparisons (see also PIMS paragraph 24).

22. The most important source documents for the ratios which follow are (a) the organisation's Balance Sheet, which shows its overall assets at a particular point in time, and (b)
the annual Profit and Loss Account, which shows income and expenditure over the
period of the preceding year. The main features of each are as follows:

❶ **The Balance Sheet**. This is comprised of the following:

Current assets (inventories, trade debtors, cash)

Fixed assets (tangibles – land, equipment etc, long-term investments)

Liabilities (**Ordinary funds** – shares, reserves; **Current liabilities** – creditors, short-
term loans; **Long-term loans** – mortgages, debentures, etc.)

❷ **The Profit and Loss Account**. Typically this comprises details of:

Operating income

Cost of sales

Gross profit

Administration and other costs

Trading profit

Interest received

Profit

Taxation

Dividends

Retained profit

23. The most important ratios to feature in strategic discussions will include most, if not all,
of the following:

❶ **Return on Investment (ROI)** – this is the universal concept for assessing the viability
of a business. The way in which it is measured varies, but two useful measures are
ROTA (Return on Total Assets) and ROE/ROSC (Return on Equity/Return on
Shareholders' Capital). These can be summarised as follows:

a) **Return on Total Assets** $= \dfrac{\text{Profit } before \text{ interest and tax}}{\text{Total assets}} \times 100\%$

ROTA measures the rate of return (before tax and interest) earned by the total
assets of a company, and is a useful indication of the efficiency of use of those
assets, because it is based on the three main operating variables – total revenue,
total costs and assets employed. Firms are usually looking for an average return
of about 15%, and anything over 18% would be regarded as very satisfactory.

b) **Return on Equity/Return on Shareholders' Capital** $= \dfrac{\text{Profit } after \text{ tax}}{\text{Net worth}} \times 100\%$

This is probably the most widely-used ratio in business finance. It measures the
absolute return to the shareholders for their investment. Net worth comprises
the Ordinary Fund (ordinary shares, capital reserves and revenue reserves). It
can also be measured by subtracting total liabilities from total assets. A large
company is likely to look for a return of some 30%, a small company might
expect about 18%, and any company earning a return of less than 10% is in

danger of failure. A healthy **ROE/ROSC** leads to a high share price and is likely to attract new funds, which in turn provide opportunities for further growth and profit increases.

❷ Return on Capital Employed $= \dfrac{\text{Profit } before \text{ tax}}{\text{Capital Employed}} \times 100\%$

This measures the return from the Capital Employed in the business by taking pre-tax profits as a percentage of the combined capital of the Ordinary Fund (share-holders' capital) plus Long-term Loans. **ROCE** indicates the efficiency of the use of the long-term funds available to the business. (See example in Case-study 6.)

❸ Profit margin/Margin on Sales $= \dfrac{\text{Profit } before \text{ Interest and Tax}}{\text{Sales}} \times 100\%$

This is often called the net profit margin. A profitable company would be looking for a return something in excess of 10%. If the margin on sales is multiplied by the value of Sales divided by Total Assets, the result figure produces the Return on Total Assets referred to in (1) above.

❹ Current ratio $= \dfrac{\text{Current Assets}}{\text{Current Liabilities}}$

This ratio simply compares Current Assets with Current Liabilities, and is a favourite with banks. A result of at least 1.0 would be looked for, but most compa-nies would expect a ratio of about 1.3 times.

❺ Gearing ratio (Leverage) $= \dfrac{\text{Short \& Long-Term Debts}}{\text{Capital Employed}}$

This refers to the extent to which a business is relying on external sources of funds. A business which is highly geared is operating on a high proportion of external borrowing. The term 'leverage' is used in the United States. (See examples in Case-studies 7 and 11.)

❻ Quick ratio/Acid test $= \dfrac{\text{Current Assets} - \text{Inventories (stocks)}}{\text{Current Liabilities}}$

This is a short-term liquidity ratio. Only a strongly-performing business will produce a figure of 1.0; the majority will end up with a figure of less than 1.0 times.

❼ Earnings per share $= \dfrac{\text{Profit after Tax}}{\text{No. of Ordinary shares issued}}$

This is one of the most widely sought features of company performance (expressed in pence), and the year on year changes for any one business are important indica-tors of how well it is doing. The EpS is not helpful for inter-firm comparisons because the number and denomination of shares varies between companies, and it is thus difficult to compare like with like. (See examples in Case-study 2.)

8 **Price/earnings ratio** = $\dfrac{\text{Market price per share}}{\text{Earnings per share}}$

This ratio is dictated not by the firm's performance directly, but by the market's view of the attractiveness of the business. That is to say it is *investors* who determine the price-earnings ratio. If, for example, a business has a market price per share of 250 pence and is earning 20 pence per share, it has a P/E ratio of 12.5.

9 **Market to Book Ratio** = $\dfrac{\text{Market capitalisation}}{\text{Total Ordinary Funds}}$

This ratio, according to Walsh (1993) 'Gives the final and, perhaps, the most thorough assessment by the stock market of a company's overall status'. This ratio is one of the six key financial parameters of 'excellence' used by Peters and Waterman (1982). It is derived from the worth of the company's shares in terms of their current market price per share multiplied by the total number of shares, which give the market capitalisation. This sum is then divided by the total ordinary funds (ordinary shares plus capital and revenue reserves) to give a ratio of around 1.0 times – greater if the company is valued highly by the investing public, or less if it perceived as unsatisfactory.

10 **Administration effectiveness** = $\dfrac{\text{Cost of administration}}{\text{Sales}} \times 100\%$

This is one of a number of managerial ratios which some organisations employ to test their efficiency in different aspects of their operations (e.g. administration costs, labour costs, etc.). This example takes administration costs as a percentage of sales, and is likely to be helpful to senior management when analysing trends in administration costs over a period of years.

24. The **PIMS** programme (Profit Impact on Market Strategy) started life as a corporate appraisal technique in the American General Electric Company in the late 1960s/early 1970s and has developed since then into major research and evaluation programme based at Harvard University. A sizeable database of details of some 3000 businesses, of whom about two-thirds are American, has been built up and is quarried by researchers investigating links between strategy and performance/strategy and profit/market share and key ratios and so forth. It is mentioned here because of its concerns with *future* performance (chiefly described in terms of Return on Investment and Return on Sales (see above), and its assumption that studying the *past* can provide clues to the future. However, its main position in this book is in the chapter on reviewing strategy (Chapter 15).

25. **Computer modelling/econometrics**: Econometrics is the study of economic variables and their various inter-relationships using computer modelling to ask 'What if …?' type questions. Many organisations will not carry out such work themselves but buy in the results obtained by specialist consultancies/analysts. These studies can be useful when trying to determine the future economic environment of an organisation. They are more accurate when forecasting medium rather than long-term outcomes. Computer modelling is used extensively in other forms of planning, especially in the design, control and

review of large-scale projects. These situations are usually operational in nature rather than strategic.

26. The forecasting techniques described so far have all relied heavily on quantitative approaches. This chapter draws to a close by outlining the qualitative approaches that have not already been described (i.e. BPEST and SWOT analyses). These remaining techniques are Scenario development, Delphi and Brainstorming, which can be summarised as follows:

Scenario development: This involves taking a set of important variables (e.g. introduction of a new product-range, estimated level of sales, possible reactions of competitors) and arriving at an agreed likely outcome. Around this desired outcome two other sets of conditions and outcomes will be constructed – one a pessimistic view, and the other an optimistic one. The pessimistic scenario may infer tougher competition, weaker take-up by the customers and so on; the optimistic view may point to a relatively 'greenfield' market, with no immediate active competition, and may show an enthusiastic take-up by customers. The three alternative scenarios together with their supporting evidence are discussed by the senior management with a view to arriving at the best assessment of the future, and thus the basis for a key strategic marketing decision.

Delphi technique: This is a method of forecasting which uses a panel of experts (both from within and external to the organisation) to examine particular issues, in which the individual members comment on them independently of the others involved. The panel then discusses the individual results, rejects some and recycles others as commented on for a further independent assessment by each member. Eventually a synthesised forecast emerges which is put before the senior management strategists for inclusion in their selection of key decisions for the future.

Brainstorming: This technique is widely used as a method of generating ideas, but can be applied to forecasting. The process involves a selected group of employees, in this case managers, who are presented with a problem or issue (such as the likely impact of new technology on company distribution methods) and asked to generate as many ideas or comments about it in a given period of time. It is an important feature of brainstorming that no ideas or comments are rejected, or even judged in any way, during the meeting. Once a list of ideas or comments has been drawn up, then the group itself, or a senior sub-group, will go through them systematically rejecting, qualifying or accepting each point.

27. Once the various forecasting techniques have been applied to future outcomes, there is likely to be a gap between what the organisation wants to achieve (e.g. in terms of Return on Sales) and what is projected by forecasts based on *current* performance. Gap analysis attempts to identify the nature of the problem and suggest ways in which strategy can be changed in order to close the gap.

Gap analysis

28. The essential performance gap that business enterprises need to spotlight is the gap between the results they have set for themselves and the results that are forecast if existing strategy is continued. In an ideal world, where there were no changes in either external conditions or internal performance capacity, there would be no gap. As indicated in Figure 5.3, the forecast outcomes over the next five years will follow the pattern of the past to produce a straight-line progression in profits as a percentage of sales.

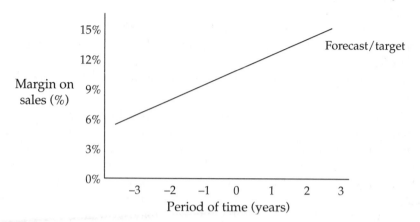

Figure 5.3 Margin on sales forecast in conditions of stability

29. A much more likely situation is where there have been changes in the *external* environment (for example, increased competition, improvements in computer-based technology, take-overs in supplier firms). This scenario is likely to produce a forecast that pitches the return on sales at a much lower percentage than the original target. By clarifying the situation graphically, the enterprise's management can see the size of the gap and the trend indicated by it (see Figure 5.4).

Figure 5.4 Margin on sales forecast in changing external conditions

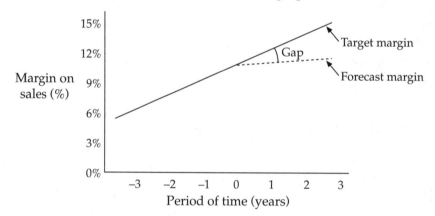

30. An analysis of the performance gap can produce a number of conclusions:

   ❶ The original targets may have been over-optimistic.

   ❷ Past performance may have benefited from lack of competition.

   ❸ Costs of supplies may have been increasing slowly but significantly.

   ❹ Existing strategy is no longer viable in the face of changing conditions.

Performance gaps need to be identified for all the key areas of business performance. Typically these are: sales targets, profit margins, revenue targets, cost targets, market share and earnings per share. Whatever the reasons for the gaps that emerge, the result is a challenge for strategic management – to devise and implement a successful new strategy designed, among other reasons, to bring targets and forecasts together. The central problem of formulating strategy forms the subject of the next chapter.

References

1. Porter, M.E. (1980), *Competitive Strategy*, The Free Press.
2. Peters, T. (1988), *Thriving on Chaos*, Macmillan.
3. Cole, G.A. (1997), *Personnel Management: Theory & Practice*, (4th edn.) Letts Educational.
4. Walsh, C. (1993), *Key Management Ratios*, Pitman Publishing.
5. Buzzell, R.D. & Gale, B.T. (1987), *The PIMS Principles – Linking Strategy to Performance*, The Free Press.

Questions for reflection/discussion

1. Given that forecasting is concerned with predicting a future which by definition is uncertain, how much emphasis should an organisation's senior management place on its findings?

2. On what key aspects of performance are the following organisations likely to focus their forecasting activities:

   ❶ A manufacturer of washing machines and similar goods?

   ❷ A life assurance company?

   ❸ A major national charity?

   ❹ A further education college?

3. Which forecasting techniques would you expect the above four organisations to employ, and why?

4. What is the role of the following in the forecasting process:

   ❶ Balance Sheets?

   ❷ Profit and Loss (Revenue & Expenditure) Accounts?

5. Which key ratios are likely to be investigated in a forecasting exercise for:

   ❶ a young, innovatory company in the healthcare equipment field?

   ❷ an established grocery retail chain?

   ❸ a distributor of luxury motor–cars?

6 Formulating a strategy

Introduction

1. This chapter looks at how organisations of different kinds establish the pattern of decisions, or strategy, that is aimed at achieving the goals and aims they have set for themselves. Previous chapters have examined the processes that senior managers set in train in deciding mission statements, setting key goals and aims, assessing their internal strengths and weaknesses, taking stock of the external environment (especially in relation to the competition), and attempting to forecast likely future developments. Those previous activities are aimed at answering such questions as 'What do we want to achieve in this organisation?', 'What is happening in and around our organisation now?' and 'What things are likely to change in the near future?'. Now we come to the two more vital questions: 'So, what do we want to do in the light of what we have discovered?' and 'What steps must we take to build on the preparatory work we have just completed?' It is time for decision-making, time to make choices between alternative ways forward and time to focus the organisation's priorities.

2. Strategy formulation can take place at more than one level in an organisation, depending on its size and shape. A large, divisionalised company, or a diversified company, for example, would have to plan strategy on at least two, and possibly three, levels. These would be (a) **corporate** level (i.e. covering the whole business network, or group of businesses), (b) **business unit** level (i.e. covering the principal, or strategic, business units which make up the organisation), and (c) **functional** level (the basic operating level, which may be product/service-based, geographic or specialist). A company organised on unitary lines would normally formulate strategy at the corporate and business unit levels, where the latter would encompass profit and/or major cost centres within the business. Only a small or medium-sized business is likely to be able to rely solely on a corporate level approach. This chapter is concerned mainly with the corporate and strategic business unit levels, since at the functional, or operational, level the issues are more about strategy implementation in the short-term than long-term strategy formulation.

3. The period covered by a corporate strategy may range from 3 to 5 years, although some organisations may employ a much longer time-span (e.g. in electricity generation and pharmaceutical development). Many organisations review their strategy regularly, especially at business unit level, rolling it forward from one year to the next with appropriate changes of emphasis and direction, as necessary. This chapter locates strategy formulation (i.e. making strategic choices) in the overall strategic planning process, summarises some leading examples of strategic alternatives, and discusses some of the theorists' views about strategic choices.

Strategic choices – the key alternatives

4. A basic model indicating the place of strategic choice in the overall process of strategic management is shown at Figure 6.1. This suggests that choices are made in the light of the organisation's goals and aims, and the evaluation of its internal and external environments. The chosen strategies are intended to meet the principal goals and aims of the organisation in terms of direct stakeholder satisfaction. Direct stakeholders, as was noted in Chapter 1) are those who have a prime stake in the organisation's results

(such as customers, shareholders, suppliers). The fact that some strategic choices are aimed at deflecting the competition (indirect stakeholders) is implied in the results to be achieved for direct stakeholders, but is not stated expressly here. The extent to which goals are attained provides feedback for the organisation's senior management, and may lead to appropriate redefinition of goals and aims, and then on to a repetition of the whole process. The manner in which organisations manage this process will vary. Some will be highly organised and rational in their approach; others will manage the process of making strategic choices rather more intuitively; and some will just be swept along by it, reacting to changing circumstances by the 'seat of their pants'. The intention in this chapter is to examine the process mainly from a rational perspective, but with some intuitive elements. Completely intuitive or tacit approaches are not easily identifiable and are therefore not included.

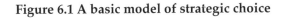

Figure 6.1 A basic model of strategic choice

5. Models of any kind are a *representation* of what is happening in reality. They do not tell the whole truth, but are a useful guide to it. In focusing on strategic choices – on the grand plan itself – we are looking at how an organisation proposes to move itself forward over the next few years. In reality the truth is usually less tidy than representations suggest, and it will be noticed that, in some of the examples discussed later, there is often a confusion between goals/aims and strategies. For example, some business enterprises consider gaining market share to be a strategy, whereas it is more accurate to consider it as a goal or aim. Typical goals/aims for a business enterprise include: profitability (expressed as Return on Investment, etc.), growth (such as in sales, assets, earnings per share, etc.), market share (percentage), market leadership), and provision of value for customers. Public sector organisations are likely to include such aims as: provide efficient service to the public (reduced waiting times, number of clients handled, etc.), and provide an optimum service within budget. Such aims indicate what these organisations want. Strategic choice (that is, deciding the strategy itself) is how they translate wants into desired outcomes.

6. Peters (1987), in typically emphatic manner, asks 'What is a good strategic plan? There is none. But there is a good strategic planning process'. In his view 'good' means fresh, succinct, open to debate by all and where the emphasis is on developing strategic skills (e.g. proactivity, imaginative risk-taking). He is careful to point out, however, that financial and growth targets should be set at a conservative level, and that there must be an adequate support infrastructure (distribution, after-sales service, employee skills and so on).

7. What are the principal strategic options open to business organisations? They include the following:

❶ Consolidation (i.e. following previous strategy)

❷ Market penetration (a similar approach, i.e. build on current position)

❸ Market development (i.e. seeking new markets)

❹ Product/service development (i.e. develop new products/services)

❺ Diversification (i.e. branching out with new products/services in new markets)

❻ Price leadership (i.e. offering the keenest prices in the market)

❼ Differentiation (i.e. developing a product or service that is seen as unique in the industry)

❽ Niche strategy (i.e. developing a distinctive marketing mix aimed at a specialist market)

❾ Growth via acquisitions and/or joint ventures

❿ Divestment (i.e. selling off part of the business/subsidiaries, etc.)

⓫ Withdrawal (i.e. selling up entirely/closing down/liquidation).

The object of these strategies (apart from withdrawal) is twofold – *firstly*, to ensure the general health and survival of the business, and *secondly*, to attain increased growth and prosperity.

8. A business enterprise can develop strategies in all of its main functional areas. For our immediate purposes, however, we will just concentrate on four areas – *product* strategies, *market* strategies, *financial* strategies and *'general'* strategies (a mixture of personnel and others). The examples given below may be based on present strategies, but more often will represent new strategies. Many businesses aim to proceed with a clutch of different strategies under each heading, and try to ensure that their overall approach is both consistent and feasible. They are likely to choose between two or more alternatives under each category:

Product strategies:
(We intend to:)

❶ maintain existing products

❷ develop a range of new products

❸ focus on product quality and value-for-money

❹ continuously improve product performance

❺ deliberately build in obsolescence/short shelf-life into our products

❻ employ the latest technology in production and distribution processes

❼ systematically reduce unit costs across our product-range

❽ rigorously drop unprofitable/badly-received products from our range

❾ maintain inventories at lowest possible levels.

Market strategies
(We intend to:)

❶ concentrate on current markets

❷ seek to develop new markets at home and overseas

❸ concentrate on identifying and supplying specialist market segments (niches)

❹ maintain existing brands

⑤ develop new brands (or a range of own-branded goods)

⑥ continuously strive for a price advantage over our competitors

⑦ concentrate on providing value for our customers

⑧ increase the proportion of our marketing expenditure allocated to advertising

⑨ constantly promote the company's reputation for quality/reliability, etc.

Financial strategies
(We intend to:)

❶ increase our level of borrowing (gearing) to fund new developments

❷ seek further share issues on the UK stock market

❸ maintain our present level of dividends to shareholders

❹ reduce the extent of debtors' liabilities

❺ increase the proportion of retained profits

❻ maintain tight budgetary control over expenditure

❼ acquire suitable companies and/or negotiate joint ventures to achieve desired market position.

General strategies
(We intend to:)

❶ retain and develop a skilled core of personnel

❷ buy in temporary and/or casual staff when required

❸ provide continuous training and updating of managerial staff

❹ encourage share participation amongst all core employees

❺ constantly update mechanisms for facilitating strategic change and developing learning throughout the organisation

❻ always present the organisation as honest, fair-minded and conscious of its obligations to society at large.

9. Each of the principal strategies can be seen as a choice between a range of further options between two strong polar positions. Most business enterprises opt for one polar position or the other, but some adopt half-way positions, which Porter (1985) calls *'being stuck in the middle'*, which he personally views as an unsatisfactory situation. The portfolio, or selection, of options made by a firm may not always be consistent, and Rosabeth Moss Kanter (1989) points out that tension may exist between different strategies and this is a cause of problems for firms.

'Corporations, too, face escalating and seemingly incompatible demands:

- Get 'lean and mean' through restructuring – while being a great company to work for …

- Encourage creativity and innovation … 'and stick to your knitting'.

- Communicate a sense of urgency and push for faster execution … but take more time to deliberately plan for the future.

- Decentralise to delegate profit and planning responsibilities to … autonomous business units. But centralise to capture efficiencies and combine resources …'

Some of these tensions will undoubtedly be present in the list of principal strategies and their polar extremes which are summarised as follows in Figure 6.2:

Figure 6.2 A range of strategic options

Generic choices

1. Match competition at every point (e.g. via differentiation/costs) ←——→ Ignore the competition

2. Adopt risk-taking strategy ←——→ Adopt no-risk strategy

3. Continuous responsiveness to market (customers) ←——→ Unresponsive to market

4. Grow from within (organic) ←——→ Grow through acquisition

5. Maintain strong ethos ←——→ Accept vaguely felt organisational ethos

6. Develop business internationally ←——→ Develop locally/nationally

7. Encourage pervasive use of new technology ←——→ Adopt cautious view of new technology

8. Maintain centralised control ←——→ Decentralise control of business or group

Product-market choices

1. Specialised range of products/services ←——→ Broad range of products/services

2. Market leadership ←——→ Market follower

3. Enter new markets ←——→ Stay in present markets

4. Maintain market orientation ←——→ Maintain product orientation

5. Adopt competitive pricing ←——→ Adopt independent pricing

6. Emphasise high quality product/service ←——→ Sustain adequate quality

7. Set supplier standards ←——→ Accept suppliers' standards

8. Proactive use of technology ←——→ Reactive use of technology

Financial/organisational choices

1. Adopt cost leadership strategy ←——→ Accept average costs

2. Emphasise investment in the business/operations ←——→ Accept minimum investment demands

3. Develop in-house support services ←——→ Buy in support services

4. Develop and train own staff ←——→ Buy in staff as required

5. Maintain current structure ←——→ Restructure organisation

Strategic choice in practice

10. In practice, companies tend to select just a few items from the alternatives referred to in Figure 6.2. These items represent the cornerstone of their strategy. The following examples are taken from recent public statements of three well-known UK companies – British Telecommunications plc (high-technology communications), Unilever PLC (retail conglomerate), and the John Lewis Partnership plc (high street retailer).

- **British Telecommunications plc:**

    'As far as our strategy is concerned, we can look at it in two parts: defensive in the home market and attacking internationally ... We compete effectively at home ... by:

    – offering new products and advanced network services ...

    – encouraging greater use of our network by innovative marketing and pricing ...

    – controlling our costs ...

    – improving the quality and value for money of the products and services we offer ... we intend to lead in our chosen markets.'

    (Report to Shareholders, February, 1994)

- **Unilever PLC:**

    'Unilever's strength has always been built on a substantial investment in brands. It is a cardinal principle that in boom or recession investment in underlying research, in product innovation and in marketing support will be consistent ... Brand equities are the most valuable assets in our stewardship. They are the foundation of past success and the key to future prosperity ...'

    (Annual Review, 1993)

- **John Lewis Partnership plc:**

    This retail business dates back to the 1860s, when John Lewis bought his first store in London's Oxford Street. From its earliest days the firm adopted certain basic principles – complete honesty in trading, good value for customers, and a wide assortment of stock. Later (1920s) were added 'the clear identification of the market', and 'the consistent, steady unflurried application of trading policy to that market', together with the introduction of profit-sharing amongst the 'partnership' (i.e. employees as well as owners). Another innovation at the time (late 1920s/early 1930s) was the policy of *'Never knowingly undersold'*. This was originally (and still is) a discipline on the buyers to purchase good value at a keen price, but was extended to include an open offer to customers that they could obtain a refund of the difference if able to buy the same goods at a lower price elsewhere. It is a salutary reminder to present-day readers to know that strategic management did not begin in the Business Schools of the Western world, but has been at the heart of many a successful business for a hundred years or more! Of course, the fact that certain strategies worked 50 or 100 years ago does not necessarily mean that they are still viable today, but neither does it mean that they should be ignored in our post-industrial, high technology society.

Theoretical models of strategy

11. There have been several theoretical models of strategic choice proposed by academics and consultants, of which the most widely-quoted are the following:
    ❶ Ansoff's product-market strategies
    ❷ Porter's generic strategies
    ❸ The Boston Consulting Group's portfolio framework.

    More recently (1991) the work of Mintzberg has also contributed to the debate about making strategic choices. These, and other contributions, will be summarised in the following paragraphs.

12. Igor Ansoff (1965), in a seminal text on corporate strategy, saw strategy as being a rule for making decisions. He took the view that strategy is about means not ends. Thus strategic decisions are a means by which organisations attempt to meet their (strategic) objectives. Although Ansoff is quite clear about the interrelationship between strategy and objectives, he believes it is important to keep them separate (see discussion of this point in Chapter 1). Strategic decisions, according to Ansoff, are to be distinguished from administrative (structural) decisions and operating decisions (tactical). The first group focus on product-market decisions, the second focus on organisational and infrastructure decisions, and the third on budgeting, scheduling and controlling decisions. The product-market decisions lead to a matrix of four generic strategies, which have become extremely well-known (Figure 6.3). In his original matrix, Ansoff uses the two parameters of Product – Mission and Present – New to produce four generic strategies. In effect Mission refers to the Market, and this is how the matrix in its basic form is described here. The option referred to as Diversification is further expanded by Ansoff, and will be described shortly.

13. The basic matrix adapted from Ansoff's original is as follows in Figure 6.3:

Figure 6.3 Product-market growth strategies
(adapted from Ansoff, 1965)

	Present products	New products
Present markets	Market penetration	Product development
New markets	Market development	Diversification

The model indicates four principal product-market strategies, which can be summarised as follows:

❶ **Market penetration**, i.e. where the business aims to focus its activities on increasing its market share by exploiting its present product range in its present markets. (An example of market penetration in a niche market is described in Case-study 12.) This strategy can be called a **Consolidation** strategy, where the *maintenance* of market share rather than *growth* is sought; a consolidation strategy is more likely to adopt defensive measures compared with a penetration strategy. (Case-study 2 is an example of a consolidation strategy.)

② **Market development**, i.e. taking present products into fresh markets, and thus focusing activities on market opportunities and competitor situations. An example is BMW's treatment of the Rover Group (See Case-study 3).

③ **Product development,** i.e. introducing new products into existing markets, and thus focusing on developing, launching and supporting additions to the product range. (See example of Marks & Spencer plc described in Case-study 1.)

④ **Diversification**, i.e. branching out both into new products and new markets. This strategy can be further sub-divided into horizontal diversification, vertical integration, concentric diversification and conglomerate diversification.

14. Diversification strategies are aimed at extending the core business of the enterprise. They achieve this in the following ways:

- **Horizontal diversification** – this occurs when an enterprise takes over a business of the same type and with a related technology, for example, where a road haulage company buys out another in order to expand its operations in its core business. The take-over of Rover Group by BMW is relevant here, since one of the major attractions of Rover was the Land Rover/Range Rover range of off-road models which BMW did not have (See Case-study 3).

- **Vertical integration** – in practice this refers to the take-over of either a supplier firm or a distributor firm, and is sometimes called a chain integration. When some UK building societies decided to buy out estate agent chains as a means of expanding their business, they were engaging in vertical diversification. Such a step is not always successful, and some of the estate agents who were acquired at that time have been divested (i.e. sold off!) at a considerable loss to the original purchasers.

- **Concentric diversification** – this occurs when an enterprise takes over another of a similar type with strong connections to one or other of its features. It is arguable as to whether this is truly a form of diversification.

- **Conglomerate diversification** – this is where an enterprise takes over another in a completely new product-market situation. Most conglomerate organisations (e.g. BAT, LONRHO and Hanson Industries) have developed by making a number of such additions to their original business. Hanson, for example, at one time contained the following kinds of business operations in the UK and USA – coal mining, industrial chemicals, health products, tobacco products, propane gas distribution, house-building, aggregates and roadbuilding products and jacuzzis. In its Annual Report for 1993, the group announced that it had taken over a large US chemical corporation

    '... in line with our policy to build up our existing major businesses, while continuing to seek acquisitions as opportunities arise in new industries and new geographical areas. Other 'bolt on' purchases during the year and recently announced disposals, underscore the ever evolving nature of your company.'

    This sort of statement typifies the broad-based approach of a conglomerate organisation.

15. The flip side of diversification is **divestment**, where elements of the business are disposed of. Sometimes a business group will buy up a company whose operations

eventually turn out to be incompatible with other businesses in the group, or whose performance is disappointing in some major respect. In such cases, the holding company management will decide to offload the acquisition. There are also cases where a conglomerate business buys up one of its lesser competitors merely in order to rid itself of the nuisance value. This leads to 'asset stripping', where the conglomerate body absorbs the key assets of the business into other subsidiaries, and then closes down the new acquisition. The Hanson Group (See Case-study 7) has recently divested major parts of its business.

16. A somewhat different approach to generic strategies is that proposed by Porter (1980 & 1985). In examining strategy from the point of view of what he terms 'sustainable competitive advantage', he propose three principal strategies – **overall cost leadership, differentiation** and **focus**. Like Ansoff, Porter employs a four- quadrant model, in this case using the parameters of Competitive advantage (i.e. lower cost or differentiation) and Competitive scope (i.e. broad or narrow target) as shown in Figure 6.4.

Figure 6.4 Porter's three generic strategies (1985)

Competitive advantage

		Lower cost	Differentiation
Competitive scope	Broad target	1. Cost leadership	2. Differentiation
	Narrow target	3A. Cost focus	3B. Differentiation focus

17. In Porter's view:

> 'The notion underlying the concept of generic strategies is that competitive advantage is at the heart of any strategy, and achieving competitive advantage requires a firm to make a choice ...'.

He suggests that the clearest of the three strategies is *cost leadership*, where a firm sets out to become *the* low-cost producer in its industry. Of course, to be profitable as well as to be cost-effective firms must offer customers product quality and features comparable with their competitors, as well as commanding prices about the average for the industry. The second strategy is *differentiation*, which means finding one or more unique attributes for which customers are prepared to pay a premium price, and positioning the firm to provide those attributes. This differentiation can be based on the product itself, on its delivery system or on the way it is marketed. According to Porter, a firm that can achieve, and sustain, differentiation will be an above-average performer in its industry, so long as its price premium exceeds the extra costs incurred in providing the unique features. The third strategy is *focus*. Basically this means choosing a market segment (or group of segments) with a view to attaining a competitive advantage in meeting the wants of that segment (or group). A focus strategy can be broken down into two sub-strategies, one focusing on obtaining a cost advantage, and the other based on developing a differentiation advantage. If a firm can achieve sustainable cost leadership or differentiation in its segment, and if the segment is structurally attractive, then it will become an above-average performer in its industry. Being structurally attractive means there is a reasonable balance of power between the five forces of rivals, potential entrants, buyers, suppliers and substitutes.

18. According to Porter, any firm that fails to achieve one or other of the above strategies will not obtain a competitive advantage – it will be *'stuck in the middle'*. He suggests that firms reach this predicament because they have been unwilling to make choices about how to compete. Even when they do make choices, there are still risks attached to each. For example, among the risks of cost leadership are that competitors will imitate, technology will change and it becomes difficult to sustain comparable differentiation with competitors. The risks of differentiation include imitation by competitors and the prospect that differential features become less important to customers. Also by maintaining differentiation, costs may increase proportionately faster than competitors' costs. The risks of a focus strategy include a fall-off in demand for the product in the chosen segment and an invasion of the segment by broadly-targeted competitors.

19. Mintzberg (1991) examines both Ansoff's and Porter's models of strategic choice and suggests an alternative view of generic strategies. Mintzberg sees such strategies as being divided into five groupings, which can be summarised on the basis of what might be considered the core strategic issues as follows:

❶ **Locating the core business in its network** – this includes assessing where the business lies in the production 'stream' (i.e. upstream, midstream or downstream). An upstream business is one that functions close to its raw materials (e.g. plastics, metal manufacture; road-building products, oil production and so forth); a midstream business is one that is essentially converting raw materials and parts into finished products (e.g. any manufacturer of finished goods); a downstream business is one where distribution and after-sales services are the central feature (e.g. warehousing, retailing, repair and service businesses).

❷ **Distinguishing the core business** – this entails examining the business in systems terms (input, process and output), i.e. sourcing materials, people and finance; designing and processing products and operations; marketing, selling and delivering; and supplying certain support services such as an organisation structure, legal services, etc. Mintzberg draws heavily on Porter's work here, comparing the latter's *'value chain'* (see Chapter 4 above) with his own systems approach, and re-examining the latter's use of the two concepts of competitive advantage and competitive scope.

❸ **Elaborating the core business** – this is essentially about breaking out of the existing strategic profile of the business, and Mintzberg uses Ansoff's quadrant as an example of alternative strategies to achieve this break-out.

❹ **Extending the core business** – this refers to taking the business beyond its present core, and in Ansoff's model lies in the Diversification box; Mintzberg sees extensions arising vertically, horizontally or from a combination of the two. 'Vertical' here means backwards or forwards in the operating chain (upstream or downstream), and he prefers the use of the expression 'chain integration' rather than vertical integration to describe this. Horizontal integration is what he calls just plain 'diversification', i.e. entry into a business that is not in the same chain (stream) of operations;

extensions can be achieved by internal development, full acquisition, joint ventures, licensing and franchising.

⑤ **Reconceiving the business** – Mintzberg recognises that it may seem strange to arrive at this grouping of strategies, but argues that

'... after a core business has been identified, distinguished, elaborated and extended, there often follows the need not just to consolidate but also to redefine it and reconfigure it ...'

He identifies three basic reconception strategies – business redefinition, business recombination and core relocation strategies.

20. In reviewing Porter's ideas about 'differentiation' and 'scope', Mintzberg criticises the latter's emphasis on *cost* leadership instead of on *price* leadership, which in reality is where the competitive advantage lies. He notes that '... it is the differentiation of price that naturally drives the functional strategy of reducing costs ...' Differentiation, according to Mintzberg, can be achieved on the basis of the following strategies:

❶ **Price differentiation,** i.e. simply charging less than the competition.

❷ **Image differentiation**, i.e. lending an image to a product, but without changing its basic performance. (Note: As ESSO once did with their *'Put a tiger in your tank!'* advertisement; it could be said that such differentiation is quite bogus.)

❸ **Support differentiation**, i.e. providing extra services after the sale. (Note: an example is offering easy credit facilities, free on-site maintenance, etc, or by offering a 'piggy-back' inducement in association with another supplier, e.g. 'a free safari holiday in Kenya, if you buy one of our products before the end of the month'.)

❹ **Quality differentiation**, i.e. producing a better product (such as more reliable, superior performance, etc.)

❺ **Design differentiation**, i.e. offering a product that is truly different (e.g. a camera that produces *instant* photographs).

❻ **Undifferentiated strategy**, i.e. a deliberate strategy of imitating the competition with no attempt at differentiation.

21. Scope strategies, according to Mintzberg, are essentially demand-driven (in contrast to differentiation strategies, which are supply-driven) and include the following:

❶ **Unsegmentation strategy**, i.e. attempting to 'capture a wide chunk of the market with a basic configuration of the product.' (Note: It is difficult to find a product that is not differentiated in some way in the marketplace, but items such as table salt and house bricks might be considered as the kind of basic 'no-frills' products that can be aimed at a wide market, in one case a consumer market, and in the other an industrial market.)

❷ **Segmentation strategies**, i.e. deliberately aiming to reach specific market segments or groups of segments; this is the most popular choice for most businesses. (For example, a stationery manufacturer produces certain sizes and quality of the same basic product – paper clips, writing paper, etc. – for domestic (home) use and other sizes and quality for office use.)

❸ **Niche strategy**, i.e. focusing exclusively on a single segment of the market. (For example, as in publishing academic textbooks just for business and management studies students).

④ **Customising strategies**, i.e. even more closely focused than a niche strategy, in that an individual customer becomes the segment! Mintzberg distinguishes between **pure** customisation, i.e. where a product or service is created especially for a customer, and **tailored** customisation, where a basic product is modified to meet the requirements of an individual (e.g. a standard-size suit is adapted to fit a particular customer; a new pair of spectacles is supplied with prescription lenses in a standard frame). There is also **standardised** customisation, where a customer may choose a particular product configuration from a standard range (such as when a car buyer can choose from a range of engine sizes, colours and accessories.)

22. The Boston Consulting Group (BCG), founded by Bruce Henderson, has contributed some important ideas to the debate about strategic choice. The two most important are (a) the Growth-Share Matrix, and (b) the Experience Curve, both of which are summarised and reviewed in the following paragraphs.

23. **The BCG Growth-Share Matrix** – this model of strategic choice was originally (1979) aimed at diversified companies, but was subsequently extended to encompass product portfolios, each with their different growth rates and different market share. The matrix shown in Figure 6.5 is based on three major variables: market share, growth rate and cash flow. The four alternative categories of company (or product) that emerge from the model are given the somewhat idiosyncratic labels of Stars, Cash Cows, Problem Children and Dogs. The characteristics of Stars are high-share, high-growth, but limited cash flow due to investment required to maintain growth. Successful Stars go on to become Cash Cows. The latter are businesses (or products) that have a high share but slow growth. They tend to generate a very positive cash flow, most of which can be used to develop other businesses/products. Dogs are businesses (or products) which have a low share of a slow-growth market. They may be profitable, but only at the expense of cash reinvestment, and thus generate little or nothing for other projects. Problem Children (sometimes called Question Marks) are businesses (or products) which have a low share of a fast-growing market and need more cash than they can generate themselves in order to keep up with the market. This category can become a problem unless it moves into market leadership.

Figure 6.5 The Boston Consulting Group growth-share matrix

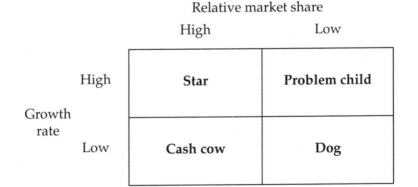

24. There have been several criticisms aimed at the Boston Portfolio, and these are twofold: first, that it is prone to oversimplification ('… easily recalled and improperly applied',

Bowman, 1990), and second, that it takes no account of other key variables such as differentiation and market structure. Seeger (1991) agrees that the Growth-Share matrix is prone to oversimplification, and suggests that some of the more superficial prescriptions that have emerged from wrongful use of the model could be overturned if the imagery was modified to 'remind the student and manager of the ... matrix's pitfalls as well as its presumptions.' For example, he suggests that Dogs are there not just to be kicked, but to 'give unquestioning loyalty to their managers, serving as scouts or watchdogs, to spread the alarm if intruders threaten ...'. This is an altogether more positive way of looking at Dogs in the portfolio, by considering how better they might be nurtured, or at least sustained, without the threat of being closed down or sold off! Seeger considers that by using a Cash Cow only for cash-flow milking, the management are wasting opportunities for developing it; he suggests that the cow might be introduced to a bull and produce a calf (and at very little extra investment!). The clear implication is that Cash Cows may have a great deal of potential synergy waiting to be exploited. Stars, according to Seeger, do not all turn out to be winners, since investment primarily on the basis of market share and growth could be unproductive if environmental conditions and the product life-cycle are not favourable. Stars tend to be judged on their past performance, whereas what is required is to judge them on their potential. Seeger has no quarrel with Problem Children, because the BCG model recommends that these be thought about, and he concludes with a thought echoed earlier (paragraph 5):

> 'No management model can safely substitute for analysis and common sense. Models are useful to managers, to the extent that they can help provide order to the thinking process. Models are dangerous ... to the extent that they bias judgement or substitute for analysis ...'

The experience curve

25. The 'experience curve' refers to a phenomenon identified by the Boston Consulting Group that, when a company's experience at producing and selling a product or service doubles, the costs of production fall by between 10-30% each time this event occurs. The relationship between costs and experience is called the experience curve, as illustrated below (Figure 6.6):

Figure 6.6 The experience curve

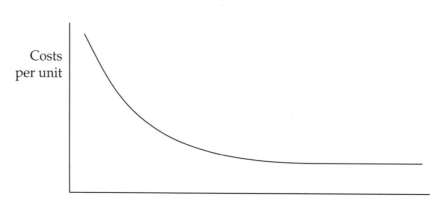

Costs per unit

Experience (cumulative units of production)

26. Bruce Henderson, who founded the Boston Consulting Group, refers to the experience curve in a text on business strategy (1984). He is particularly concerned with its application, so far as it is practicable, to an understanding of competitors' costs, which he emphasises is an extremely important variable in the competitive situation. Although he sees the curve as a useful schematic for focusing attention on the relationship between costs and experience, he is aware of its shortcomings, and urges further research into the concept. However, if the limitations of the present concept are taken into account, he suggests that it can be a useful way of predicting competitors' costs, and argues that a firm with lower costs will, other things being equal, displace its rivals. Factors that contribute to the experience curve include:

- improved labour efficiency over time
- improved production methods in the light of experience
- improved performance from existing equipment, and
- improved supplier conditions.

The attainment of lower costs enables a firm to consider the early option of price reductions on its product(s), which in turn leads, eventually, to lower prices overall as competitors also take advantage of their experience curve.

Further theoretical aspects of strategy

27. Further insights into the nature of strategy have been provided by Hofer and Schendel (1986), who studied how successful firms adapted to their environment ('survival of the fittest') compared with unsuccessful firms. Their studies emphasised the important difference between *effectiveness* (i.e. the extent to which an organisation achieves its objectives – actual versus desired outputs), and *efficiency* (i.e. the ratio between outputs and inputs). From their research, Hofer and Schendel concluded that when firms adapt to events in their *external* environment, the results are more likely to make an impact on effectiveness, whereas when they adapt their structures and ways of working (i.e. when responding to their *internal* environment), the impact is more likely to be felt on efficiency. On a day-to-day basis managers are mostly interested in efficiency, but where strategic management is concerned, it is effectiveness that is the more important, and this implies attention to the external environment of the business.

28. Hofer and Schendel separate goal-setting from strategy formulation, and they see strategy as a pattern 'of present and planned resource deployments and environmental interactions that indicates how the organisation will achieve its objectives'. For them strategy is to do with *means* rather than ends, which fits the subject of this, and the following, chapter. Their conclusions were that strategy has four components, which can be summarised as follows:

   ❶ **Scope (or domain)**, i.e. the extent of the organisation's interactions with its environment. (This could be represented by its product-market position, for example.)

   ❷ **Resource deployments**, i.e. both past and present resource and skill deployments that help to achieve organisational goals; these are also referred to as the organisation's 'distinctive competences'. (This is an implementation component – see Chapter 7.)

❸ **Competitive advantages**, i.e. the unique competitive position developed by an organisation through its pattern of resource deployment and scope decisions. (Competitive position, industry structure and so forth were looked at in Chapter 4).

❹ **Synergy**, i.e. the total effect sought by the organisation through all its strategic decision-making. (Synergy is usually expressed as the 2+2=5 effect, i.e. where the whole is greater than the sum of the parts. Different parts of the same business, or different companies within a group, can be so resourced and directed as to produce the greatest benefit for the whole. Developing synergy is a key challenge for strategic management. Not every organisation seeks to achieve synergy. Conglomerates, for example, often prefer to develop certain subsidiaries independently in order to be able to sell them off and free up cash for other purchases.)

29. Hofer and Schendel distinguish three main levels of strategy – corporate, business and functional. Each has its particular priorities and applications of the four components, as the table (Figure 6.7) illustrates. The priority of corporate level strategy is suggested, not surprisingly, as being the definition of the business (purpose, etc.), its overall growth and profit objectives, and its survival. The focus at this level is on effectiveness, which requires attention to the components of scope (domain) and resourcing. At the business level, by which they mean at business unit level (e.g. profit centres), the priority is competitiveness and the attainment of profit and growth objectives. The focus here is on both effectiveness and efficiency. The key components are competitive advantage and resourcing. At the functional (i.e. operational) level, the priority is on products and market segments, and the attainment of budget targets. The prime focus is on efficiency, and the key components are developing synergy and resourcing.

**Figure 6.7 Strategic levels – their priorities and components
(adapted from Hofer & Schendel)**

Corporate level	Business level	Functional level
Priority		
1. Define purpose/mission	1. Compete successfully	1. Product-market development
2. Set overall growth/profit objectives	2. Growth/profit objectives	2. Efficient use of resources
3. Ensure survival	3. Effectiveness and efficiency	3. Achieve budget targets
4. Effectiveness		
Components		
1. Scope/domain	1. Competitive advantage	1. Synergy
2. Resource deployments	2. Resource deployments	2. Resource deployments

30. Two other researchers, whose work is also of interest for the purposes of this chapter, are Thompson and Strickland (1990), who suggest that there are five tasks of strategic management, which they see as bringing together (a) the setting of the overall mission or goals of the organisation, (b) the establishing of business objectives, and (c), of relevance to this chapter, the strategy required to achieve the first two. The five tasks can be summarised as follows:

- Task 1 is to **define the overall business** and develop a mission (or principal goal)

  Note: this is essentially an entrepreneurial task involving vision, risk and judgement. (See Chapter 2.)

- Task 2 is to **break down the mission statement** into specific performance objectives (both long-range and short-range).

  Note: this task is also entrepreneurial, and may be considered as an element of corporate strategy by those who do not separate goal/objective-setting from strategy. Thompson and Strickland, however, see it as a separate objectives-setting exercise. (See Chapter 2.)

- Task 3 is the **crafting of a strategy**, i.e. the *'pattern of organisational moves and managerial approaches used to achieve organisational objectives … and mission.'*

  Note: here the task is to formulate plans to support organisational goals – i.e. the subject of this chapter.

- Task 4 is to **implement and execute** the strategy.

  Note: this stage is concerned with team leadership, efficiency and other operational matters. (See Chapter 7.)

- Task 5 is to **evaluate, review and adjust** the implementation activities, as necessary.

  Note: a key consideration at this point is organising the feedback of the results of the review, and the model described by Thompson and Strickland allows for feedback to connect with every previous task.

31. In discussing the issue of crafting a strategy, Thompson and Strickland distinguish four levels of strategy – corporate, business, functional and operating. These provide a useful comparison with the approach adopted by Hofer and Schendel. The former separate the operating (line operations) from the functional (specialist functions), which makes the analysis a little clearer for British readers, who are used to defining 'functional' as 'specialist' in describing the different strands of the management hierarchy. The four levels distinguished by Thompson and Strickland can each be summarised in terms of their primary focus as follows:

Corporate	• Building a portfolio of business units
	• Finding synergies among business units and converting them into competitive advantage
	• Allocating resources between and among business units
	• Reviewing, revising and unifying business unit's strategic proposals
Business	• Devising approaches aimed at gaining competitive advantage
	• Responding appropriately to changes in external conditions
	• Addressing company-specific issues and problems
	• Reviewing, revising and unifying functional strategic plans
Functional	• Set objectives to support business strategy in key functional areas such as R & D, manufacturing, marketing, sales, personnel, etc.
	• Reviewing, revising and unifying strategy-related moves by operating managers

Operating	•	Crafting specific approaches to support functional and business strategy
	•	Making provisions for attaining basic unit/department objectives.

32. Thompson and Strickland suggest that the managers responsible for devising strategy at each level have to develop a game plan to meet their objectives. These individual plans have to be pulled together into a coherent whole by means of the reviewing and revising process. They suggest that strategy-making will not usually be successful unless three important criteria are met. These are:

❶ there must be a *'goodness of fit'* between external and internal factors

❷ the strategy must create a sustainable advantage

❸ the strategy raises performance.

33. The strategic management process as proposed by Thompson and Strickland is useful for the way it shows the links between top-level strategy formulation and lower-level strategy implementation, which is the subject of the next chapter (see Figure 7.2).

References

1. Peters, T. (1987), *Thriving on Chaos*, Macmillan.
2. Porter, M.E. (1985), *Competitive Advantage*, The Free Press.
3. Moss Kanter, R. (1989), *When Giants Learn to Dance*, Simon & Schuster.
4. Ansoff, H.I. (1965), *Corporate Strategy*, McGraw-Hill.
5. Ansoff, H.I. & McDonnell (1990), *Implanting Strategic Management* (2nd edn) Prentice-Hall International.
6. Porter, M.E. (1980), *Competitive Strategy: Techniques for Analyzing Industries and Competitors*, The Free Press.
7. Mintzberg, H. (1991), *The Strategy Process – Concepts*, Contexts, Cases, Prentice Hall.
8. Bowman, C. (1990), *The Essence of Strategic Management*, Prentice Hall.
9. Seeger, D. 'Reversing the Image of BCG's Growth Share Matrix', in Mintzberg, H. (1991), *The Strategy Process – Concepts, Contexts, Cases*, Prentice Hall.
10. Henderson, B. (1984), *The Logic of Business Strategy*, Ballinger.
11. Hofer, C.W. & Schendel, D. (1986), *Strategy Formulation: Analytical Concepts*, West Publishing Company.
12. Thompson, Arthur & Strickland, A.J. (1990), *Strategic Management: Concepts and Cases*, Richard D. Irwin.

Questions for reflection/discussion

1. What product, market and financial strategies might be chosen by a firm pursuing market penetration as its overall strategy?

2. How might the generic choices in Figure 6.2 be applied to a charity for the handicapped?

3. What avenues might be open to a growing publishing business that decided it could benefit from diversification?

4. What are the risks involved in choosing a cost focus strategy rather than a differentiation strategy in order to gain competitive advantage?

5. How might synergy be realised in either (i) a functional organisation in the heavy goods manufacturing sector, or (ii) a divisionalised organisation in the fast moving consumer goods sector?

7 Implementing strategy: an overview

Introduction

1. This short chapter takes an overall view of the implementation stage of strategic management. It aims to map out the key decisions that need to be made, and the facilities that must be provided, if the strategic choices referred to in the previous chapter are to be put into effect. Most of the points raised in the chapter are dealt with at greater length in subsequent chapters.

2. Few organisations implement a strategic plan from scratch. On the contrary, it is most likely that their efforts will be directed at revising a strategy that is still in place, with all its attendant organisational and decision-making mechanisms, and with all the after-effects of decisions from the immediate past still rippling through its operations. The strategic management cycle referred to in Chapter 1 can usefully be reintroduced here (slightly adapted) to illustrate this continuous flow of strategic management activities within an organisation (Figure 7.1):

Figure 7.1 A basic strategic management cycle

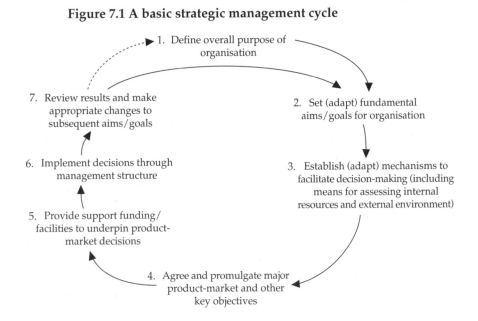

1. Define overall purpose of organisation

2. Set (adapt) fundamental aims/goals for organisation

3. Establish (adapt) mechanisms to facilitate decision-making (including means for assessing internal resources and external environment)

4. Agree and promulgate major product-market and other key objectives

5. Provide support funding/facilities to underpin product-market decisions

6. Implement decisions through management structure

7. Review results and make appropriate changes to subsequent aims/goals

3. It is easy to see from the model that implementation is as much a question of adaptation as it is of innovation. The key points on the circle of events, from the implementation point of view, are the following:

- point 3 (establishing/adapting mechanisms to facilitate decision-making)
- point 5 (providing support funding and facilities)
- point 6 (implementing decisions)
- point 7 (reviewing results).

Each of these points will be considered briefly in this chapter. Some have already been outlined in previous chapters (e.g. Chapter 3 – Assessing the Environment), and others will be dealt with shortly. First, we turn to point 3 – the establishment, or adaptation, of appropriate mechanisms to facilitate decision-making, i.e. to set up a framework within which strategic choices can be executed.

Devising a framework for implementing strategy

4. As noted at several points elsewhere in this book, the approach taken here towards strategic management assumes that it is a rational and logical process, albeit underlaid with elements of intuition. In constructing a framework for implementing the range of strategic choices referred to in the previous chapter, it is clear that reasoned and systematic approaches are not the only ways of dealing with the implementation of strategy – there is always a place for intuition, flair and imagination. However, these last three characteristics will always produce better results when developed within a rational framework of decision-making.

5. A framework for implementing strategy can be based on one or more alternative focal points. These can include the following:

    *   goals and objectives (see examples in Chapter 2) which can be used as ever-present signposts of where effort and priorities should be directed
    *   budgets and other quantifiable targets (see Chapters 8 and 15)
    *   key concerns (i.e. matters of process and outcomes commonly agreed as vital by the management of the business – see Figure 7.2 below).

    Each of the above three main alternatives contains within it both long-term and short-term aspects of strategy implementation. For, when considering how best to implement a strategy, managements are faced with more than just the longer-term, corporate, view of events. This is because implementing a strategic plan requires organisations to deal with short-term, tactical, issues at the same time. Indeed, as was noted in Chapter 1 (Figure 1.4), several strategic concerns and tactical, or operational, concerns shade into each other.

6. This shading of strategy and tactics provides the basis for a useful model for analysing strategy implementation, adapting the diagram referred to earlier in Figure 1.4. The revised diagram (Figure 7.2) shows where strategic concerns and tactical concerns feed off each other. It also indicates where the other two main focal points (goals, objectives and budgets/targets) might fit into the overall picture. The model suggested by the diagram shows strategy implementation as a combination of strategic and tactical concerns. Strategic concerns are focused on *effectiveness*, which means identifying the best market position, developing an appropriate competitive strategy, agreeing the organisation's dominant values, allocating resources (funds, people, etc.) to the maximum effect, and devising suitable financial controls to monitor progress. Tactical, or operational, concerns focus on identifying customers' needs and wants, and meeting them efficiently by optimum use of procedures and systems, and by attention to employee motivation and quality issues. In between these two sets of concerns are the overlapping concerns where strategy and tactics are difficult to separate. These include the development of marketing strategy and resourcing (people, plant and buildings , for example), the introduction of mechanisms such as management information systems and budget targets, and the management of change. Indeed it is probably more realistic to think of tactical and operational plans as forming part of a grand (total) strategy than

to view them as somehow separate. It is important to recognise this total view, even if separation helps in the early days of studying the subject to identify key issues of strategic management.

7. The revised diagram, showing the model of overlapping concerns between strategy and tactics, is shown at Figure 7.2 below:

Figure 7.2 Where strategy and tactics meet – the major concerns

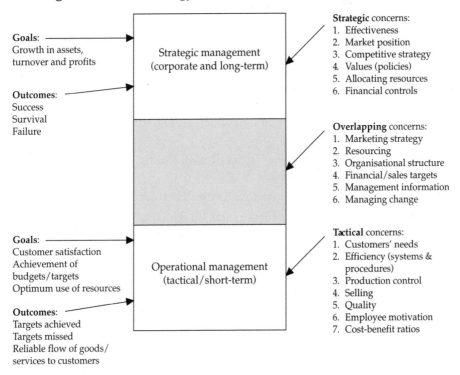

8. The diagram highlights the overlaps between strategy and tactics on such key concerns as:

   • devising a suitable marketing strategy to meet the market and competitive concerns expressed in the corporate plan;

   • deploying the organisation' human, physical and financial resources between its various units and functions;

   • devising an effective organisation structure to facilitate communication, decision-making and necessary change;

   • agreeing suitable sales and financial targets;

   • ensuring a sufficiency of management information for feedback/review;

   • preparing for, and implementing, change.

9. Mintzberg and Quinn (1991) see strategy implementation as being conducted under four key headings – structure, systems, culture and power. They take the view that strategic management is basically about balancing a number of interdependent factors. On the topic of structure, for example, they note that:

' Structure, in our view, no more follows strategy than the left foot follows the right ... The two exist interdependently, each influencing the other.'

'Structure' in this context refers to organisation structure, and 'systems' refers to the administrative procedures which help organisations function. 'Culture' is fundamentally about developing an organisation's value-system (the 'ideological glue that holds organisations together ...'). The reference to 'power' mainly concerns the allocation of authority throughout the organisation, but also to the possession of personal influence by powerful individuals or groups.

10. Mintzberg and Quinn's four headings can be compared with the so-called Seven-S framework developed by the management consultants, McKinsey & Co (see Pascale and Athos, 1981). This framework was designed to facilitate the analysis of organisations by focusing attention on seven key variables – strategy, structure, systems, staff, style, skills and superordinate goals (or shared values). These variables are sub-divided by Pascale and Athos into two categories, the first of which are the so-called 'hard' elements, which are:

❶ **Strategy** – the plan, or course of action, for allocating scarce resources over time to achieve the organisation's goals.

❷ **Structure** – the organisation structure (centralised, divisionalised, etc.).

❸ **Systems** – the formal and informal means by which information is circulated within the organisation (paper, computer files, meetings, etc.).

These are contrasted with the second category, the so-called 'soft' elements, which are:

❹ **Staff** – the organisation's personnel (all categories, including the management)

❺ **Style** – this refers to management style and organisation culture.

❻ **Skills** – the distinctive capabilities or competences of key personnel and the organisation as a whole.

❼ **Superordinate goals/Shared values** – together these represent the fundamental values or philosophy of the organisation (e.g. commitment to customers, respect for environment, drive for quality, excellence, etc.).

11. As can be seen there is much common ground between Mintzberg and Quinn and the McKinsey group, and each of the headings referred to in the above paragraph appears later in this text, together with others not specifically mentioned so far. For example, the next chapter (Chapter 8) looks at Business Planning (i.e. especially at systems), Chapter 10 considers the role and importance of Organisation Culture in strategic management, Chapter 11 deals with Managing Change, Chapter 12 outlines some of the issues involved in Quality Management, Chapter 14 examines the role of Personnel in strategic management, and Chapter 15 reviews the measurement of performance and supplies a definition of 'success'. The final chapter (Chapter 16) develops a working model of strategic management based on the key ideas described earlier in the book.

Support funding and facilities

12. Implementing strategy is not just about devising a management framework, crucial though that is. As we saw in Figure 7.1 above, a major element in the strategic management cycle is the allocation of resources amongst the strategic business units. An early stage of corporate strategic management is to decide what, and how much, to allocate to corporate and business-level units. Which corporate functions/departments (for

example, central research, management development, etc.) are to be strongly supported, and which are to be maintained in order to provide a sufficiency of service to the subsidiary units? Which strategic units are to be developed and expanded (e.g. by means of new buildings, plant and machinery etc) in pursuit of their product-market goals? Which units are to be supported enough to maintain their current, or planned, level of operations? Which units are to be run down, or sold off? Once these major decisions have been made, the corporate and strategic units concerned know what financial and other parameters they have to work to.

13. Apart from major capital projects, which are likely to be closely controlled from the corporate centre, other expenditure on resourcing will be left to the strategic business unit managers to allocate according to their priorities. Such expenditure will usually be in the form of budgets for each cost, profit or revenue centre within the unit. In generic terms expenditure is likely to be spread amongst **procurement** (purchasing) (i.e. supplies, consumables, transport, etc.), **technology** (e.g. computer networks, telecommunications systems, process controllers, electronic point of sale systems) and **personnel** (i.e. salaries, wages, pensions, recruitment costs, training and development costs, etc.). These are the major items of expenditure likely to be incurred in running operations.

Implementing decisions and reviewing results

14. The strategic management cycle (Figure 7.1) also incorporates the implementation of decisions and the review of results. Generally, decisions are likely to be carried out in the context of closely-monitored budgets and periodic (e.g. three monthly) reviews by the corporate management. However, budgets and other procedural mechanisms are operated by people. Thus implementation on this score involves issues of communication, leadership, group working and personal motivation. For summaries of these general management issues see Cole (1996). The implementation of strategy at every level is conducted against the background of the corporate and unit/functional cultures. Success in implementing a chosen strategy depends very considerably on how acceptable the **corporate** culture is to the workforce, and how well it is conceived and communicated by the top management of the organisation (see Chapter 10).

15. Reviewing results is a key element of the strategic management cycle. It is vital for the senior and top management to know how, and how well, the organisation and its various sub-units are progressing towards their intended targets. This is important to enable adaptive decisions to be made in the light of sudden or unexpected changes in business conditions. Whilst budgetary systems, for example, can add to the level of bureaucracy in an organisation, they can also play a crucial role in enabling the organisation to react flexibly to changes in its environment. This topic is dealt with in Chapter 15.

Conclusion – a working model of strategy implementation

16. On the basis of the discussion so far, it is possible to construct a working model of strategy implementation, which encapsulates the strategic and tactical concerns expressed earlier, as follows (Figure 7.3):

Figure 7.3 Implementing strategy – a working model

17. The model shows the major forces that are required to move an organisation's chosen strategy on from being an idea, or intention-in-embryo, to becoming a living creature that can make its presence felt throughout every part of the organisation. These are the forms of energy available to the organisation in pursuit of its strategy:

   ❶ the organisation structure, which provides a framework within which decisions can be formulated, considered and implemented,

   ❷ the management, which facilitate decisions, motivates employees, promotes the organisation's culture, reviews results and makes appropriate changes

   ❸ organisational and individual values, which drive the pursuit of goals and objectives, explicitly and implicitly,

   ❹ the organisation's personnel, who carry out the strategy, and deal with the changes that may occur during its implementation,

   ❺ the organisation's financial and physical assets, which can be deployed to achieve optimum synergy (i.e. where the combined effect exceeds the sum of their parts).

18. These forces represent the internal energy, or potential, of the organisation, which is available to implement its chosen strategy in pursuit of its goal to serve customers, if in the marketplace, or members of the community, if in the public arena. Much of what follows in the subsequent chapters is aimed at identifying these forces, spelling out their role, and assessing their impact on the various stakeholders.

References

1. Mintzberg, H. & Quinn, J. (1991), *The Strategy Process – Concepts, Contexts and Cases*, Prentice Hall International.
2. Pascale, R. & Athos, P. (1981), *The Art of Japanese Management*, Penguin.
3. Cole, G.A. (1996), *Management: Theory and Practice*, (5th edn.) DP Publications.

8 Business plans

Introduction

1. In this chapter we consider the content and mechanisms of the plans which put corporate intentions into effect. The context of the discussion is the principal business unit, often called the strategic business unit. Large organisations, whether in the public or private sector, are usually comprised of several principal business units, which make up the corporate whole. These units may be divisions, major profit-centres, head-quarters units, specialist functions or departments, but they all have one thing in common – they are subject to the control and direction of a corporate group (e.g. a main board of directors for a Plc). Thus, all such units have their operational (i.e. business) plans approved by a senior body within the context of an overall corporate/strategic, plan.

2. The planning horizon for a typical strategic business unit (SBU) is usually 1-3 years, unless the organisation is unitary in nature. In this case the SBU is one and the same as the corporate whole, and the horizon is likely to be longer (e.g. 2-5 years). Business organisations that operate in a turbulent industry, where change is frequent and rapid, will usually devise corporate plans that can be implemented on a rolling basis on the back of strategic business unit, or other operational-level plans. Thus, firms talk of their 'rolling five-year plan', within which their one-year business unit plans are implemented, monitored and fed back into the corporate plan.

3. The place of a strategic business unit plan in a company operating through a number of divisions and specialist units, is illustrated as an example in Figure 8.1. The process effectively begins after the key strategic choices have been made at corporate level.

4. The diagram shows that once the key strategic choices have been made at corporate level, then objectives can be set for the SBU, the major allocations of resources by the parent body can be made, policies put in place and review procedures agreed. This enables the senior management team of the SBU to flesh out the detail of its objectives, allocate its resources among its line and functional units, set and agree detailed budgets and reaffirm the company's policies. Specific targets for the line and functional units are agreed and budgets are implemented, monitoring and feedback mechanisms are set in place, and results are fed back regularly to SBU and corporate level to complete the planning cycle.

5. Thompson and Strickland (1990) suggest that the implementation stage of strategic management is primarily administrative, and is basically a question of ensuring a good fit between the chosen strategy and 'the way the organisation does things'. Another way of looking at this point is to consider implementation as an interplay between several forces, of which the chosen strategy is the centrepiece (see Figure 8.2). It will be noticed that this model is very similar to the one that concluded the previous chapter (see Figure 7.3)

6. Figure 8.2 implies that implementing a strategy requires an organisation to achieve its objectives fairly as well as efficiently. Thus the organisation structure, and any adaptation that might be made to it, is there to ensure the efficient co-ordination of effort between the various functions and activities that are taking place in the organisation. Ideally structure should act to facilitate (i.e. to smooth the path of) all the major communication and decision-making processes of the organisation.

Figure 8.1 The strategic business plan – an outline

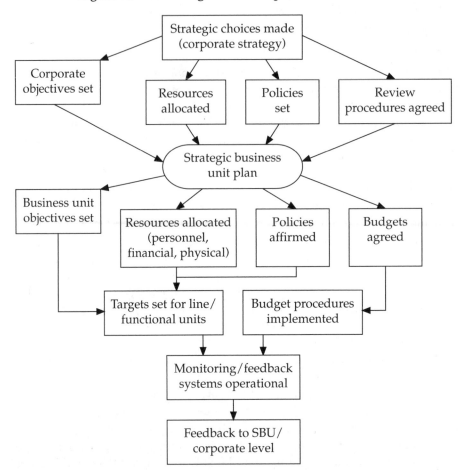

7. Budgetary procedures, and the budgets themselves (see below) have the function not only of identifying priorities (targets) and allocating resources, but also of enabling those resources to be shared out with a reasonable degree of fairness. Thus, through the organisation's budgetary mechanisms, individual line and functional managers can be given rational explanations for their unit's allocations, and have access to procedures that can modify their budget provisions, including obtaining further funding, where they can justify them. In organisations adopting zero based budgeting, all budgets are drawn up from scratch, with every manager having to justify or explain afresh each major item of expenditure or revenue. This approach to budgeting avoids reliance on the previous year's performance as the main guideline for reaching forecasts about next year's estimated costs and revenues. However, compared with traditional approaches, it does require greater discipline and more attention to detail among the managers involved.

8. Personnel skills are a vital factor in the implementation of a strategy, for they are what an organisation must harvest in order to achieve its particular reputation and perceived competencies in the marketplace. Together with motivation, skills are what organisations need in order to meet the challenge of change. In the final analysis, organisations *are* people. If people decide that they cannot, or will not, commit themselves to organisa-

Figure 8.3 The basic budget cycle

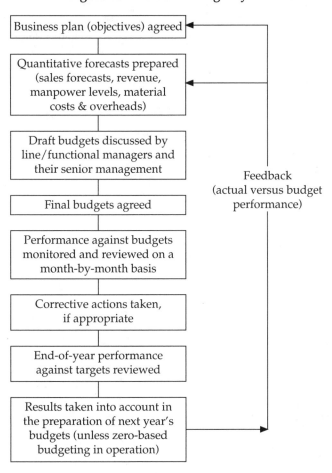

15. Once overheads have been accounted for it is possible to arrive at the *trading profit margin* (i.e. profit before tax and depreciation). The master budget that is eventually drawn up represents the profit and loss forecast for the year in question. An example of the format of a typical profit and loss forecast is shown at Figure 8.4.

Once a set of budgets has been agreed and consolidated into a master budget, the centre-piece of the business plan has been put into operation. Most organisations review progress against budget on a monthly basis, or at least quarterly. The usual areas of concern are budgeted revenue targets and budgeted costs, both direct and indirect. As the year progresses changes may need to be made to the budget figures in order to deal with unexpected external influences or to switch funds between subsidiary budgets, or from one budget head to another (a process usually called *virement*). The key point is that budgets are there to *assist* the management process not to act as barriers to the achievement of objectives.

Figure 8.4 Profit and loss forecast – typical format

	January		February		March	
	Budget	Actual	Budget	Actual	Budget	Actual
Sales						
less:						
Direct labour costs						
Cost of materials						
Total						
Gross Profit						
less Overheads:						
Salaries						
Rent, rates etc						
Insurance						
Transport						
Heating/lighting/power						
Postage						
Telephone						
Printing/stationery						
Professional fees						
Interest charges						
Total Overheads						
Trading Profit/(Loss)						
less: Depreciation						
Net Profit/(Loss)						

Cash flow forecasts

16. Another important aspect of business planning is to develop a cash flow forecast to track the movement of cash in and out of the business over the budgetary period. A cash flow forecast is usually set out on a monthly basis, showing cash sales, cash from debtors, and capital introduced into the business *less* the various payments that have to be made during the course of the year (e.g. payments to creditors, employees' salaries, office overhead costs, interest charges etc). An outline of a cash flow forecast is shown at Figure 8.5.

As a working document, the Cash Flow Budget is intended to provide a detailed, month-by-month, picture of the movement of funds in and out of the organisation. A sufficiency of cash, which is literally the life's blood of the system, is vital for every business. Even if a business is fundamentally profitable, it cannot survive without sufficient cash (liquidity) to pay wages and salaries and meet its obligations to suppliers. Numerous businesses have collapsed, even though profitable and with a good product, because they have experienced a 'cash crisis' and have been unable to meet their debts. A major responsibility of strategic management is to ensure that there is a safe cash balance available during the implementation of a strategy, and that the proportion of the organisation's wealth tied up in capital items, stocks, work-in-progress and property does not squeeze out its demands for cash. Hence the need, when assessing company performance, to ensure sufficient liquidity (see Chapter 15).

Figure 8.5 Outline of a cash flow budget

	January		February		March	
	Budget	Actual	Budget	Actual	Budget	Actual
Cash sales						
Cash from debtors						
Sale of assets						
Loans received						
Total Receipts (a)						
Less payments:						
Cash purchases						
Payments to creditors						
Wages/Salaries						
Rent/rates						
Repairs etc						
Insurance						
Telephone						
Postage						
Stationery						
Transport						
Loan repayment						
Interest						
Bank charges						
Professional fees						
Other						
VAT payable (or refunded)						
Total Payments (b)						
Net Cash Flow (a - b)						
Opening Bank Balance						
Closing Bank Balance						

17. Capital budgets are another example of budget planning. In this case, however, the focus in not on the normal running of the business but on the provision of funds for specific projects (for example, new buildings and plant, innovatory projects, special management development programmes). It is a useful way of separating out one-off, or extraordinary, expenditure from the regular costs of operations.

References

1. Thompson, A. & Strickland, A. (1990), *Strategic Management: Concepts and Cases*, Richard D. Irwin.
2. Hrebeniak, L. & Joyce, W. (1984), *Implementing Strategy*, Macmillan.

Questions for reflection/discussion

1. Who benefits, and how, from the monitoring of budgets and targets?
2. How would you rank the key forces mentioned in Figure 8.2, and how would you justify your ranking?

3. How does zero-based budgeting differ from traditional approaches to budgeting? How far do you agree that it brings benefits to managements rather than extra bureaucracy?

4. In what circumstances might a manager want to seek virement of his/her budget allocation? Give some examples.

5. Why is it important to keep a close eye on cash flow in a business?

9 The international dimensions of strategy

Introduction

1. In a major trading nation such as the United Kingdom, few companies can afford to ignore the international dimensions of their marketplace. For several decades now large multinational corporations, mostly from North America and Europe such as Ford, Shell, BP, Texaco, Unilever and Coca Cola, have established operations on a worldwide basis, often taking with them their own management styles and business attitudes. In recent years these have been joined by a number of major Japanese companies, mostly in electronics and motor vehicle manufacture, such as Nissan, Sony, Honda, JVC and Toyota. The Japanese have established production facilities as well as marketing and distribution operations overseas, both in the USA and in Europe.

2. Other international influences, especially on British companies, include the changing and developing nature of the European Union (EU), which, with its movement towards free trade, is slowly but surely increasing the competition in UK domestic markets as well as in the EU itself. On the other hand the EU is also increasing opportunities for combinations of European companies to work together in joint ventures, such as aircraft development (such as Airbus Industrie, Panavia). Nowadays, the costs of many industrial developments are so high that individual businesses cannot undertake them on their own. Aircraft development and production is one such industry, and in addition to mainly European joint ventures, such as the European Airbus (civil airliners) and Eurofighter (military), there are growing collaborative ventures with other nations. For example, McDonnell Douglas in the United States collaborates with British Aerospace in the design and manufacture of military aircraft such as the British Harrier jump-jet. British Aerospace has also sought joint ventures in its regional jet-liner business, and reached agreement with Taiwan Aerospace Corporation for the joint manufacture and marketing of its BAe 146 series of regional jets.

3. Such agreements not only enable development and manufacturing costs to be shared, but also provide market entry opportunities for the leading partner. The pay-off for the receiving company (or nation) includes:

    ❶ the creation of jobs in high technology areas

    ❷ an influx of valuable technical and systems know-how

    ❸ the prospect of either earning foreign currency, or engaging in barter-type deals (especially where the business or state corporation concerned has something valuable to bargain with, e.g. oil, minerals and fresh foodstuffs)

    ❹ the prospect of building on the experience of operating large-scale collaborative projects to developing a national industry.

    Even a company as large and powerful as BP (British Petroleum plc), which is the third largest oil producer in the world, cannot undertake safely on its own all the development projects that it perceives as contributing to its global competitive advantage. Thus it looks for joint ventures, perhaps through part-ownership, perhaps by means of a collaborative project, to further its work in various parts of the world. For example, BP

Exploration, one of its three core businesses, obtained such agreements in nations as diverse as the USA, Colombia, Vietnam and Papua New Guinea.

4. Another important development in the world economy is taking place in the so-called Pacific Basin, where relatively undeveloped nations such as South Korea, Taiwan and Malaysia are joining their smaller but experienced rivals from Hong Kong and Singapore to supply high quality goods at very competitive prices to the Western nations. Such goods range from ships and motor cars to electrical goods and clothing. Together with Japan, such a grouping provides a major challenge to the UK and its European neighbours, as well as to the other major world economic grouping – the North Americas (the United States, Canada and Mexico). The nations of the Pacific Basin have shown themselves capable of manufacturing goods to the highest of standards and at a lower level of costs than their counterparts in Europe and North America. They have thus become an attractive prospect for Western firms wanting to share production costs and development risks, whilst gaining possible new markets. Since most of the goods manufactured in that area are exported to developed nations, there is considerable benefit to the host nation in terms of overseas earnings and/or preferential trade deals.

5. Finally, there are the activities of businesses, which, while not international conglomerates, are major international companies in their own right, such as British Airways, Singapore Airlines, Cunard and TWA. The activities of such companies are as much constrained by national politics as they are by competitive pressures. However, due to the enormous increase in demand for air travel, airline businesses, in particular, are beginning to benefit from a reduction in controls by national governments all over the world. Deregulation, or the so-called 'open skies' policy, is gradually being extended from the USA and UK domestic markets to Europe as a whole (via the EU). It is likely that this process will continue apace, enabling airlines to compete freely on routes, both regional and international. Because of the costs and sheer scale of global air transport operations, there is a growing trend towards mergers and joint agreements between existing carriers. British Airways, for example, already has global alliances with USAir, Qantas, TAT European Airlines and Deutsche BA, which are intended to provide a 'network fit' in which route structures complement each other. Such alliances enable the participants to gain access to routes and/or markets which are at present denied to them because of current restrictions imposed by the nations concerned. Other benefits include access to development finance and a share in a larger market. Deutsche BA, formed by British Airways and a consortium of German banks, purchased Delta Air, a niche carrier, principally serving a local business market until linking up with British Airways, the world's leading international air passenger carrier. Following the purchase, Delta's fleet expanded significantly, staff numbers doubled in 12 months and passenger numbers rose from under 700,000 to over one million in less than two years.

International competition

6. One effect of the international dimension of business is that the concept of the *domestic* market becomes less significant. For many companies the *world* is their marketplace. Such companies have to think globally, even if they have to act locally in their markets for the purpose of delivering their corporate strategy. Another effect lies in the cost differences between producing nations. Most of the countries in the Pacific Basin, for example, can produce highly competitive products for sale in the West, because they currently have the twin advantages of (a) access to new microelectronic-based tech-

nology, and (b) far lower labour costs than Western companies. Thus shoes, clothing, ships and motor-cars can be produced at relatively low cost, but at a very acceptable standard for Western markets. If goods can be produced more cost-effectively in Malaysia, for example, why should a large international company need to continue to produce them in high-cost areas, such as Europe? The truth is that whereas in the past century people bought their finished goods from the factories of Europe and the United States, now they are increasingly likely to buy them from factories in the Far East. The developed economies are moving steadily away from manufacturing into services, and into what some have called the 'information economy'.

7. The resulting competition from both old-established and new rivals in manufacturing affects British companies in several ways:

- Firstly, it forces them to compete fiercely at home on differentiation, where a distinct competitive advantage can be gained due to close contact with customers and a better understanding of their specific value requirements.

- Secondly, it forces them to compete as closely as possible on price, where the main aim is to minimise the cost disadvantages through increased efficiency.

- Thirdly, it forces them to consider how they themselves might find competitive advantage overseas by taking advantage of the lower labour costs in competitor nations.

Thus, opportunities for investment overseas have to be considered, as well as joint ventures or other collaborative efforts with existing indigenous companies. Given that entry barriers to competitor nations are generally very high, such steps are not always available, but there is a growing world movement to facilitate the expansion of world trade by removing trade and other restrictions on international operations, for example by means of GATT – the General Agreement on Trade and Tariffs. UK companies, and their counterparts in the world's trading nations, have opportunities to lobby diplomats and governments to this end.

International business and the impact of technology

8. A crucial factor in the development of world trade is ease of communications. In recent years enormous strides have been made in the development of global satellite communications, electronic mail, facsimile transmissions (fax) and other products of microelectronic technology. Today, telephone, fax, computer and video links are possible between large numbers of nations. Markets, and information about them, have never been so accessible in communications terms. Thus, bids can be scrutinised, contracts agreed, orders made, and payments confirmed all at very short notice. Such technological developments have also helped international commodity trading and money markets to improve the speed and efficiency of their services to the international trading community, all of which helps to facilitate the growth of world trade. Companies that wish not only to survive, but also to thrive in world markets ensure that they take every possible advantage of the increasingly sophisticated and ever-cheaper forms of electronic technology that are available to poorer and richer nations alike.

9. Strategic management on a global basis calls for microelectronically-based communications systems, and the skills to establish and apply them. Companies not only have to invest in the new technology as it becomes available, but also have to search constantly for the most appropriate software systems and organisational forms for their

decision-making requirements. As multi-media forms of communication become increasingly possible, it will soon be feasible for individual directors and their lawyers to conduct negotiations across the globe using video links, computerised graphics and excellent sound facilities. The business world at least will indeed become a smaller place!

The Single European Market

10. The greatest influence on UK management policies over the next few years will be the opening up of the Single European Market, which was inaugurated in January 1993. This has considerable implications for the British economy, particularly for the management of business and public sector organisations. Britain's participation in the European Union (EU) means that its own laws (and customs) can, and will be, affected by EU laws, guidance, codes of practice and administrative decisions. Although individual countries will be permitted to retain, or develop, certain local practices (the notion of 'subsidiarity'), the overall intention of the underlying legislation (the Treaty of Rome) is to work towards the harmonisation of business and economic practices between all the EU nations. In this situation, the key issue for all concerned is how to balance local (i.e. national) wishes with acceptance of EU-wide policies and practices, at a time when there will be increased competition in home markets as a direct result of the lifting of trade barriers within the Union.

11. Whereas in other parts of the world, regional co-operation is by means of trade agreements, the European model, as evidenced in the EU, is intended to achieve close political union internally, as well as to develop trade both internally and with the world-wide community. Already, in Europe, the laws of the EU take precedence over those of its members on certain issues affecting the management of enterprises (such as equal opportunities legislation). Under EU law, an **Article** is directly binding on member states, and a **Directive** requires a member to introduce its own legislation, whilst not being directly binding.

12. An example of an Article is Article 117 of the main Treaty, which aims to promote the harmonisation of improved living and working conditions for workers. Within the context of this binding legislation, discussions have particularly centred on the EU's so-called 'Social Charter', which many UK business organisations object to on the grounds that it is too prescriptive and inflexible, and will lead to increased labour costs at a time when international competitors are reducing theirs. The fact is that, whilst there are several common *problems* faced by managers in the EU (e.g. encouraging greater job flexibility in production, managing employee relations in times of economic and technological change, achieving greater efficiency with smaller workforce and so on), the *solutions* to them are quite varied, as each country follows its own preferred pattern of handling competitiveness, productivity, and employee relations.

13. The emphasis in the UK's enterprise economy has been to break down large organisational structures in favour of smaller units with delegated powers, and to encourage individual as opposed to state initiatives and responsibility. Whilst some decentralisation of business and state enterprises has also taken place in many EU countries, there is nevertheless a greater emphasis on community affairs and a more regulated partnership between governments, employers and trade unions than in the United Kingdom. Thus there are several issues on which British and other EU opinions are likely to vary, and the so-called 'social' aspects of business and economic activities provide a case-in-point.

Japanese management practices

14. There has been great interest worldwide in the phenomenal success of Japanese enterprises in securing such a significant proportion of world trade. In Britain, also an island nation, this interest has more than been awakened by the considerable investment in the British economy by major Japanese firms. The latter have introduced a number of Japanese management practices into their UK-based organisations, some of which have led directly to efficiency savings over earlier practices (e.g. development of core workers supported by part-time/casual (non-core) workers; insistence on non-specialised career paths and job flexibility for core workers; team-working seen as essential; single status working conditions; a respect for the company culture; and meticulous attention paid to production planning and quality). Other practices, such as the employment of a central core of workers with guarantees of secure employment, and the attention paid to employee selection and training, are seen as less effective in that they can *reduce* flexibility and/or raise labour costs.

15. Some of the above practices have been incorporated into the personnel policies of Japanese companies in Britain, and they appear to have worked successfully. No employment guarantees were given, but unions were recognised, single status applied, and thorough training provided, including key worker visits to Japan to the parent company. A particularly significant advantage for employers in the British context was the acceptance of job flexibility after training.

16. Japanese firms investing in Britain have undoubtedly been able to take competitive advantage of a situation in which entry barriers have been reduced due to:

    ❶ government policy of attracting foreign investment in the UK economy

    ❷ high unemployment in the areas selected for investment

    ❸ availability of enterprise grants from the government

    ❹ diminished trade union power due to changes in the law and high unemployment.

    The investing firms have nevertheless won the support of the British workforce, who have demonstrated their ability to collaborate positively with the Japanese styles of management to produce quality products efficiently.

17. The pay-off for the Japanese companies who have invested in Britain is that they have been able to provide themselves with regional manufacturing bases from which to launch their products into Europe at a time when that continent is steadily becoming one vast market. Part of the price of that advantage has to be paid for in accepting a gradually higher proportion of British and/or EU supplied parts in finished manufactured goods. Toyota, for example, not only produces body shells and assembles cars at its Derbyshire factory (an investment of over £800m), but also supplies engines for one of its major models from another factory in Deeside. Increasingly, other parts are also being supplied from a UK or European source. Manufacturers who can claim that '80% of our leading models are built with UK/European-made engines and parts' are clearly heading for a competitive advantage over those whose finished products still rely heavily on parts made in Japan. Ultimately, car manufacturers, such as Honda, Nissan and Toyota hope to be thought of as British as Fords or Vauxhalls (both American-owned companies).

Multinational enterprises

18. The Japanese investment in Britain has been undertaken by large business corporations rather than small companies, and this is typical of internationalisation in business. There are three principal strategies that a national firm can adopt in relation to overseas markets:

     It can export its goods or services from the home base, as in the cases of a supplier of Scotch whisky, or Irish peat, or architectural services. This approach works best where there is no real substitute product (or service) available locally.

    ❷ It can establish franchise arrangements, where the local franchisee takes responsibility for sales and specific (local) aspects of marketing, leaving the parent company to provide the business framework and the brand name, and thus achieve significant investment without excessive capital outlay and minimising local/national bureaucracy. Examples of this approach include the McDonald's fast food chain, the Pizza Hut chain and Hertz Car Rentals. This kind of approach favours *service* industries rather than manufacturing, although the latter can produce goods under licence from a parent company. Industrial examples include aircraft, tractors and so forth.

    ❸ It can set up manufacturing plants or business centres in the overseas countries making the same, or similar, goods (or services) as in the home country. For example, as in Toyota's motorcar manufacturing operations in the UK, and the Coca Cola Company's bottling plants in India. Service examples include major accountancy firms with overseas offices, and management consultancies with bases overseas. The advantage of this approach, which gives multi-national status, is that the organisation concerned is able to make use of local labour and local businesses/suppliers in making the goods or supplying the services. This is often welcomed by nations who (a) have insufficient employment opportunities for their own nationals, and (b) are keen to support investment in their national economy by overseas companies.

19. One American writer (Korth, 1985) sees four stages, or degrees, of internationalisation ranging from domestically-based reactive trading with foreign countries to full-blooded multinational operations on a global scale. Only in the later stages of international trading do companies actually invest in foreign countries. Such investment plays an important part in the shaping of company business strategy, even though headquarters is still in the home country. Full multinational status is likely to confine the influence of headquarters to that of a holding company, since it is the international divisions that are responsible for the success of the company's overall product-market strategies.

20. The sheer size (and wealth) of multinationals means that they can have a significant effect on their host nations. Many such companies have total sales well in excess of the Gross National Product of many of the world's nations. For example, the large oil firms, Exxon and Shell, are larger in economic terms than nations such as South Africa, Austria and Argentina. Most of their effects on their hosts are likely to be beneficial, for they include:

    • provision of capital investment in major economic activities that would be beyond the scope of the nation concerned
    • contribution to the creation of jobs, usually in the context of high unemployment
    • making available a wider range of products to customers
    • introduction of new technology

- supply of scarce skills and passing them on to nationals
- usually a contribution to social needs (e.g. road building, water supply plants, power generation)
- improvement to the nation's balance of payments following the export of goods and services.

21. Nevertheless, the power of multinationals to influence national economies due to the extent of their investment in host nation cannot be denied, and it is always open to such large enterprises to threaten to remove their operations to another country at relatively short notice, which is a powerful sanction on the host. However, the evidence seems to be that most hosts at government level are willing to take the risks since they perceive the benefits as outweighing the costs. Others may feel some reservations. Local suppliers, for example, who have come to depend on the multinational's business for their very existence know that any decision to move out would be disastrous for them. A clear strategic option for such businesses is to aim to widen their customer base, so as not to be reliant on just the multinational's custom.

References

1. Korth, Christopher M. (1985), *International Business, Environment and Management*, 2nd edn, Prentice-Hall.

Questions for reflection/discussion

1. What advantages would a manufacturing company expect to gain from an investment in production facilities overseas?
2. To what extent can governments (a) encourage, and (b) hinder the development of world trade? Give examples from your reading.
3. Why is it important for firms pursuing a strategy of international expansion to understand the implications of micro-electronic technology for communications and decision-making?
4. What benefits may be experienced by a nation that encourages overseas investment in its economy?

10 Organisation culture and strategic management

Introduction

1. In the opening chapters of this book, there were various references to the significance of corporate culture in the process we call strategic management. In Chapter 1 it was noted that Mintzberg (1991) referred to strategy as 5 Ps, of which one – perspective – was basically concerned with aspects of culture, especially the ingrained way of looking at the world that dominates many organisations. It was also noted in that chapter that Johnson and Scholes (1993) identified two approaches to strategy which centre around the notion of culture – one they called simply 'a cultural view', and the other they called 'a visionary view'. The whole concept of values and vision was implicit in Chapter 2, which dealt with organisational purposes and goals. Several examples of mission statements were put forward in that chapter, and could usefully be referred to again during the reading of the present chapter. Subsequently, in Chapter 7, a number of other references were made to aspects of culture. Mintzberg (1991), for example referred to the implementation of strategy under four key headings, of which one was 'culture'. Reference was also made to the 7-S framework developed by the management consultants McKinsey & Co as a way of examining organisations, one aspect of which was 'superordinate goals or shared values'.

2. The concept of corporate culture is such a powerful phenomenon in organisations that it deserves a chapter in its own right. Corporate culture is a central feature of strategic management. Indeed, it would not be putting it too strongly to say that it is an organisation's culture which is given expression by its corporate strategy. Given that there are a number of ways of expressing the concept, it will be useful to provide our own working definition of corporate culture, or organisation culture, as follows:

> 'In an organisation the term 'corporate (or organisation) culture' refers to the dominant values at work in the organisation. These are variously referred to as 'the company ethos', the 'organisation culture' or 'our values'. The corporate culture usually includes the dominant management style active in the organisation. The values embodied in an organisation's culture usually focus on its relationships with customers, the community, and employees as well as defining its attitude towards quality, safety and ethical issues. Some of these values may be written down and others implied in behaviour.'

3. The above definition stresses the shared nature of corporate culture. It is a phenomenon that is caught just as much as it is taught. It is more than just the sum of the values and attitudes of individual employees, some of whom, in fact, may not share the values promulgated on behalf of the organisation. For example, individual civil servants in the UK have been known to leak information quite deliberately to the press, even though the ethos of their calling is to maintain confidentiality ahead of any public announcements made by their Ministers. To take another example, more than a few trade union leaders at shopfloor level some 10-15 years ago were actively working against the interests of their employers by insisting on *their* rights being considered before all others. As a result of this 'anti-company culture', several major British industries, such as machine tools,

motor–car manufacture and shipbuilding, suffered grievous losses of production, and lost their market share to American, Japanese, Korean and Polish competitors.

4. In some organisations culture is acquired as a result of professional standards (for example, engineering quality standards in Rolls-Royce, and respect for probity and trust in accountancy firms). In others it develops from the philosophy of a powerful group of managers or owners (such as in Hewlett Packard and J Sainsbury plc). In yet others it is the product of the vision of one person (e.g. Steve Jobs of Apple Computers, and Richard Branson of the Virgin Group). Mintzberg and Quinn (1991) see culture as concentrating on

> 'the collective interest and the building of a unified organisation, through shared systems of beliefs, habits and traditions.'

When such beliefs and habits are in rich supply in an organisation, then, according to Mintzberg and Quinn they become an *'ideology'*, of which the key feature is its unifying power.

5. Peters and Waterman (1982), in their study of excellence in American companies report how

> 'we were struck by the dominant use of story, slogan and legend as people tried to explain the characteristics of their own great institutions. All the companies we interviewed, from Boeing to McDonald's, were quite simply rich tapestries of anecdote, myth, and fairy tale ... these stories ... appear to be very important, because they convey the organisation's shared values, or culture.'

So important was culture that they concluded that

> 'the dominance and coherence of culture proved to be an essential quality of the excellent companies'.

This latter point is significant, for it is the coherence of the shared values, even more than their dominance, that produces what we have chosen to call 'culture'. Thus, culture does not merely equate with the power that certain charismatic individuals (or groups) might possess. Sometimes the personal power of individuals can make it difficult for a coherent culture to emerge, as could be said in the case of Robert Maxwell's empire in the 1980s. Another implication of Peters and Waterman's findings is that 'culture' is less written down than talked about. However, judging by the amount of written material circulating in major British companies about their mission and strategic objectives, it seems that when 'culture' is seen as an issue requiring attention rather than a concern to be shared, then written reinforcement may be used more often by the senior management.

6. Edgar Schein (1985), in his fascinating text on organisation culture, provides a definition of 'culture' that seems very appropriate for a strategic management context, as follows:

> '... a pattern of basic assumptions – invented, discovered, or developed by a given group as it learns to cope with its problems of external adaptation and internal integration – that has worked well enough to be considered valid ... and to be taught to new members as the correct way to perceive, think and feel in relation to those problems.'

Schein's definition is useful to our discussion here, because he suggests that culture is a pattern of *assumptions*, and by implication, therefore, culture itself may be implicit rather than explicit. However, much is likely depend on how confident the top management are about the commitment of their middle managers and other employees to the culture they wish to see as dominant. The suggestion that such assumptions may be invented or developed implies that dominant individuals can decide to promote them throughout the organisation, so that they become part of its folklore. The suggestion that they can be *discovered*, implies that there are also other culture-forming forces at work in the organisation (for example, professional standards, employee attitudes, managerial experience). Schein makes the valuable comment that the development of culture is part of the learning experience of the organisation, and in relation to strategic management his reference to coping with the problems of external adaptation and internal integration could not be more apt. Finally, his definition is useful for the suggestion that culture is something that newcomers are expected to acquire.

7. Although Schein emphasises the implicit aspects of culture, it must also be recognised that it has important explicit features (e.g. mission statements, publicity brochures, company rules, etc.). In fact, it is usually the case that an organisation will have a two-tier set of values and assumptions within its ranks. At one level is the explicit company culture as propounded in public statements, training courses and in the dominant management style. At another level, there are implicit assumptions, often held by individual operational and functional units, which may not always be consonant with corporate values, and indeed may sometimes be working against them. Clearly, a strong organisation culture requires the sort of consensus that enables emerging (and probably unofficial) cultural values to be absorbed quietly and effectively into the overall (and official) culture of the organisation. A weak organisation culture is one where either there is little or no *explicit* manifestation of values and assumptions, or where the explicit and the implicit assumptions are at odds with each other.

8. It is no surprise, in the light of the above, that researchers such as Goldsmith and Clutterbuck (1984), and Peters and Waterman (1982) are able to point out that winning, or successful, companies in the UK and America have found the knack of harmonising the implicit with the explicit, the unofficial with the official, the emergent with the status quo. Japanese companies have also established a reputation for being strong on culture. This has been achieved by emphasising a unique company philosophy based on policies such as group working, open communications, and concern for employee welfare. Together with a respect for customer requirements and product quality, these cultural norms have enabled Japan to build itself into one of the most powerful trading nation in the world, despite the physical limitations of its geography and its relatively small population.

9. Culture both contributes to, and is influenced by, change in the organisation. Rosabeth Moss Kanter (1984), in her influential study of change in major American companies, found that companies with an 'integrative' approach to change (that is, dealing holistically with problems, trying out new ideas, seeing change as an opportunity rather than a threat) were better able to handle innovation than firms with a 'segmentalist' approach (seeing the organisation and its problems as segmented/compartmentalised, and unwilling to alter the overall structure). These two approaches are themselves indicative of different cultures at work in the organisations concerned.

According to Moss Kanter, one of the key ways of overcoming resistance to change in an organisation is to encourage a 'culture of pride', where achievements are highlighted and experienced innovators are used to act as internal consultants throughout the organisation.

10. There are several means by which both business and not-for-profit organisations can nourish their culture, including the following:

❶ by recruiting people (especially managers) who will fit into their way of looking at things

❷ by ensuring that all new employees undergo an induction into the company

❸ by providing regular training and development for employees

❹ by emphasising key aspects of culture (e.g. quality, customer care, pride in the job, respect for clients' confidentiality, safety-consciousness, etc.) by means of company bulletins, notices, newsletters and annual reports

❺ by ensuring that managers and supervisors emphasise cultural norms in the course of everyday tasks.

❻ by capturing emergent values or assumptions and either putting them at the disposal of the whole organisation, if they are acceptable, or by stamping them out, if they are considered to be damaging

❼ by adopting a 'zero-base' approach to culture (that is, to question every assumption anew at periodic intervals).

11. Peters (1987), in his prescriptions for success, stresses the importance of developing an inspiring vision. He suggests that visions are not only strategically sound, but also aesthetic and moral, and argues that inspiring visions have to fulfil a number of criteria, which can be summarised as follows:

❶ they must be clear and challenging – and focus on excellence

❷ they have to make sense in the marketplace (e.g. by stressing quality, service, responsiveness and so on)

❸ they should be stable, but not complacent, and should be challenged frequently, though only changed marginally

❹ they should act both as beacons (focal points for action) and controls (guiding people's decisions)

❺ they should first aim to call forth the best from their own employees before focusing attention on the customers' needs

❻ they should *'prepare for the future, but honour the past'*

❼ they should be lived out in details not broad strokes (i.e. culture is more than just a set of exhortations, and examples of culture in action need to be seen by those concerned).

12. Schein, in the work already quoted, suggests that culture has a life-cycle and thus matures and develops over time (see summary in Cole, 1997). Briefly, Schein suggests that organisations pass through their own life-cycle – from Birth and Early Growth through Mid-life to Maturity and eventually either to Destruction or Transformation. At each of these major periods, culture plays a different function. For example, at Birth culture acts as the glue of the organisation, holding the organisation together; during Mid-life the dominant culture begins to weaken and is subject to change; at Maturity culture can either be transformed in an evolutionary way, or subject to a revolution, in which former ways (and people) are swept away, and a completely new culture develops.

13. Goldsmith and Clutterbuck (op. cit.) concluded their study of winning firms in Britain by asking the question 'Can corporate culture be changed?' The answer, they suggested, is 'yes', and point out that culture in companies such as J Sainsbury and Marks & Spencer, whilst recognisable in terms of their owner-founders, nevertheless has changed to reflect modern values. Culture is thus constantly evolving. In the light of their findings, they suggest a number of guidelines for companies wishing to change their culture. These include:

❶ identifying the existing culture, spotlighting any discrepancies between departments or functions, and developing a *'unity of perception'*

❷ identifying the most appropriate culture given the markets served by the company, and especially noting whether cost or quality is the key criterion for customers

❸ assess what organisational changes may have to be made to accommodate the new culture

❹ assess what personnel changes may be required, especially in terms of top management commitment to change.

14. The repercussions of implementing the shared values of an organisation do not end just in the internal manoeuvring of the organisation – for example in influencing the managers, supervisors, rank-and-file employees, and even shareholders. The implementation of a culture has implications also for customers and clients, for suppliers, for creditors, for competitors and the community at large. For example, customers can learn what to expect from a firm (e.g. in terms of product quality, after-sales service, range of products, etc.); suppliers can learn what standards will be expected of them, and also what treatment they will receive (for example, in terms of settling invoices); creditors can assess the firm's likely response to paying its debts responsibly; competitors can learn what competitive advantage is being gained by the pursuit of a particular culture (e.g. price leadership, product quality, product safety or reliability etc); the community can understand what is driving the company in its external relations (e.g. attitude towards toxic waste, treatment of staff, support for local community projects).

15. Most major companies tend to end up with what might be described as a core and cluster approach to culture, that is to say they have over the years adopted certain core values (e.g. service quality or price competitiveness), which form the heart of their corporate culture – the core - yet at the same time they are adding and removing other values – the cluster – in order to maintain a culture that is responsive to change (e.g. by removing a men-only tradition for certain positions). Changing aspects of culture is not easy. New ways of looking at things are not automatically welcomed by managers and other employees. If there is to be a harmonising of company culture and individual viewpoints to form a strong culture, then much work has to be done. The subject of change is another important issue for strategic management, and will be dealt with in the chapter which follows (Chapter 11).

References

1. Mintzberg, H. in Mintzberg & Quinn (1991), *The Strategy Process*, Prentice Hall International.
2. Johnson, G. & Scholes, K. (1993), *Exploring Corporate Strategy*, Prentice Hall.
3. Peters, T. & Waterman, R. (1982), *In Search of Excellence*, Harper Collins.
4. Schein, E. (1985), *Organisational Culture and Leadership*, Jossey Bass.
5. Goldsmith, W. & Clutterbuck, D. (1985), *The Winning Streak*, Penguin Books.

6. Moss Kanter, R. (1984), *The Change Masters – Corporate Entrepreneurs at Work*, Allen & Unwin.
7. Peters, T. (1987), *Thriving on Chaos*, Macmillan.
8. Cole, G.A (1997), *Personnel Management – Theory & Practice* (4th edn.), Letts Educational.

Questions for reflection/discussion

1. Discuss how an organisation culture comes about. What influences are the most significant, in your opinion?

2. In what ways might (a) individual values, and (b) the attitudes of work groups conflict with the dominant ethos of an organisation? Give some examples from your reading or your own experience.

3. How might a 'culture of pride' be introduced into an organisation you are familiar with?

4. Discuss whether it is possible for employees to be trained in the organisation's culture? Consider also whether training can only deal with the *explicit* aspects of culture.

11 Managing change and innovation

Introduction

1. Change, especially in the sense of *improvement*, is at the heart of strategic management. Every strategy developed by an organisation's senior management is aimed at strengthening and developing its performance, as well as sustaining and nourishing its very existence. The process of strategic management referred to in the opening chapter (see page 4) indicates these twin elements. The basic cycle of strategic management illustrated in Figure 1.1 refers to the definition of purpose and goals, the establishment of decision-making mechanisms, the development of means of assessing the environment and the installation of a review process. All of these activities are aimed at sustaining and nourishing the organisation by setting in place a structure and systems designed to underpin performance. Subsequently, by defining and promulgating key objectives (the chosen strategy) and implementing these through the organisation structure, the management is positioning the organisation in its chosen markets with a view to strengthening and developing its performance.

2. Some organisations change largely in response to *external* circumstances – this is often called 'reactive change'. Others change principally because they have decided to introduce change – this is usually known as 'proactive change'. Some organisations are conservative in outlook, seeking little by way of change; others are entrepreneurial in outlook, always on the look-out for new opportunities and challenges. Strategic management, as can be seen from previous chapters, is a process that combines a number of these varying attitudes towards change. Once an organisation's senior management begins to think strategically, it follows that some changes will be made because of changes in the external environment, and are hence reactive. Other changes, however, will be introduced (proactively) because they are seen to be useful in their own right and not because they have been dictated as a result of external pressures. Beyond these basic changes, an organisation can choose to adopt a more or a less conservative/entrepreneurial view of its strategic direction, depending on its culture and management style.

The effect of environment on change

3. Some organisations are so placed, in terms of the simplicity of their structure, the relatively unchanging nature of their products or services, and the relative stability of their markets, that change is a slow and generally evolutionary process. By comparison, other organisation may find themselves coping with a major internal re-structuring process against the background of a turbulent external environment, where decisions are often crisis-driven and the pace of change bewildering. Examples of stable organisations, experiencing little by way of major change, include the British Broadcasting Company (national broadcasting services), the Co-operative Funeral Service (burial and funeral services), and the Kellogg Company of Great Britain (production and marketing of breakfast cereals). These organisations offer a predictable service or product in a relatively stable market. Organisations currently in a volatile situation include IBM (facing intense worldwide competition from rival manufacturers), the P & O Ferries group (facing regional competition from cross-channel ferry rivals, the airlines and the railways with the opening of the Channel tunnel), and British Aerospace plc (this major contrib-

utor to the armaments/military aircraft industry has been challenged in its strategic position by the collapse of the former Soviet Union, and the consequential ending of the so-called 'Cold War').

4. What are the factors that make for a volatile and turbulent environment? They can be divided into two categories for our purposes: (i) external factors, and (ii) internal factors as summarised below.

Factors in the external environment

These can be analysed under the BPEST heading referred to in Chapter 3 above, and the following are likely to have an impact:

Business
- Activities of competitors jockeying for advantage in the market place
- Takeover bids launched against the company by rivals or conglomerates seeking to add to their portfolio of companies
- Suppliers going bankrupt, or experiencing major production problems
- Suppliers exerting pressure on the company due to their bargaining strength

Political
- Government action against the industry (e.g. by withdrawal of licences)
- Government action to promote the industry or the company (e.g. by removal of tax/regulatory barriers)
- Government action to encourage overseas investors (e.g. by offering tax incentives, greenfield sites, etc.)
- Trade agreements between nations that restrict/open up exports, etc.

Economic
- Sudden increase/decrease in price of raw materials
- Sudden changes in price/supply of oil and other fuels
- Changes in purchase tax, VAT, Corporation Tax, etc.
- Unforeseen collapse/escalation of key currencies

Social
- Changing attitudes towards unsocial hours at work
- Disillusionment with factory life
- Increased expectations of rewards for work achieved
- Demand for greater consultation/involvement in workplace decisions
- Expectation of greater support for families at work (e.g. crèche provision, flexible working, etc.)
- Changing attitudes towards the acquisition and development of key skills (e.g. in the sciences and engineering)
- Development of anti-work culture in sections of society
- Lack of suitably able people to develop required skills

Technological	• Impact of the latest technological developments on existing systems
	• Additional training requirements brought about by new technology
	• Increased reliance on outside experts due to constantly-changing state of technology
	• Increased pressure to adapt work schedules and jobs to fit in with new technology
	• Costs of keeping up-to-date to maintain competitive advantage.

5. Some factors in the internal environment (e.g. technology) overlap with others in the external situation. The internal list is likely to include the following: **people** (i.e. personnel), **structure**, **systems**, **technology** and **functions** (such as finance and marketing). These are summarised as follows:

Factors in the internal environment

Personnel	• Inappropriate/ineffective people in key posts (senior or junior)
	• Unwillingness to accept change in certain units/functions
	• Dissatisfaction with the rewards system
	• Key individuals using their power against the corporate interest
	• Mistakes made by staff in key positions
Organisation structure	• Existing structure not meeting pressures of strategy implementation
	• Too many organisational layers, leading to stifling of managerial initiative and slow decision-making process
	• Head office exercising too much power over operational decisions
	• Insufficient collaboration across departmental or functional boundaries, leading to lost opportunities and unnecessary duplication of effort/resources
	• Establishment of new cost/profit centres leading to tension between centres
Systems	• Inadequate procedures for tracking progress of products/service
	• Over-complicated documents, leading to customer and/or staff errors
	• Insufficient systems for reviewing quality and reporting problems /solutions
	• Inadequate forecasting methods, leading to undesirable variances between actual and budgeted performance
Technology	• Novel introduction of micro-processor controlled equipment into production areas
	• Major change in hardware or software applications in offices, especially where an earlier system is being replaced
	• Inadequate attention paid to the people's reactions to the introduction of new technology and/or revision of current technology, leading to increased work errors, more waste, reduced employee commitment and increased time spent on re-training

Financial	• Cash flow problems in key areas and/or throughout the operation Inadequate control of debt/credit
	• Unexpected increase in costs of capital projects leading to switching of funds between sector budgets and slowing down of developments in the losing sectors
Marketing / sales	• Marketing research failing to acquire early notice of key developments in consumer tastes/competitor behaviour and so on
	• Sales personnel failing to meet agreed targets
	• Sales so successful that production cannot keep pace with orders
	• Public relations department contribute to successful launch of new product range/new logo, etc.
	• Public relations department succeed in offending the public/fail to reassure the public following an unhappy event (accident, evidence of fraud, etc.).

Organisational change

6. Change generally implies innovation, in the basic sense of introducing something new into an environment. This includes the rearrangement of jobs, roles, and structures. It also includes rearranging systems, since the process of change itself is an innovation. Indeed, it is this aspect of change which has attracted the most attention from researchers. What are the key variables that have to be considered when looking at organisational change? They include the following:

- **Organisation structure** (including tasks and roles)
- **People** (including Skills, Management Style and Leadership)
- **Systems** (administration procedures, production systems, computer networks, budgetary control systems, etc.)
- **Technology** (office technology, communications technology, etc.)
- **Organisation mission and goals** (including strategy)
- **Organisation culture** (including sub-cultures/alternative cultures)
- **External environment** (see BPEST list above).

In addition to the above must be added issues such as resistance to change, organisational development, and the role of change agents.

7. Over thirty years ago Burns and Stalker (1961) conducted their famous enquiries into the management of innovation, and identified what they termed 'mechanistic' and 'organic' systems of organisation. **Mechanistic** systems of organisation had the following characteristics:

- specialised differentiation of tasks
- precise definition of rights, obligations and technical methods of functional roles
- an hierarchical structure
- a predisposition towards vertical interaction between people in the structure
- a tendency for operations to be dominated by superiors

- an insistence on loyalty to the concern and obedience to superiors

Such systems were seen by the authors as being appropriate for conditions of stability. They have come to be associated with modern concepts of bureaucracy.

Organic systems of organisation, by contrast, were seen as suitable for changing conditions. They displayed the following characteristics:

- individual tasks subject to adjustment and interaction with others
- a network structure (as opposed to an hierarchy)
- a predisposition towards lateral communication within the structure
- communications tend to consist of information and advice rather than instructions
- commitment to the organisation's tasks seen to be more important than loyalty and obedience.

8. Burns and Stalker saw the two systems as being at opposite ends of a continuum along which other forms could exist. They recognised that organisations could move from one system to another, and that the two systems could co-exist in different parts of the same organisation. These two dominant organisational types have been confirmed time and time again by subsequent researchers, including current exponents of organisational change such as Rosabeth Moss Kanter and Tom Peters (see below). The point is that these organisational types have a considerable bearing both on the kind of strategies developed by organisations, and in the way they manage the change required to bring those strategies to fulfilment. Mechanistic organisations (i.e. organisations that are *seen as*, and probably *designed as*, mechanisms by their owners and/or senior managers) are likely to emphasise control, predictability and authority levels. Organic organisations (i.e. organisations that are treated as dynamic organisms, and organised accordingly by their owners/managers) are likely to minimise the number of controls, whilst permitting risk-taking, and emphasising personal responsibility.

9. Moss Kanter (1984), in her in-depth study of change in major US companies, identified two quite different ways in which companies approached innovation. One approach, which she called the *'integrative'* approach, described firms who were observed to deal holistically with problems, were willing to try out new ideas, prepared to push the organisation to its limits, and generally saw change as an opportunity rather than a threat. The other approach, by contrast, compartmentalised problem-solving, saw the organisation as a collection of segments rather than as organic whole, dealt with change within segments/compartments and was unwilling to alter the balance of the overall structure. This approach she called the *'segmentalist'* approach. It soon became clear to her that innovation – the introduction not just of new products and new technology, but also of *new ideas and practices* – was much better handled by integrative companies than by the segmentalists.

10. The most important motive for innovation in a business enterprise is, according to Moss Kanter, to improve the organisation's ability to meet and satisfy customer needs. For companies to become integrative they need to develop three new sets of skills in their managers. These can be summarised as follows:

   ❶ Power skills – i.e. skills in persuading others to invest time and resources in new (and perhaps risky) initiatives
   ❷ Skills in managing problems arising from team-working and employee participation

❸ An understanding of how change is designed and constructed in an organisation.

The way in which 'successful' companies handle change has been a focus of interest for a number of other researchers, including Peters and Waterman (1982), Goldsmith and Clutterbuck (1985), and Clifford and Cavanagh (1985), whose findings are referred to shortly.

11. Whilst covering much of the same ground as Moss Kanter, Peters and Waterman, (1982) used the concept of 'excellence' as the central feature of their study of 43 of the largest US companies. 'Success' was defined as a mixture of above average growth rates and financial returns together with a reputation for *continuous innovation in response to changing market situations*. Success, it was pointed out, was not meant to imply perfection. The two authors were experienced management consultants, working for the well-known consultancy company, McKinsey & Co. They used their experience of analysing client organisations to devise a model for use in their excellence survey. The model focused on the following characteristics of business organisations: **structure, strategy, systems, management style, skills, people, and shared values (i.e. culture)**. This is the Seven-S framework referred to in earlier chapters.

12. As a result of their studies, Peters and Waterman, identified eight attributes of excellence, which, although they do not refer specifically to managing change, are certainly descriptions that apply to organic types of organisation rather than to mechanistic, or bureaucratic, types. The eight attributes can be summarised as follows:

❶ The excellent organisations have a bias towards action (i.e. once a problem has been identified and analysed, people are expected to come up with solutions).

❷ These organisations listen to their customers – customer service is foremost.

❸ They encourage internal autonomy and entrepreneurship (and are prepared to tolerate the inevitable failures that will occur).

❹ Employees are held in high esteem, but in a performance-conscious environment; expectations are high.

❺ They emphasise the organisation's basic values (culture) and demonstrate their commitment to them.

❻ They stick to what they know (acknowledging that what they know increases over time).

❼ They avoid complex structures; divisionalised structures are the most likely; corporate/headquarters staff are kept to the minimum.

❽ Control is loose yet tight; it is loose in that decision-making is pushed downwards, but tight in that certain core values/practices are insisted upon (e.g. attention to quality, information feedback, etc.).

An important conclusion reached by Peters and Waterman was that there was invariably one strong individual at work in the crucial early stages of developing a culture of excellence.

Managing strategic change

13. In the process of managing change at the strategic level, the companies that have been successful have shown an ability to harness the external forces bearing on them and their own internal strengths. Goldsmith and Clutterbuck, for example, noted that:

'In trying to isolate what our top companies did that enabled them to innovate where it matters, we came across five recurrent themes. These were by no means universal, but they do seem to represent a basic approach to the fostering of innovation. Those themes were:

- absence or removal of barriers to change
- natural curiosity about how things are done elsewhere
- international perspective
- directed research and development
- role of the chief executive.

14. The absence or removal of barriers to change included organisational structures that facilitated the flow and implementation of ideas, for which there were high incentives if things went well, but low punishment if they went badly. Other significant factors were clear objectives, direction and guidance from senior management, and enough growth in the firm to enable people not to worry about losing their current job, since another would be available as a result of change.

15. On research and development, Goldsmith and Clutterbuck found that in the top companies it tended to 'revolve around defined market needs and to be closely targeted in matters such as end price.' The role of the chief executive and/or senior management is critical too. They noted that where the chief executive showed himself genuinely interested in innovation, then others would respond. The involvement of the senior management was seen as particularly important in technological innovation in order to provide consistent direction to R & D and Marketing. This avoided situations where the two functions might set themselves different goals and thus be at odds with each other!

16. Clifford and Cavanagh (1985) in the United States looked at the changes involved in small companies becoming mid-sized companies. The latter, who formed the focus of the research, were selected on their successful growth record (growth in earnings, assets and return on equity and so forth). One of the key features about these businesses was their attitude to innovation:

    '… their successful pursuit of innovation is focused at least as intensively on inventing
    new ingenious ways of doing business as on turning out breathtaking new products.'

The so-called 'winning' companies demonstrated six distinctive characteristics of organisational behaviour in making the transition from small to medium-sized. These were:

❶ They instilled 'a strong sense of mission and shared values' – and worked constantly to reinforce them.

❷ They paid 'relentless attention to business fundamentals' (i.e. to support priority aspects of the business, be that research & development or advertising; to specify what financial and other information needed to be reported on and reviewed regularly, and to provide it in a disciplined and very focused way; to keep a constant eye on developments in the external environment, especially amongst competitors and in the government domain).

❸ They treated bureaucracy as 'an arch-enemy'.

❹ They encouraged experimentation:

    One important way the winning performers encourage experimentation and
    innovation is by sending strong, consistent signals that – as long as experiments meet the

test of commonsense reasonableness – failure won't be punished. The greater sin is not trying at all.'

⑤ They studied their customers with a view to getting inside their mind.

⑥ They relied heavily on selecting the best staff, motivating them and retaining them if they did well. This operated from top to bottom, for example the chief executive took on the role of chief personnel officer.

17. Moss Kanter (1989) comments on the bureaucracy that large corporations are heirs to, and suggests that they need to become more athletic if they are to meet the challenge of the nineties. She suggests that the demise of bureaucracy and hierarchy is imminent. She sees what she terms 'post-entrepreneurial organisation' as:

> '... a fundamentally different set of organising principles from bureaucracy, a different way of conducting corporate life ... Whereas bureaucratic management is inherently preservation-seeking, entrepreneurial management is inherently opportunity-seeking.'

She suggests that post-entrepreneurial organisations are more person-centred than position-centred, and that they value individual contribution rather than status. She sees post-entrepreneurial management as creation-oriented, seeking innovation as well as efficiency, rather than repetition-oriented, seeking efficiency through doing the same thing time and time again. The former is likely to be results-oriented rather than rules-oriented.

18. Moss Kanter is aware that the new calls to creativity, risk-taking, personal responsibility and collaboration across functional/departmental boundaries have their disadvantages. It is possible, she states, that where strategic changes are handled badly, they can lead to excessive in-house competition (e.g. if a competitor is taken over), rivalry between individuals (e.g. under pay-for-performance conditions), reduced opportunities for promotion (e.g. due to reduction in hierarchical levels), rivalry between decentralised units/departments, as each tries to better the others in obtaining scarce resources from the corporate centre, and short-term asset-shuffling, leading to job losses. There are clearly dangers of a 'dog-eat-dog' attitude developing within organisations undergoing change, and this raises a number of ethical issues.

19. To avoid poor management of change, Moss Kanter suggests that there are seven skills and sensibilities (including ethical ones) which must be cultivated. These are as follows:

❶ Managers must *'learn to operate without the might of the hierarchy behind them'*.

❷ They must know *'how to compete in a way that enhances rather than undercuts co-operation'*.

❸ They must *'operate with the highest ethical standards'*.

❹ They have to acquire *'a dose of humility'*.

❺ They need to develop *'a process focus'* (i.e. execution of plans may matter more than creating them in the first place).

❻ They must become *'multifaceted and ambidextrous'* (i.e. able to work across functions/units, to be flexible, to make connections with the skills of others).

❼ They must *'gain satisfaction from results and be willing to stake their own rewards on them'*.

20. It is interesting to compare Moss Kanter's views of the business athletes of the nineties with the 'excellence' sought of management by writers, such as Peters (1988). In his book, *Thriving on Chaos*, he proposes a number of prescriptions for managing change, innovation and survival. The title of the book is intended to show that the external environment is turbulent and unstable, and that managements have to develop a suitable strategy for change if they, and their firms, are to survive and win. Whilst he proposed 45 prescriptions for excellence, he notes that excellent firms probably don't believe so much in excellence as in constant improvement and constant change.

21. His 45 prescriptions are developed under five different headings, of which the first is *Creating Total Customer Responsiveness*. Here he suggests that firms should concentrate on finding appropriate market niches – differentiation is the order of the day. Having found the niche, meet the customer's needs with top quality products/services, provide superior service, develop responsiveness, become internationalist and create uniqueness (make your product or service stand out among the competition). Listening to customers is a vital element here; others include making more positive use of manufacturing and marketing functions. Such attributes are those which have already been adopted by many leading Japanese firms, and some are featured in Deming's Fourteen Points for Quality (see Chapter 12).

22. Peters' second heading is *Pursuing Fast-Paced Innovation*. The main point here is that innovation should be pursued in small starts. Big firms have to tackle innovation as if they were small firms. Thus there is an incremental approach to change – little by little, but ever onward. Innovations should be tested (piloted) before introduction; success should be rewarded and used as a model for others; failures should be tolerated, especially what he calls 'fast failures', since there is much to be learned from failure. Overall, the organisation should aim to create a corporate capacity for innovation.

23. The third heading is *Achieving Flexibility by Empowering People*. This word 'empowerment' is also used by Moss Kanter. It implies allowing, indeed encouraging, employees at all levels to share in the decision-making processes of the organisation. Thus, firms should do all they can to create opportunities for people to participate fully in the running of the operation, providing incentives, recognising successes, providing training and reducing the amount of supervision and other traditional controls. These policies are increasingly features of many renewed companies.

24. The fourth heading is entitled *Learning to Love Change: A New View of Leadership at All Levels*. This is mainly about management style. It proposes that managers should be single-minded about their pursuit of key values in order to provide a stability of purpose and vision, but should be willing to listen, to delegate and to defer to the front line (i.e. to adopt a participative style). Many of the ideas in this section overlap with those concerning empowerment.

25. The last heading is concerned with *Building Systems for a World Turned Upside Down*. This is concerned mainly with control systems, and Peters' exhortation is to measure what is important (e.g. product quality, customer satisfaction as well as financial situation) and keep the measures as simple as possible. He suggests that a new look should be taken at such controls as Management by Objectives (MBO), Employee Appraisal and Job Descriptions with a view to encouraging self-control and flexibility. Information, Authority and even Strategic Planning should be decentralised (i.e. by means of 'bottom-up' planning), and, surprisingly, he proposes that organisational goals should be conser-

vative, by which he means not timid goals but achievable ones. This fits in with his idea of incremental steps towards change. Finally, on the issue of trust, he urges everyone to practise total integrity, i.e. to honestly practise living up to commitments both inside and outside the firm.

26. Peters (1988) book has the sub-title 'Handbook for a Management Revolution', and it is true that many of the ideas and practices that he and other current exponents of innovation, quality management and corporate excellence, are proposing are destined to bring about the collapse of mechanistic forms of organisation. What is notable about these proposed changes in the management of organisations is that:

   ❶ decentralisation is likely to increase

   ❷ decision-making is likely to be diffused throughout the organisation

   ❸ stability will be maintained chiefly through vision and values (i.e. company culture)

   ❹ innovation will be encouraged, but in manageable amounts, on a more or less continuous basis

   ❺ mistakes will be dealt with as positive forms of learning

   ❻ corporate decisions and strategies will be directed fundamentally at serving the customer

   ❼ this sense of the customer will be employed *within* firms (i.e. each employee is the customer of another)

   ❽ whilst mistakes and failures will be accepted as part of the drive towards excellence, the emphasis on total quality will be stronger as the organisation strives to 'get it right first time'

   ❾ the overall impact on organisation structures will be a move away from mechanistic forms in favour of organic structures.

Resistance to change

27. Much of what has been said earlier in this chapter has focused on the positive aspects of change. It is important to recognise, however, that most people need to be *persuaded* of the need to change. There are difficulties that have been pointed out, especially where change has been handled badly. In any case there is little point in 'change for change's sake', and people need to know the reason why. Some people fear change. The reality is that every human group has simultaneously within it pressures that keep it together and provide it with stability, and others which provide the spur for change and adaptation. Kurt Lewin (1951) illustrated the dilemma neatly with his classic notion of 'Force-field theory', see Figure 11.1. This theory suggests that all behaviour is the result of an equilibrium between two sets of opposing forces (what he calls 'driving forces' and 'restraining forces'). Driving forces push one way to attempt to bring about change; restraining forces push the other way in order to maintain the status quo.

28. Generally speaking, human beings seem to prefer to use driving forces to bring about change. They want to 'win' by exerting pressure on those who oppose them, but, as Lewin's model suggests, the more one side pushes, the more the other resists, resulting in no change. The better way of overcoming resistance, therefore, is by focusing on the removal, or at least weakening, of the objections and fears of the resisting side. Thus the initial policy should be not 'How can we persuade them of *our* arguments for change?',

but rather 'What are *their* objections/fears, and how can we deal with them?' It is noticeable in studying the results obtained by Peters and Waterman, Moss Kanter and others, that the principal approach to change is to reduce opposition rather than try to impose new ways of working.

Figure 11.1 Force-field theory (after Lewin)

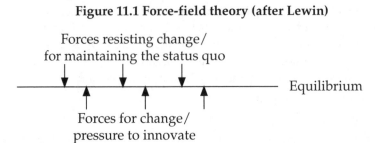

29. For example, in dealing with issues of resistance to change and overcoming inertia ('roadblocks to innovation'), Moss Kanter (1984), in her earlier work on change management, suggests a number of actions that can be taken:

   ❶ As a prerequisite to change, top management must be personally committed to supporting innovation and must learn to think integratively.

   ❷ A 'culture of pride' should be encouraged within the organisation, in which achievements are highlighted and where experienced innovators serve as consultants to other parts of the organisation.

   ❸ Access to power sources (management committees, etc.) should be enlarged to improve support for innovatory/experimental proposals.

   ❹ Lateral communication should be improved. Cross-functional links should be developed, and staff mobility should be encouraged.

   ❺ Unnecessary layers of hierarchy should be reduced (i.e. a flatter structure should be aimed for) and authority should be pushed downwards ('empowerment' of staff).

   ❻ Information about company plans should be more widespread and given as early as possible to enable people to contribute to change before decisions are made (for instance, by means of task-forces, problem-solving groups, etc.).

30. The management of innovation and change is a challenge to the senior management of every organisation. It is particularly important at the strategic level to:

   ❶ identify priorities and targets
   ❷ provide adequate resources to carry them out
   ❸ allow for mistakes within reason
   ❹ develop positive employee attitudes towards change
   ❺ provide appropriate means of learning.

The last two points have particular relevance for the Personnel/Human Resource function, and will be considered separately in Chapter 14. In concluding this chapter on change, one final point is emphasised: in today's highly competitive market-place, made even more complex by the activities of governments and pressure groups, firms must learn to adapt or they will die.

References

1. Burns, T. & Stalker, (1961), *The Management of Innovation*, Tavistock.
2. Moss Kanter, R. (1984), *The Change Masters – Corporate Entrepreneurs at Work*, Allen & Unwin.
3. Peters, T. & Waterman, R. (1982), *In Search Of Excellence: Lessons from America's Best-Run Companies*, Harper & Row.
4. Goldsmith, W. & Clutterbuck, D. (1985), *The Winning Streak*, Penguin Business.
5. Clifford, D. & Cavanagh, R. (1985), *The Winning Performance*, Sidgwick & Jackson.
6. Moss Kanter, R. (1989), *When Giants Learn to Dance*, Simon & Schuster.
7. Peters, T. (1988), *Thriving on Chaos – Handbook for a Management Revolution*, MacMillan.
8. Lewin, K. (1951), *Field Theory in Social Science*, Harper.

Questions for reflection/discussion

1. Why is the management of change so important for strategic management?

2. What *political* and *technological* factors are the most likely to cause turbulence in the external environments of:

   a) a financial services industry?

   b) an oil extraction industry?

3. *'Organisational change is influenced more by the organisation's culture than by the external environment.'* Discuss this assertion in relation to an organisation you are familiar with.

4. What are the most significant *disadvantages* of change, when handled ineffectively by senior management? How could these have been avoided?

5. How far can an organisation go in dismantling a bureaucratic structure without causing the collapse of its communication and decision-making channels? Consider in the context of an organisation you know from personal experience.

12 Managing quality

Introduction

1. One of the most consistent themes to be found embedded in mission statements, goals and objectives is that of 'quality'. Organisations both business and public sector have been keen to stress their attention to product quality and/or quality of service not just in their external public statements but also in the way they implement their chosen strategies internally. In fact no business strategy will succeed fully in today's competitive conditions unless it gives adequate priority to quality issues. This chapter examines what is meant by 'quality', if and how it differs from the equally popular concept of 'value', and how it is put into practice.

The concept of quality

2. The concept of 'quality' is rather elusive, mainly because it is a term which expresses a relative, even though noticeable, difference between one thing and another – be that a product, commodity, or service of some kind. In judging quality, we normally have some implicit standard in mind, for example an 'acceptable' design or even 'the best possible' design. Either way, we are seeking a product or service that fulfils our particular purposes. Generally quality is also judged in relation to price. Thus, we look for an acceptable standard of product within a certain price-range. Customers, wherever they are, want satisfaction. If they are buying a product they obviously want it to be fit for its purpose, and they want it to be safe, reliable and probably durable too. And they are influenced by price. Most people want to own a car, but not everyone wants a Rolls-Royce, or an expensive executive model. They will be quite happy with a standard middle-range vehicle. However, they do want it to be reliable, safe and economical. In the past many manufacturers were unable even to guarantee these three features. Nowadays, all manufacturers have to provide these, and many other standard features, in order to maintain their sales against the competition. These considerations are extremely important in deciding a product-market strategy, and can mean all the difference between success and failure in achieving strategic objectives.

3. In the case of a service, people are looking for factors such as availability, reliability, effectiveness (fitness for purpose) and courtesy. They may also be influenced by price. Thus, in looking for a suitable family dentist, parents will want to know that the dentist is fully-qualified and competent, that they can book an appointment without having to wait weeks or months, that any fears their children may have about visiting the dentist will be dealt with sympathetically, and, finally, that the cost of treatment will not be prohibitive. Time-standards are a key aspect of quality, especially where a service is concerned, and so in judging the standard of a restaurant, we usually take into account speed and efficiency of service as well as the quality of the food. It is clear that the concept of 'quality' in our thinking is linked to a number of important variables that, as consumers or end-users, we look for, implicitly or explicitly, when we purchase goods and services. These variables can be demonstrated in the following figure (Figure 12.1):

Figure 12.1 Key elements in the concept of quality

4. The use of the term 'quality' to describe what users want from goods and services is somewhat of a catch-all to describe a number of important characteristics that are perceived to make the difference between something that is just acceptable and something that is exactly what the user requires. It is easy for organisations to make pious statements about 'quality', and even easier for people to nod their agreement. However, if the word is to have any lasting meaning, and if the concept is to have any long-term value for strategic management purposes, it is essential to break it down into its major components, or elements. Thus, issues of fitness for purpose, reliability, availability and price all play their part in determining what 'quality' truly means in a given set of circumstances.

The concept of value

5. One other aspect of quality is 'value'. Many firms advertise the desirability of their products and services in terms of their being 'good value'. It is possible to say that 'value' is yet another ingredient of quality, closely allied to the idea of acceptable price-range, for it is certainly true that most customers are seeking good value, whether they are buyers purchasing goods for Marks & Spencer's, or individuals purchasing a motor-car. However, value can also be considered as an independent concept, just as overarching as quality, and not merely an element of it. From this viewpoint 'value' can be defined as

    'the perceived worth to the customer of a particular product or service. It is the customer's overall conclusion about the particular marketing mix (product, price, promotion and distribution) that is on offer.'

So, the concept of 'poor value', for example, is generally associated with an adverse relationship between price and other features of the product or service. One of the selling features of the subscription magazine service (*Which*) offered by the consumer advice organisation, the Consumers' Association, is precisely its ability to help consumers distinguish good value products/services (Best Buys) from poor value ones. Poor value products may still incorporate sound design features, and are to be distinguished from dangerous or badly-designed products, but their better features are outweighed by the price being asked and are thus perceived as insufficiently attractive.

6. The concept of value is referred to frequently by Porter (1985) in his discussion of competitive advantage, and he sees it as follows:

    'Competitive advantage grows fundamentally out of value a firm is able to create for its buyers that exceeds the cost of creating it. Value is what buyers are willing to pay, and superior value stems from offering lower prices than competitors for equivalent benefits or providing unique benefits that more than offset a higher price.'

    Porter's meaning hovers somewhere between value as defined above (i.e. perceived worth) and value defined as profit or margin. Indeed, Porter refers specifically to margin in his describing his model of the 'value chain', which will be considered shortly. The question of who gets what proportion of value is determined, according to Porter, by the structure of the industry (power of buyers, suppliers, etc. – see Figure 4.1, Chapter 4).

7. Porter's idea of a 'value chain' is introduced as a tool for analysing the main strategic activities of a firm that contribute to competitive advantage. The idea is based on a systems approach to strategic activities (i.e. input – process – output), and is illustrated in its generic form in Figure 12.2.

Figure 12.2 Porter's generic value chain

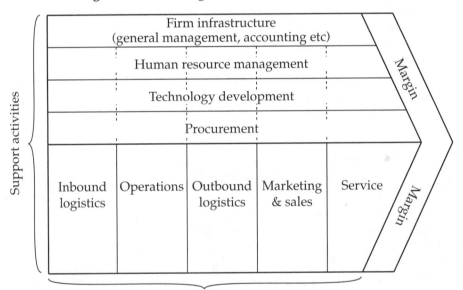

Primary activities

The thinking behind the model, in its application to a manufacturing concern, can be summarised as follows:

Competing in any industry involves five generic (strategic) activities:

❶ **Inbound logistics** i.e. materials handling, inventory (stock) control, warehousing and other functions related to raw materials and parts;

❷ **Operations** i.e. machining, testing, assembly, packaging and other functions related to turning out finished goods;

❸ **Outbound logistics** i.e. order processing, warehousing, delivery operations and other functions related to the distribution of finished goods;

❹ **Marketing & sales** i.e. advertising, pricing, promotion, sales and other functions related to the satisfying of customers' needs and wants;

❺ **Service** i.e. after-sales support (installation, training, maintenance and repair, etc.).

In addition to these primary activities are four generic support activities, as follows:

❶ **Firm infrastructure**, i.e. activities that support the entire chain, including overhead costs, such as corporate finance, management accounting, general management, etc.;

❷ **Human resource management**, i.e. employee recruitment, selection, training, etc.;

❸ **Technology development**, i.e. product development, process development, software applications, research and design;

❹ **Procurement**, i.e. the purchasing of goods and services on behalf of the firm.

The total cost of all the above activity groups subtracted from the total value (revenue) generated by them produces the **margin**. As Porter puts it, 'Margin is the difference between total value and the collective cost of performing the value activities'.

8. Porter refers to one further dimension to his model, and that is that each of the primary and support activities can be sub-divided into three different types of the activity – **direct, indirect** and **quality assurance**. Within operations, for example, some activities are directly involved in creating value for the ultimate buyer (e.g. machining), while others are indirectly involved in this function (e.g. equipment maintenance). Quality assurance includes activities such as inspection and testing.

Although the example used here is based on manufacturing, the model can be applied equally to a service industry.

9. One final point about Porter's concept of the 'value chain' is that each firm is also part of a wider value chain by virtue of its links with suppliers, dealers and buyers. This wider chain is called the 'value system' by Porter, and an understanding of the value chains of other key players in the system is vital for strategic management. Thus awareness of the value system becomes an important part of the external environment discussed in Chapter 3 above, and in Porter's view is an essential element in gaining and sustaining competitive advantage.

Quality in theory and practice

10. A number of definitions of 'quality' have been put forward. Oakland (1993), for example, sees it simply as *'meeting the customer's requirements'*, or, even better, *'delighting the customer'*. This latter notion of quality has been taken up recently by a number of consumer-oriented businesses such as the W H Smith Group plc, for example:

'Our Vision for the Group

We are in business to delight our customers. We will do this by offering them memorable products, good value for money and legendary service.'

(W H Smith Vision Statement, 1993)

What exactly constitutes a memorable product, or legendary service, might be hard to define, but it is clear that, in principle, W H Smith's customers are to be treated as special people who will be listened to and dealt with fairly. Part of this fair treatment will be supplied by providing 'good value'.

11. It may be less easy for some businesses to delight their customers, especially in situations where the basic quality of the product (e.g. drinking water) is taken for granted by consumers. However, Anglian Water plc as an example of such a business, aims to provide 'high quality' drinking water through 'our continuing commitment to quality, reliability and value …'. In this example, the test of *'high quality'* is linked directly to achieving better than the legal minima of limits on nitrates, pesticides and bacteria present in drinking water. Most of the quality standards for water, and all those relating to the healthiness of water, are set by national and international requirements. In such an operation customers are much more likely to be aroused when their water supply fails, or, through some accident, becomes highly polluted – usually a very rare occurrence in developed countries. It is essential in such an industry to ensure the provision of a first-class delivery and after-sales service, since these are often the most noticeable features of quality to the average consumer. Not surprisingly, therefore, considerable strategic effort is put into improving water supply systems (which involves considerable capital expenditure) and dealing promptly with emergency repairs.

12. Another example, where quality is uppermost in people's minds, is in food preparation and sale. J Sainsbury plc, like other food retailers, pays particular attention to product safety and freshness, as well as to taste and flavour. Since most of their raw food and much of their branded products are bought in, the control of quality from suppliers is critical. In 1992 the company introduced a Product Management System for controlling suppliers' standards. This sets particular standards in a variety of products. In support of its strategy of constantly improving supplier quality, Sainsbury's has set up a shellfish cooking plant in Grimsby, where imported products such as tiger prawns from Thailand, lobsters from New England and fresh mussels from Ireland can be cooked under conditions specified by the company, prior to delivery to stores the following day. The company reports that:

> 'Last year we spent £30 million on maintaining and improving our food safety chain. We strengthened links across the world with research institutes, thereby gaining access to the most sophisticated technology. Our strategy allows us to take the initiative by identifying emerging technical issues and managing them effectively in partnership with our suppliers.'

(J Sainsbury plc – Annual Report & Accounts, 1993)

13. In the light of the above examples of quality in practice, the earlier definitions of such quality gurus as Joseph Juran, W. Edwards Deming and Philip Crosby can be seen in perspective. Deming and Juran applied and developed techniques such as **statistical process control** (see note below) to the post-war industries of Japan. They showed that, by paying attention (a) to the continuous improvement of production processes, and (b) to the importance of gaining employees' commitment to the idea of quality – at every stage of production – it was possible to achieve consistently high standards of finished goods at a price the customer was more than willing to pay in order to secure reliable and acceptable performance.

[Note: statistical process control is the name given to a number of techniques, usually based on random sampling, for identifying the inputs and outputs of a production system and comparing them with the standards required, often by use of control charts. The factors selected for analysis are usually grouped under the headings of machines, materials, methods and people.]

14. Juran (1980), in particular, showed that at least 85% of failures in production could be laid at the door of management, and that much of this situation had arisen because managements were prepared to accept that present performance could not be improved upon, rather than thinking all the time of how it could be improved. Given the day-to-day pressures of a production unit, it is not surprising that many managers are unable to move beyond short-term 'crisis' management. Juran argued, however, that it is essential to look further ahead in order to prevent problems occurring in the first place. Developing this attitude leads to what he termed *'management breakthrough'*, which is a core feature of his ideas on total quality. In essence, he was urging managements to stop trying to cure the *symptoms* of production problems, and concentrate instead on identifying and tackling their *underlying causes*. Juran's definition of quality sees it predominantly as *'fitness for purpose or use'*.

15. W. Edwards Deming (1986), who is considered by many to be the godfather of Japanese industrial success, saw quality as aiming at *'the needs of the consumer, present and future'*. In the immediate post-war period, after Japan had suffered great devastation of its industries, Deming persuaded the Japanese Union of Scientists and Engineers (JUSE) to try his approach of looking at products from the *customer's* point of view, and then meeting customer requirements in close collaboration with suppliers. A further key point in Deming's approach was his emphasis on the need to gain both managerial and employee commitment to engage in a process in which quality was paramount. Thus the total quality approach was born – an approach based not just on statistical process control and similar quantitative techniques but also on a positive attitude towards quality at every level in the organisation. It was the adoption of this approach as a key business strategy which led Japanese manufacturing firms out of their industrial mediocrity of the 1960s/70s into their present position as world renowned manufacturers of the highest quality.

16. Another American, Crosby (1979) saw quality primarily as *'conformance to requirements'* and introduced the idea of 'zero defects'. He proposed fourteen steps that management could take to improve quality throughout the business. These mostly concentrated on raising awareness about quality and gaining collaboration for the achievement of zero defects. Thus, he too was aware of the strategic importance of gaining employees' commitment to quality.

17. Deming's work led him also to promote Fourteen Points for Total Quality Control. These have been extremely influential in guiding firms on the strategic aspects of quality. They also give considerable insight into his arguments for a total quality approach, and can be summarised as follows:

   ❶ Create and publish for all employees a statement of the company's mission (aims and objectives) and ensure that managers constantly demonstrate their commitment to it.

   ❷ Everyone from top management down must learn the new philosophy (i.e. of continuously improving customer satisfaction).

   ❸ Employ inspection primarily for improving production processes rather than for detecting and correcting errors.

   ❹ Award business to suppliers on the basis of consistent quality and reliability of their product as well as on price (which is secondary).

⑤ Continuously aim to improve the production system.

⑥ Ensure adequate training both of employees and suppliers (so that all parties know what is expected of them).

⑦ Introduce participatory leadership style in order to achieve employee co-operation

⑧ Develop climate of trust between management and employees, and between groups (including avoidance of approaches such as Management by Objectives (MBO), which is based on fear, according to Deming!)

⑨ Develop an across-the-board approach to co-operation and teamwork.

⑩ Cease all exhortations and slogans! Instead provide the *means* to improve customer satisfaction.

⑪ Eliminate numerical quotas for production in favour of instituting methods for improvement; eliminate MBO.

⑫ Remove barriers to workmanship by providing adequate training and equipment and encouraging pride in own work.

⑬ Encourage education and self-improvement at every level (including training in statistical process control techniques).

⑭ Create a climate where quality improvement is embedded in the organisation's culture from top to bottom.

18. In view of the above statements it is not surprising that Deming's approach emphasises:

    * top-management commitment
    * the development of a longer-term (i.e. *strategic* view) of quality rather than a short-term one
    * the need for managements to persist in the face of initial setbacks on the road to total quality
    * encouragement to developing quality *at source*
    * a ban on emphasising output at the expense of quality.

    Deming's approach tends to lead to a three-tier system of quality management where (a) top management is responsible for the quality of the aims, objectives and *fundamental strategy* of the organisation; (b) middle management is responsible for the *implementation* of those aims and objectives, in line with the overall policy on quality; and (c) where work-groups are responsible for *results*, within a continuous framework of improvements to production processes.

19. Specifically Japanese influences on quality were led by Professor Ishikawa, who in the early 1960s introduced the idea of Quality Circles (i.e. where small groups of workers gather regularly to discuss operational quality issues, especially identifying problems and finding and implementing solutions). The idea arose from his interest in the training of supervisors in the quality process, where he realised that if the work-groups themselves participated in the process it would provide a means of securing quality standards at the workplace, and provide a system for giving feedback to supervisors and managers on quality problems. The strongly participative nature of Quality Circles aids the process of gaining every employee's commitment to quality. However, such groups are not intended to be ends in themselves but are an integral part of a total quality control approach, including the use of statistical quality control.

20. In a total quality approach, especially where 'just-in-time' (JIT) systems are being implemented (this refers to stock/parts ordering, where suppliers – internal or external – have to supply on request at short notice, i.e. to be just in time for use in the production process), an important lesson for Quality Circles is that their output is not passed on to the next process group until it is asked for. They in turn are not required to accept components, parts, etc. from their 'suppliers' until they are ready for them. Thus, each work-group has to learn to react to the needs of their 'customers'. This idea of everyone being a supplier and a customer of someone else in the organisation, is a key feature of a total quality approach and a fundamental aspect of production strategy in many firms.

21. Collard (1989) reports a spokesman for JUSE stating that today in Japan quality control has the following principal features:

    • Quality control is company-wide.

    • Quality control audits are carried out both within the organisation and with suppliers.

    • Regular training is given in aspects of quality (and especially in statistical techniques) throughout the company.

    • Quality Circles underpin the whole programme.

    • Statistical methods are applied to production processes.

    • Nationwide quality activities (conferences and so on) are held for management and employees.

    From the above comments, it is clear that Japanese companies have adopted a vertical approach to quality as an essential part of their production and marketing strategies.

22. National encouragement for quality programmes in the UK is spearheaded mainly by the development of International and British Standards e.g. BS5750 for quality systems. The Standards do not go quite so far as total quality management in that they are aimed at encouraging frameworks for developing quality systems rather than being concerned, for example, with gaining employee commitment to total quality. Many British Standards are now superseded by International (ISO) Standards.

ISO 9002 – formerly British Standard 5750

23. The Standard is not concerned with setting specific quality standards, but is a framework for the establishment of a quality management system. Organisations (e.g. see Case-study 13) seeking to obtain ISO 9002 have to demonstrate to the external assessors that they have the following key features of a quality system:

    • a senior manager responsible for quality, who is charged with ensuring that ISO 9002 standards are met

    • documentation to support quality procedures, processes, organisation and so forth

    • the system planned and developed across all other functions

    • the planning of quality that addresses issues of updating techniques and ensuring adequate equipment, personnel and records

    • design and development planning that is adequately resourced and documented with adequate control of the interfaces between disciplines

    • a co-ordinated system set up covering the total production process, in which all control functions are described and accounted for

- control in writing of the quality system to be applied by suppliers, including reference to purchasing data, inspection of purchased products
- establishment of procedures and work instructions, including customer specifications, in a simple form which covers every phase of manufacture, assembly and installation
- procedures for inspection of, and tests on, incoming goods
- procedures and records covering control, etc. of measuring and test equipment
- written control procedures to establish quickly whether a product has not been inspected/been inspected and approved/been inspected and rejected
- system established to enable prompt and effective corrective action to be taken where non-conformance to specification is found
- written procedures and instructions regarding the movement of the product as it passes through the plant
- detailed records are available to demonstrate that customer quality requirements are being met (including audit reports, etc.)
- effective internal quality audit systems are installed
- adequate training is provided
- clear statistical procedures for monitoring quality standards are operated.

24. The emphasis in the above British Standard is on the procedural aspects of installing a quality management system. It enables the basis of such a system to be established, but this has to be built on by means of communication measures and motivational and training programmes aimed at capturing the spirit of total quality throughout the whole organisation. Nevertheless, many UK firms, and government agencies too, are insisting that their suppliers conform to ISO 9002 as a minimum indication of their commitment to, and capability in, quality management.

25. Quality management begins with a consideration of the customers, be they internal employees, other businesses or members of the public. As Figure 12.3 indicates, the whole process is cyclical. Initially, customer wants and needs have to be translated into specifications of one kind or another. These specifications need to be developed and tested. Resources and operational plans have to be drawn up. Then production (or delivery, if a service) can begin. The process of production (or delivery of a service) must be assessed and monitored at every stage in order to see where improvement can be made. Once the customer has received the goods or service, procedures need to be in place to deal with after-sales problems or queries, and to assess the level of customer satisfaction. Then the quality process can begin all over again – in a total quality management system (TQM) it is a cyclical process which never stops.

26. The cycle forms the basis of a strategic approach to quality founded on studying the needs of the customer. As Oakland (1993) puts it:

> '... consumers place a higher value on quality than on loyalty to home-based producers, and price is no longer the major determining factor in consumer choice.'

The latter sees TQM as the way forward for firms wishing to make the most of quality as a strategic issue, for in his words it is:

'... a comprehensive approach to improving competitiveness, effectiveness and flexibility through planning, organising and understanding each activity, and involving each individual at each level. It is useful in all types of organisation.'

Figure 12.3 The quality management cycle

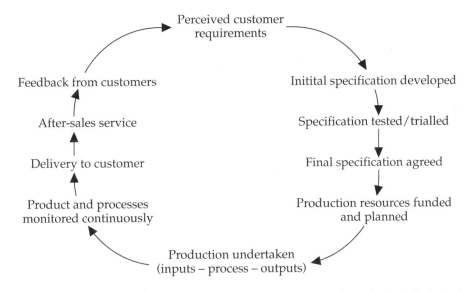

The basic requirements of a total quality management system, as described by Oakland in the book just quoted, fit very closely with the fourteen points proposed by Deming (see paragraph 15 above), and his ideas on analysing each activity endorse those put forward by Porter in his discussion of the value chain.

27. In the final analysis, a total quality management system should set out at least the following standards for itself:

❶ The aim of the system is *prevention* of errors, not their detection and correction.

❷ Every person's motto should be 'Right first time!'.

❸ Management must be totally committed to the total quality policy.

❹ The ultimate purpose of the system is to meet customer requirements – quality is defined by the customer.

❺ Each employee is a customer to every other employee.

❻ Quality implies continuous improvement.

❼ Quality assurance must be installed to review and measure performance, including all the quality processes involved as well as the delivery of the final product, or service.

❽ Quality is everyone's responsibility (including suppliers).

28. The importance of quality management in achieving business success can hardly be denied. Peters and Waterman (1982) found quality to be an important element in the pursuit of excellence:

'The excellent companies were, above all brilliant on basics ... They insisted on top quality. They fawned on their customers.'

In developing their eight characteristics of excellent companies, the authors highlighted such quality features as: (a) getting close to the customer by providing *'unparalleled quality, service and reliability'*; (b) achieving productivity through people – *'the excellent companies treat the rank and file as the root source of quality and productivity gain.'*; (c) being value-driven, i.e. harnessing the corporate culture, especially in relation to such factors as quality, service and value.

It is unlikely that all firms will behave so deferentially towards their customers that they will fawn on them. However, it is clear that, to survive in a competitive business today, all firms must at least listen rather more closely to their customers than in the past, and that they must incorporate that listening into their strategic planning processes.

References

1. Porter, M. E. (1985), *Competitive Advantage*, The Free Press.
2. Oakland, J.S. (1993), *Total Quality Management*, Butterworth Heinemann.
3. Deming W. Edwards (1986), *Out of the Crisis*, MIT Press.
4. Juran, J. (1980), *Quality Planning and Analysis*, McGraw Hill.
5. Crosby, P.B. (1979), *Quality is Free*, McGraw-Hill.
6. Collard, R. (1989), *Total Quality – Success Through People*, IPM.
7. Peters, T. & Waterman R. (1982), *In Search of Excellence*, Harper & Row.

Questions for reflection/discussion

1. What are the key quality features that individual customers are likely to look for when buying expensive finished goods?

2. What quality features might be sought by a civil engineering contractor when purchasing gravel and sand for a major motorway construction project?

3. How would you define the term 'value', and how would you distinguish it from 'poor value'?

4. Which of Deming's Fourteen Points do you consider to be the most important when applied to a service industry?

5. To what extent is Quality Management in manufacturing a matter of giving *services* to the customer rather than providing goods of some kind?

13 The role of the marketing function in strategic management

Introduction

1. The role of the marketing function in strategic management is central. This is because the marketing function acts as a bridge, or channel of communication, between the organisation and its customers. Customers, or rather the needs and wants of customers, are the very reason for existence of business organisations. No business can succeed without raising sufficient revenue from the sale of its goods or services to its customers. Marketing strategy, therefore, has to be at the centre of corporate strategy. Of course, marketing departments do not just deal with customers and their needs. They have to interpret those needs to colleagues in other functions – design and development, production, distribution and so on. They also have to explain to customers what is, and what is not, possible in meeting all their requirements. Finally, the marketing staff are responsible for obtaining customer feedback on the standard of goods or services provided by the organisation.

2. It is worth reminding ourselves what marketing is about, where is its primary thrust and how it fits into the other major functions of a business. Marketing, according to the UK Chartered Institute of Marketing is defined as follows:

   'Marketing is the management process responsible for identifying, anticipating and satisfying customer requirements profitably.'

   In every sense marketing is a powerful influence on all the other functions in a business organisation. In many cases it is also the driver of those other functions. Non-business organisations (such as charities and public services) may not be affected quite so strongly by their marketing wing, but nevertheless will still be energised by the reactions of those they serve, or seek to persuade. Charities, for example, need to be aware of changing attitudes towards issues they are promoting; if they fail to notice that public sympathy is falling away from their particular area of interest, they may be taken by surprise when donations drop and projects have to be abandoned. Such organisations also have to be aware of how best to capture public opinion in their publications and media advertising. The International Red Cross, for example, is engaged in projects all over the world and needs to know where, how and when is the best moment to ask for donations and physical aid for crisis areas as different and far apart as Bosnia and Rwanda.

3. The above definition of marketing can be analysed further by considering Kotler's (1993) definition of marketing management:

   'Marketing management is the analysis, planning, implementation and control of programs designed to create, build, and maintain mutually beneficial exchanges and relationships with target markets for the purpose of achieving organisational objectives. It relies on the disciplined analysis of needs, wants, perceptions and preferences of target and intermediary markets as the basis for effective product design, pricing, communication and distribution.'

Much of what Kotler has included in his definition is undertaken as part of the strategic management process. The principal difference being that the latter encompasses a wider range of issues than just marketing, such as growth and profit targets, capital investment, acquisition strategy, organisational structuring, optimising employee skills, and funding.

4. The marketing perspective that has come to be called 'the marketing concept' is just as applicable today as it was when it was first introduced in the 1950s. This view of the marketing function is based on the fundamental importance of customers and their needs/wants. It assumes that strategic management must focus on the needs and wants of customers as its first priority, and this echoes the comment by Peters and Waterman (1982) quoted in the last chapter (paragraph 28), that the excellent companies *'fawned on their customers'*. The marketing concept also assumes that marketing activity takes place throughout the organisation, and is not just the preserve of planners or specialist marketing personnel. Interestingly, the Institute of Marketing definition of marketing mentioned above refers to marketing as a *'management process'*, thus implying it is not just the specific concern of a few, but is a generic activity. Marketing in fact is carried out at every level. For example, all the following are fulfilling a marketing role (i.e. endeavouring to satisfy customer needs and wants):

❶ senior managers engaged in an assessment of strategic business options

❷ specialist marketing staff engaged in analysing market conditions

❸ production managers discussing modifications with customers

❹ personnel specialists recruiting people to the organisation

❺ van drivers making deliveries to customers.

5. In one sense, it could be said that strategic management itself is a marketing function *par excellence*, for it:

❶ defines the objectives designed to satisfy customer needs and wants

❷ sets out a programme (strategy) for achieving them

❸ ensures the allocation of resources to support the strategy

❹ strives to obtain the commitment of all employees to the service of the customer

❺ establishes review and feedback mechanisms to ensure that plans are being achieved

❻ ensures that the customer's changing requirements are monitored and fulfilled.

However, it is also important to recognise that strategic management is not only concerned with customer needs and wants, vital though these are. It also has to balance the varied, and sometimes conflicting, interests of a much wider range of stakeholders, both direct and indirect (see Chapter 1 paragraphs 28-30). Marketing, by comparison, focuses principally on just one group of stakeholders, variously called customers, clients, patients, consumers or end-users.

6. For the purposes of this text, we shall examine the strategic role of the specialist marketing function at two levels – first, at the level of corporate strategy, and second, at the Strategic Business Unit (SBU) level. As mentioned in Chapter 6 (paragraph 2), there are several levels at which corporate strategy can be developed, but for the purposes of analysis it is simpler to assume two levels – corporate level and strategic business unit level. The main differences between these two are summarised in the following paragraphs, but, as was pointed out in Chapter 1, and illustrated in Figure 1.3, there are

invariably overlapping concerns between strategic activities and lower-level (operational) activities. This point is particularly important in unitary companies, where corporate strategy and operational concerns are almost certain to overlap.

7. **Corporate-level strategy** – this refers to strategy that encompasses the whole organisation, and is usually to be found in two distinct settings:

    ❶ one in which a corporate headquarters, or holding company, makes certain major decisions (e.g. defining the core business, establishing major performance goals, allocating funds between units, prioritising R & D etc.), which are binding on subsidiary units (SBUs), and then leaves the latter free to take responsibility for more local issues (e.g. market segmentation, pricing, quality,etc.);

    ❷ one in which a unitary organisation formulates (and subsequently implements) a strategy for the entire business.

    In both cases, the major *strategic* attention is on satisfying primary (direct) stake-holders, such as shareholders, creditors and customers by:

    ❶ setting out such targets as percentage Return on Investment, Current Ratio, and Gearing Ratio (see Chapter 5), which are of major interest to shareholders and creditors,

    ❷ stating intentions regarding acquisitions, new capital investment and other strategic plans aimed at improving the service to customers.

8. **Strategic business unit-level strategy** – this refers to a situation where a semi-independent/semi-autonomous unit of an organisation, which may be a subsidiary company, or a division of a large company, or some other major unit, is empowered to make key decisions about current and future strategy *within the framework of the overall corporate strategy.* The focus of SBU strategy is likely to be on such concerns as competitive strategy, market share and allocation of human, material and financial resources between operational or functional areas. Decisions in these matters will be planned to meet the sort of performance and other targets mentioned in the previous paragraph.

9. Both the above levels of strategy are concerned more with strategy formulation than implementation, although, as was indicated in Chapter 7, there comes a point when strategic and operational concerns overlap. Ultimately every organisation has to be involved in executing its chosen strategy, and ultimately every step towards implementation will involve grass-roots operations. Thus, in a real sense, strategic management is a vertical process that affects every organisation from the main board directors down to the individual employee at the point of sale.

Marketing at the corporate level

10. In Chapter 1 a number of definitions of strategy were given. These were summarised into a working definition (Chapter 1, paragraph 5), which can now be adapted and extended as follows:

    Strategic management is a process, directed by top management, but engaged in throughout the management structure, which is aimed at determining the fundamental aims or goals of the organisation, including those concerned with satisfying customers' legitimate needs and wants, and ensuring the attainment of those fundamental aims and goals through the adoption of adequate decision-making mechanisms and the provision of adequate resources in support of a planned direction for the organisation over a given period of time.

This revised definition includes additional references to such issues as:

1 the legitimate needs and wants of customers

2 the provision of adequate resources

3 the planned direction of the organisation

4 the inclusion of every level of management in the strategy process.

These additions are important in the context of marketing and its role in the strategy process, because (a) they stress the central place of the customers – at least insofar as they seek goods and services of a *legitimate*, and not of a criminal kind – and (b) they make explicit the intention to drive the organisation in a certain direction (e.g. position in the market place). They also imply that the resourcing of strategic choices, whilst decided by top management, is carried out by managers at every level.

11. The role of marketing at a *corporate* level is basically to contribute, where applicable, to the development of the following aspects of corporate strategy:

- **product strategies** (e.g. maintenance or development of present products, innovation strategy, differentiation strategies)
- **market strategies** (e.g. market penetration, development of new market, segmentation strategies, diversification strategy, niche markets and so on)
- **brand strategies** (e.g. supporting existing brands, introducing new brands)
- **pricing strategy** (e.g. competitive pricing, premium pricing, differential pricing)
- **performance goals**, such as Return on Investment, Margin on Sales, etc.
- **total quality management** (e.g. product, delivery, service, etc.)
- **the adoption of the marketing concept** across the organisation.

In short, the ultimate role of marketing at corporate strategy level is to ensure, so far as possible, that the business is set on the right lines in terms of its products, its markets, its treatment of customers, and the value that can be generated by the firm's activities. In this way marketing contributes to the overall strategic purpose of the business, that is to achieve its mission to its customers, employees, shareholders and the other stakeholders in its chosen field of operations.

12. The contribution made by marketing *specialists* to the development of strategy at corporate level is usually in the form of such activities as:

1 supplying intelligence about the market, the industry and the competition

2 providing feedback on customer satisfaction levels

3 putting forward proposals for continuing or revising product-market strategies

4 giving advice on 'value-for-money' and 'quality' issues.

Peters and Waterman (1982) point out that excellent companies stay close to their customers, and that they are *'obsessed with service'*. Such contacts are usually made, and sustained, by marketing personnel. Marketing people tend to understand better than most others in the organisation that customers do not buy products, but *services*, or what are more accurately termed *'benefits'*. Clifford and Cavanagh (1985), in their study of medium-sized companies in the USA, also point to the importance of marketing issues. Winning performance was achieved by firms whose strategy was one of market-driven innovation (new markets, products, services, methods). These firms emphasised supplying value for their customers rather than being over-concerned with price, costs or scale. As Clifford and Cavanagh put it:

> 'The winners almost always compete by delivering products and services that provide superior value to customers rather than ones that just cost less. In fact 97 percent of our survey respondents reported that value rather than just price was a basis for their success.'

13. A comparison between corporate (strategic) management and strategic marketing can be illustrated in the following diagram (Figure 13.1), which shows stage-by-stage the main concerns of each:

Figure 13.1 Comparing corporate and marketing planning

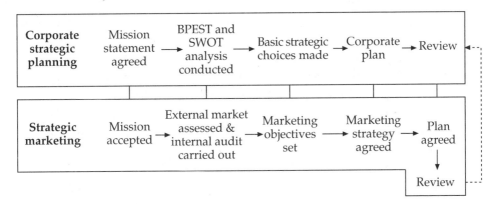

The diagram shows the common ground between BPEST and SWOT analyses and the exercises carried out by marketing, often at one and the same time as part of the corporate exercise. In the strategic marketing assessment of the *external* market, such issues as the size, nature and level of demand in the market will be analysed, alongside an assessment of the competition and the life-cycle of the industry, or of major products within it. In assessing the internal marketing situation, particular attention will be paid to general issues concerning the marketing mix, the performance of sales and other staff, and the status of quality throughout the business.

14. The assessments lead on to decisions about marketing objectives, especially the key product-market objectives that the business wishes to pursue (for example, revenue targets, margins, market share, market position – leader, follower, etc.). The strategy selected to attain these objectives is likely to support a number of routes forward, depending on product types, differing market conditions between geographical areas and other factors. Thus, for some products/markets/divisions a market penetration strategy might be promoted; in others a market development strategy might be followed; in others, a strategy of phased withdrawal may be planned. Ultimately, whatever the strategy, detailed plans, sales forecasts and budgets will be drawn up to provide a support framework within which implementation can take place. This stage will involve co-operation between marketing and the other key functions (production, R & D, personnel, finance and accounting). The process then goes into a review stage to provide feedback on performance, and to enable strategy modifications to take place, if necessary.

Marketing at the strategic business unit level

15. Whereas the corporate strategic decision-making process produces the grand plan for an organisation, and thus deals principally with general issues of product-market strategy, the decision-making process at the level of the Strategic Business Unit (SBU) also has to produce, and implement, a strategy aimed at gaining and sustaining competitive advantage. The specific concerns that are dealt with at SBU level include the following:

- decisions about market segmentation (i.e. specifying segments of a total market which will be provided with a particular marketing mix, taking account of the activities of competitors in the same market)
- decisions about the marketing mix for each product or product-range (including brands)
- establishment of sales and revenue targets.

These concerns give rise to further decisions, principally about the marketing mix, affecting:

- products (quality, variety, features, brand name, packaging, etc.)
- pricing (basic, premium, loss-leader, etc.) and discounting/credit etc
- promotion (advertising expenditure, media, personal selling, sales promotion activities, publicity, etc.)
- availability and distribution (stocks, distribution channels, agents, mail order, transport, warehousing, etc.).

16. Other marketing concerns likely to be addressed at SBU level include:

- market research (desk/field research, customer surveys, etc.) and analysis
- competitor analysis (direct competitors, potential entrants to market etc)
- structure, staffing and cost of marketing department/function (including sales)
- internal marketing audit (marketing department performance, sales performance, etc.)
- regulating conflicting priorities between marketing and other functions, especially production and R & D.

Some of these concerns are clearly prime on implementation rather than formulation of strategy, for example, organisation structuring, staffing and auditing of the marketing department or function. However, as explained earlier, strategy formulation activities always tend to shade into issues of implementation (operations) in SBUs and unitary companies. Undoubtedly, marketing specialists play as much a key role in the implementation of strategy as they do in its formulation.

17. Morden (1993), looking at the above issues from a marketing viewpoint, neatly summarises the relationship between strategic marketing planning and the corporate strategic plan. In the diagram that follows (Figure 13.2), Morden shows market research as following strategic choice, but it is important in the context of this book to note that market research also *precedes* strategic choice. It is useful to point out that the diagram shows links between the planning of the marketing mix (product, price, etc .) and other functional planning (e.g. production planning, inventory scheduling, physical distribution, etc.). Finally, the feedback elements should be noted. Marketing to a considerable extent lives or dies by the quality and quantity of the feedback it can provide to the rest of the organisation. It is an important lesson for other functional groups.

Figure 13.2 Strategic marketing planning and implementation (from Morden, 1993)

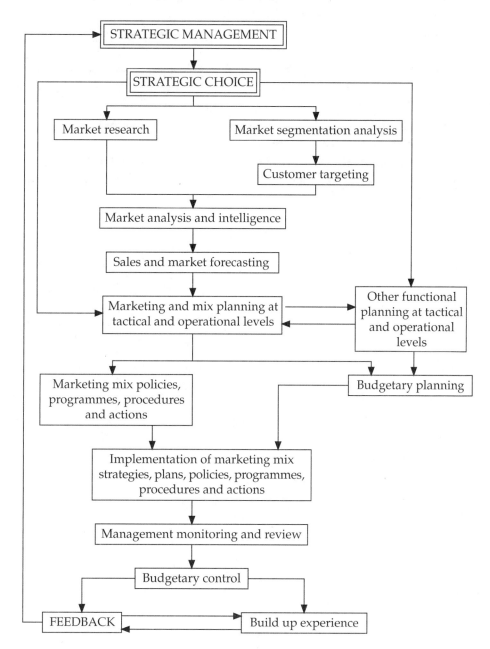

References

1. Kotler, P. (1993), *Marketing Management – Implementation ...*, Prentice Hall International.
2. Peters, T. & Waterman, R. (1982), *In Search of Excellence*, Harper Collins.
3. Clifford, D. & Cavanagh, R. (1985), *The Winning Performance*, Sidgwick and Jackson.
4. Morden, A. (1993), *Elements of Marketing* (3rd edn), D P Publications.

Questions for reflection/discussion

1. To what extent is it likely that adherence to the 'marketing concept' could put an organisation's various stakeholders at odds with each other?

2. In what ways might marketing strategies differ as between corporate and strategic business unit levels?

3. It has been suggested that corporate strategic management defines the business, its marketplace and its values, while strategic business units define the company's competitive stance, and implement it. How far is this true, in your opinion?

4. To what extent is it reasonable to suggest that the link between marketing strategy and overall corporate strategy lies in the concept of 'value'?

5. What is the marketing function's role in supplying feedback to the senior management for the purposes of strategic planning? What advantages might marketing specialists have over other members of the organisation in supplying feedback?

14 The role of personnel in strategic management

Introduction

1. In earlier references to stakeholders, employees were described as direct stakeholders, i.e. a group that is directly affected by the decisions made on behalf of the organisation. It was also suggested (Chapter 1 paragraph 29) that employees could be considered a dependent category of stakeholder. Employees are individuals who, over a given time, invest a large proportion of their lives in their organisation. Thus, much of their personal lives (for example, as breadwinners), as well as their role as employees, depends on the success or otherwise of the corporate strategy adopted by their employer. In this situation one obvious role for personnel (or human resource) management is to ensure the fair treatment of employees as important stakeholders in the organisation. To this extent personnel managers are assuming a protective role towards employees. However, as noted elsewhere (Cole, 1997), there are several other stakeholders who have an interest in the personnel and human resource activities carried out in the organisation. As Figure 14.1 shows, these include other managers, customers, suppliers and governmental bodies.

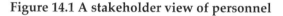

Figure 14.1 A stakeholder view of personnel

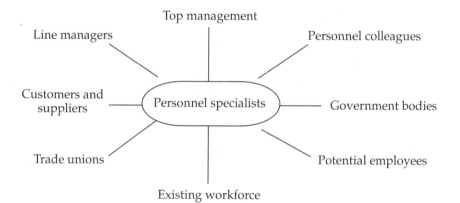

2. What expectations might these various stakeholders hold? They can best be summarised under the following two categories, depending on whether their involvement with personnel is direct and indirect. First, we list (Figure 14.2) those stakeholders who are **directly involved**, and suggest the contribution they might reasonably expect from personnel specialists:

3. As the list shows, most of the stakeholders directly involved are internal stakeholders, but two are external – trade union officers and potential employees. The influence that the latter can bring to bear on the organisation depends primarily on the demand for the kind of labour that they represent (i.e. a scarce category of personnel, skills in short supply and so on). Trade union officers have less influence nowadays in British industrial relations, due partly to legal changes and partly to economic changes. However,

where they represent groups that are powerfully placed logistically, such as railway signalmen or air traffic controllers, they are capable of exerting pressure on employers on behalf of their members. Potential employees may have some influence to the extent that, where they too possess special skills or experience, they can command premium employment conditions over other employees.

Figure 14.2 Stakeholder expectations of personnel – I

Stakeholders	Expectations of the personnel function
Line managers	• Advice and guidance on personnel policy/company culture
	• Appropriate, timely and cost-effective services (recruitment, training, welfare, etc.)
Top management	• Contribution to formulation of mission statements and major strategic goals
	• Major contribution to organisation values (e.g. human relations policies)
	• Development of effective personnel objectives designed to facilitate achievement of strategic goals
	• Major contribution to the management of change during implementation of strategy
	• Effective and efficient personnel resourcing within the organisation (e.g. human resource planning, recruitment)
	• Provision of effective measures to support management succession plans and management development
	• Provision of adequate training and career development facilities for all employees
	• Provision of efficient compensation systems for employees
	• Provision of adequate welfare and counselling services for all employees
Personnel colleagues	• Adequate guidance on personnel policies and practices
	• Adequate consultation about human resource matters
	• Flexibility within guidelines when dealing with line personnel needs
	• Support from Personnel Director when implementing policy in line units
Trade union officers	• Bona fide consultation and negotiation agreements
	• Fair treatment for union members employed by the organisation
	• Reasonable access to management and members
Existing workforce	• Acceptable pay and working conditions
	• Adequate consultation facilities
	• Efficient administration of personnel services (especially pay and benefits)
	• Fair and efficient grievance procedure
	• Adequate training, development and career opportunities
	• Fair treatment within the organisation's disciplinary procedure
	• Efficient and sympathetic welfare service
Potential employees (e.g. interviewees)	• Efficient and fair recruitment and selection procedures
	• Adequate information about the organisation, vacancies, etc.

4. Top management's influence will undoubtedly be the greatest, primarily because they will need to keep a tight rein on personnel costs, which are such a large proportion of total operating costs. The extent to which the corporate personnel function is accepted by *other* stakeholders depends largely on how far it can meet their legitimate objectives and preferences within the strategic framework of decisions and policies laid down by the Board of Directors. Some conflict of interests is inevitable between corporate and line/strategic business unit management, depending especially on the degree of change introduced by strategic decisions and their impact on the relative power of key individuals. The issue of resistance to change was referred to in Chapter 11, and is discussed below in relation to personnel management.

5. Next we consider (Figure 14.3) stakeholders who are **indirectly affected** by personnel management in the organisation, and note their likely expectations.

Figure 14.3 Stakeholder expectations of personnel – II

Stakeholders	Expectations of the personnel function
Customers	• Availability of the organisation's goods or services (i.e. no disruption) • Quality and reliability of the organisation's output (i.e. skilled employees) • Effective and pleasant after-sales service (i.e. effective staff training) • Efficient and pleasant handling of enquiries or queries (i.e. effective staff training)
Suppliers	• No unexpected interruptions to the supply chain due to strikes or other industrial action by employees • Efficient handling of transactions by the purchasing and other staff, including use of information technology, where applicable • Courteous treatment of enquiries by own staff
Government bodies	• Adherence to legislation (e.g. health and safety, employment laws) • Adherence to codes of good practice in employment (e.g. in equal opportunities, disciplinary procedures) • Provision of adequate information for local/regional/national labour market (e.g. new jobs, redundancies) • Collaboration with government statistical services • Cooperation with schools, colleges and local education authorities in terms of work experience, careers advice and so forth.

6. The above category is composed entirely of *external* stakeholders, of whom customers and government bodies are likely to be the most influential on personnel issues. The demands made on an organisation's personnel/human resource policies by external stakeholders can often provide a useful lever for the personnel function in getting its policies and practices accepted by line units and other functions. For example, in situations where improved attitudes towards service quality are being sought by the top management of a hotel chain, personnel management's training role can be aided by the production of evidence about customers' preferences, and used to persuade staff of the need for change.

7. In assessing these various, and sometimes conflicting, stakeholder interests from a strategic viewpoint, it is certain that top management's expectations will be the most

significant, at least in the long-term. This is because personnel/human resource management has a powerful role in the underpinning of corporate strategy through its responsibility for supplying, training and developing the organisation's most valuable (and usually most expensive) resource – people. This is quite separate from its role as an advocate for employees. Porter (1985), looking at the world from the point of view of competitive advantage, puts it this way:

> 'Human resource management affects competitive advantage in any firm, through its role in determining the skills and motivation of employees and the cost of hiring and training. In some industries it holds the key to competitive advantage.'

Sainsbury's, to take a practical example, expresses its view of personnel as follows:

> 'Sainsbury's considers people to be its most valuable asset. The management of human resources through the recruitment, training and retention of staff are vital to the company's continued growth, hence the importance of the Personnel Division in the company's overall strategy.'

(J Sainsbury plc, Information Pack, October 1991)

8. Significantly, human resource management (HRM) is one of the important support activities in Porter's model of the value chain (see Chapter 4 paragraph 19). He acknowledges that HRM supports the entire value chain as well as individual primary and support activities. It permeates the entire chain, according to his view, but can lead to inconsistent policies because of its dispersed nature. A key point in developing any personnel strategy is to ensure the consistency, as well as the fairness, of personnel policies throughout the organisation. Such policies are themselves an important reflection of the organisation's culture and value-system, for which the top management are the guardians. Indeed some personnel commentators (such as Purcell, 1985) see the cultivation and dissemination of corporate philosophy as a core function of central personnel departments.

9. Where does personnel/human resource management fit into the cycle of strategic management? Its primary focal points are three, shown in Figure 14.4 as a modified version of the model of strategic management proposed in Chapter 1.

10. Although personnel/human resource management plays an influential role at every stage of the cycle, there are three principal points of entry for the purposes of the discussion here – one, straddling the mission setting and goal-setting stages; another at the key objectives-setting stage, and one more at the implementation stage. In Chapter 1 reference was made to strategic issues (paragraphs 23-24), many of which are relevant to the personnel/human resource function. These include issues concerned with purpose, goals and values, as well as issues such as organisation structure, decision-making mechanisms, and the need for the renewal and replenishment of resources (including human resources). Specific questions raised in the earlier chapter, and relevant to the discussion here, included:

   ❶ *'How effective are our present organisation structures, and will they suffice for the future?'*

   ❷ *'What kinds of people should we be employing to meet future demands on the organisation?'*

   ❸ *'What personnel and training development might be required?'*

   ❹ *'Where do we stand in terms of senior management succession?'*

Figure 14.4 The personnel role in the strategic management cycle

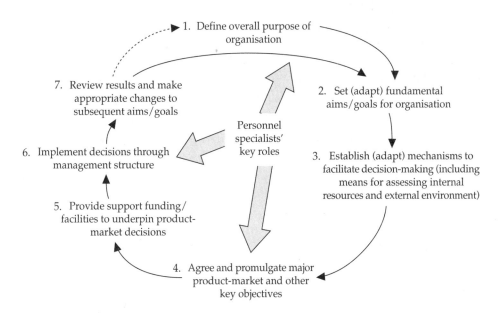

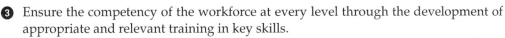

1. Define overall purpose of organisation

2. Set (adapt) fundamental aims/goals for organisation

3. Establish (adapt) mechanisms to facilitate decision-making (including means for assessing internal resources and external environment)

4. Agree and promulgate major product-market and other key objectives

5. Provide support funding/facilities to underpin product-market decisions

6. Implement decisions through management structure

7. Review results and make appropriate changes to subsequent aims/goals

Personnel specialists' key roles

11. These sorts of questions give rise to key personnel goals such as:

   ❶ Ensure that organisation structures facilitate operations, provide for adequate decision-making channels, and encourage delegation of responsibility.

   ❷ Ensure an adequate and suitable supply of personnel committed to the organisation and its objectives.

   ❸ Ensure the competency of the workforce at every level through the development of appropriate and relevant training in key skills.

   ❹ Ensure a supply of experienced and well-trained managers ready to step into more senior posts.

   These broad goals will eventually be expressed in more measurable objectives, taking account of numbers and time, for example. Both goals and objectives will be sustained by personnel strategies aimed at their fulfilment.

12. Relevant strategies that could be applied to the above examples include:

   ❶ Use internal and/or external change agents to review the organisation structure, suggest appropriate measures, and implement them in collaboration with line and functional managers.

   ❷ Establish a central personnel group to advise on recruitment, selection and induction of all categories of staff, and to assist line departments in executing their own needs.

   ❸ Establish a system whereby line and departmental managers can arrange internal or external training for their staffs.

   ❹ Devise and maintain a management succession plan as part of a management development system incorporating adequate on and off–the-job training.

Personnel and the implementation of strategy

13. The implementation stages of corporate strategies usually involves both specialist human resource personnel and line managers. So long as adequate policy guidelines exist, it should be possible to ensure that fairness to employees and consistency of treatment is applied across the management structure. Examples of policies that might be applied to the strategies mentioned in the previous paragraph include:

 'No organisational changes will be implemented without thorough consultation and discussion with those directly affected'.

❷ *'All job vacancies will be advertised internally before the company seeks recruits from outside.'*

❸ *'Every new staff member, and every person appointed to a new post internally, will be entitled to expect a period of induction training in their new position.'*

❹ *'All employees are to be encouraged to participate in the training opportunities offered by the company, which will be available to all regardless of length of service, seniority, race or sex.'*

❺ *'The management succession plan will be completed by appropriate senior managers primarily on the basis of appraisal reports conducted within the company's staff appraisal scheme.'*

14. In considering personnel's impact on the implementation of corporate strategy, it is useful to reconsider the model of strategy implementation used in Chapter 7 (see Figure 14.5 below). The diagram shows the relationship between strategic choices, which drive implementation, and a number of key internal factors – the organisation structure, managerial leadership, the organisation's culture/value-system, personnel skills, and financial and physical resources. Figure 14.5 also indicates quite clearly that there are personnel/human resource management implications in most of these key factors. Indeed, only the financial and physical resources factors have no direct personnel implication, but even they are affected by recruitment and training.

Figure 14.5 Internal factors influencing strategy implementation

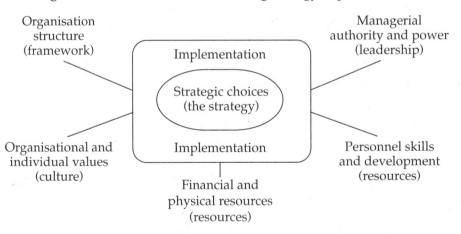

15. Organisational structure is important because it determines the extent to which delegation is encouraged (and hence people empowered), and decision-making facilitated. Culture is important because it determines the spirit in which a strategy is formulated

and executed. Managerial leadership is vital, for without this no strategy can be implemented effectively and efficiently. These are three aspects of the strategic management process which are fundamentally personnel-oriented, and in which personnel specialists and other managers involved in human resource management have a key role to play. They are also aspects of strategic management which are the most likely to be the cause of (and, paradoxically, the source of greatest resistance to) significant change in the organisation. On the resourcing side of strategy, the whole issue of acquiring, retaining and developing sufficient and suitable employees is, of course, central to personnel management.

16. It is not surprising, in such circumstances, that those who have made a study of specific organisations, especially when analysing strategic outcomes, have pointed out the significance of personnel and human resource related factors. For example, Peters and Waterman (1982) include the following personnel-related characteristics in their summary of eight characteristics of excellence. These were:

 Productivity through people:

> 'The excellent companies treat the rank-and-file as the root source of quality and productivity gain. They do not foster we/they labour attitudes or regard capital investment as the fundamental source of efficiency improvement.'

2 Hands-on, value-driven:

> 'Every excellent company we studied is clear on what it stands for, and takes the process of value shaping seriously ... The specific content of the dominant beliefs of the excellent companies is ... narrow ... including ... 1. a belief in being best ... 3. a belief in the importance of individuals ... a belief that most members of the organisation should be innovators, and ... the willingness to support failure.'

3 Simple form, lean staff:

> 'The underlying structural forms and systems ... are elegantly simple. Top level staffs are lean ...'

17. Similarly, in another text, Peters (1988) includes five groups of prescriptions for excellence, of which two are strongly-related to human resource management:

1 *'Achieving Flexibility by empowering People'*, i.e. allowing, indeed encouraging employees at all levels to share in the decision-making processes of the organisation.

2 *'Learning to love Change'*, i.e. developing a new view of leadership which embraces change and adopts a participative style.

The research conducted by Peters and his colleagues shows the importance of the internal factors affecting strategy that were referred to in Figure 14.5. This raises another question – 'What about the influence of *external* factors on strategy implementation?'

18. In conducting a BPEST or a SWOT analysis (see Chapter 3), it is certain that some personnel-related issues will be identified. These are most likely to include the following:

- the state of the labour market, i.e. the pool of potential employees in the community (which is becoming increasingly international, e.g. the European Union)
- the demand (current and forecast) for the organisation's goods and services

- demographic changes (e.g. increasing proportion of elderly in the population, development of immigrant centres of population, de-population of areas of declining industryand so on)
- government legislation and policy on labour, commercial and fiscal matters (e.g. encouragement of inward investment into areas of high unemployment, national training programmes for unemployed, restrictions on/latitude towards trade unions, changes in personnel on-costs such as National Insurance, etc.)
- rapid technological developments in key areas of business activity (e.g. new telecommunication equipment, improved computer software, novel applications of microprocessor technology to key production processes)
- action by competitors on personnel matters (e.g. pay/benefits improvements, provision of crèche facilities, greater use of part-time/casual labourand so on)
- trade union policies and actions (e.g. greater willingness to seek legal redress on labour disputes, increased militancy in pursuit of pay claims/opposition to redundanciesand so forth).

19. These key external factors affecting how, and how successfully, a strategy is implemented, can be set out diagramatically, as in Figure 14.6.

Figure 14.6 Personnel aspects of strategy implementation

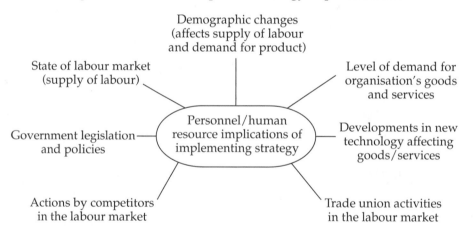

20. Some of the alternatives that might flow from the impact of the above factors on personnel strategy include the following:
   ❶ Buying in trained and experienced staff or hiring inexperienced staff and training them in-house
   ❷ Staffing line units to meet extra demand or contracting out to others
   ❸ Increasing or reducing the proportion of staff on part-time contracts
   ❹ Seeking government grants to increase production in a development area or moving production to a better labour-market area
   ❺ Continue recognising one or more unions for bargaining purposes or revoking existing recognition agreements (with due notice).

   All the above alternatives are possible personnel responses to changing conditions.

Personnel management and organisational change

21. Many of the major decisions at the heart of strategic management lead directly to significant change within the organisation. Mintzberg and Quinn (1991) point out that although 'The need for major strategic change reorientation occurs rather infrequently', it does mean moving from:

    'a familiar domain into a less well-defined future where many of the old rules no longer apply. People must often abandon the roots of their past successes and develop entirely new skills and attitudes.'

    This last point refers to a revolutionary (framebreaking) type of change occasioned by powerful forces inside or external to the organisation. Examples of influential *internal* forces include the death of a powerful entrepreneurial owner (such as the publishing tycoon, Robert Maxwell) or, on a more positive note, the arrival of a 'new broom', who succeeds in restoring the fortunes of an ailing business. Examples of powerful *external* influences include political upheaval in an overseas territory, or the discovery of unwelcome side-effects in a drug that has hitherto seemed safe and appropriate (as in the case of thalidomide).

22. Revolutionary changes, which are usually the result of a crisis, call for deep changes in one or more of the organisation's strategic areas – e.g. products, markets, financial, organisational and personnel. Thus existing products may be ceased or sold off, new markets may be entered, parts of the business may be sold off to pay creditors, the organisational structure may be turned on its head, the entire operation 'downsized'. Most change, however, is generally more evolutionary in nature, and occurs incrementally during the life of an organisation. Therefore, only moderate changes need be made to the product-market strategy, to financing arrangements and to the organisational structure, for example. It is also worth remembering, however, that organisational activities are not just about dealing with crises. Most of such activities, on the contrary, are what have been described by systems specialists as 'steady state' activities, that is, routine, non-threatening, familiar activities. Handy (1993) points out:

    'The steady state often accounts for 80 per cent of an organisation's personnel. It includes the infrastructure of the organisation – the accounting system, the secretarial system, the office services section. It includes ... most of the production component ... sales activities ... but not the marketing activity.'

23. Handling change, including tackling resistance to change, is an aspect of strategic management where personnel/human resource management skills can play a key role. The topic of change was considered at greater length in Chapter 11, and could be usefully revisited at this stage. In Chapter 11, use was made of the McKinsey Seven-S Framework, which, it will be recalled, contained the following key elements: **strategy, structure, systems, staff, style, skills, shared values**. These headings provide a useful tool for analysing the personnel implications of change in an organisation. In the examples which follow, typical questions relating to each of the seven elements are listed. Against each question are set out (a) examples of the strategic options that might be available, and (b) suggestions as to how personnel might be involved. The options presented in the table below (Figure 14.7) all have personnel/human resource management implications, and are an indication of the importance of having a *corporate* perspective on personnel, as well as ensuring the diffusion of human resource management throughout the organisation.

Figure 14.7 Personnel implications of strategic change

Element	Typical questions	Strategic options	Personnel implications
Strategy	1. What changes are we under pressure to make?	Reduce costs Price leadership Withdraw from market/segment	Staff training Staff redeployment Redundancies
	2. What changes can be introduced at our own initiative and pace?	Attack new segments Increase R&D effort Diversify	Marketing training Recruit scientists etc Management training
Structure	1. How effective are our present structures?	Maintain Reduce hierarchy	Continue routine training Redeployment/retrain Redundancies
		Establish project teams	Team training
Systems	1. How effective are our present systems (by category)?	Revise/replace Maintain	Staff training Update staff handbook Continue routine induction training
	2. How efficient are our present systems (by category)?	Improve Maintain	Staff training/induction Continue as now
Staff	1. Have we enough of the right people in the right jobs?	Increase staff Maintain current level	Recruitment and selection Induction/job training Recruit as required Career development Wage/salary planning
	2. Are staff performing to the required standards?	Emphasise quality	Appraisal schemes Management development Staff training
Style	1. Is our preferred style operating in practice?	Emphasise mission	Induction/training Staff handbook
Skills	1. Are present talents and skills identified?	Emphasise quality Support promotion	Personnel records Pay structure Supervisor training
	2. What new skills are required?	Product development Emphasise quality	Recruit skilled staff Job training
Shared Values	1. How relevant are our present values?	Restate mission Revise mission and/or key policies	Induction training Staff handbook Personnel policies
	2. How well are staff adopting/promoting our culture?	Emphasise mission Emphasise policies (e.g. customer service, product quality, etc.)	Train/induct as now Staff handbook Management/supervisor training Staff training

Resistance to change

24. As noted in Chapter 11, and earlier in this chapter, change tends to produce resistance. Ansoff and McDonnell (1990), in discussing the management of strategic change, comment that:

    '... practical experience shows that significant changes in a firm's strategic orientation, whether introduced through formal strategic planning or as an informal process, encounter organisational resistance.'

    They also note that such resistance occurs whenever an organisational change introduces 'a discontinuous departure from the historical behaviour, culture, and power structure.'

    In their opinion, resistance to change is a fundamental problem of strategic management and deserves as much attention as the formulation of strategy itself. Key issues, to which they draw attention, include the size of the change, the time over which it is introduced, its impact on organisational capability, the strength of its threat to individuals' power, and its congruence with the present organisation culture. Certain mixes produce the greatest resistance, others produce minimal resistance. A major change in culture, which is seen by those concerned as politically threatening, will give rise to great resistance. By comparison, some changes can be culturally acceptable and politically welcomed, and are received positively.

25. Kurt Lewin's 'Force-field theory' (1951), referred to earlier, illustrated the opposing forces of change – *'driving forces'* and *'restraining forces'* (see Chapter 11 paragraph 27). It will be recalled that the easier way of overcoming resistance to change was to focus on the removal, or at least the weakening, of the restraining forces. Here personnel specialists can play a key role by (a) helping to identify blocking points, (b) proposing ways of easing the path of change (e.g. by means of employee redeployments, attractive early retirement proposals and so forth), and (c) providing effective training and/or re-training. In practical terms the issue is not so much a question of 'How can we persuade them of *our* arguments for change?', but rather 'What are *their* objections and fears, and how can we minimise them in a cost-effective way?'.

26. The issue of how to bring about change in organisations has been studied by a number of writers. It was mentioned in Chapter 11 (paragraph 29) that Rosabeth Moss Kanter (1984) suggested several ways in which resistance to change – *'roadblocks to innovation'*- could be overcome. These included the following suggestions of direct relevance to personnel management:

    - encouraging a culture of pride in the organisation
    - improving communication in the organisation
    - encouraging labour mobility
    - improving the dissemination of information throughout the organisation

    These points take us back to the diagram in Figure 14.5, where personnel factors such as organisation structure, managerial leadership, and culture were seen as influential in implementing strategy.

27. Lewin developed a three-stage approach to changing behaviour, which was revised, and extended, by Edgar Schein (1964), whose generic model – also in three stages – has become very well known. It comprises the following steps:

    ❶ 'Unfreezing' existing behaviour (gaining acceptance for change)
    ❷ Changing behaviour (adopting new attitudes, modifying behaviour) – this stage usually requires the services of a change agent

❸ 'Refreezing' new behaviour (reinforcing the new patterns of working).

The 'unfreezing' stage is aimed at getting people to see that change is not only necessary, but also desirable. The change stage is mainly a question of identifying what needs to be changed in people's attitudes, values, and actions, and then helping them to accept and acquire 'ownership' of the changes. A crucial role at this stage is that of the change agent (that is, a skilled person responsible for helping individuals and groups to accept new ideas and practices). The 'refreezing' stage is aimed at consolidating and reinforcing the changed behaviour by various support mechanisms (encouragement, promotion, participative management style, more consultation, etc.).

28. Other ways of dealing with change in a strategic context have been identified by Ansoff and McDonnell (1990), who compare four change methods:

- **coercive** (i.e. where top management *insists* on certain things being done)
- **adaptive** (i.e. where change is introduced gradually over time)
- **crisis management** (i.e. where everyone accepts that change is necessary, even if not particularly desirable)
- **managed resistance** (i.e. where change is introduced flexibly under conditions of moderate urgency, aiming to be fair to all).

They conclude that coercive measures have the advantage of speed, but the disadvantage of high resistance. Adaptive measures are slow but meet low resistance. Crisis management is conducted under extreme time pressures and contains a high failure risk, but meets low resistance. Managed resistance is complicated to operate, but meets low resistance, is tailored to the time available, and is capable of achieving comprehensive change. Personnel specialists are most likely to be involved in the adaptive and managed resistance processes, which are likely to include education and communication programmes. Senior line managers are more likely to take the lead role in coercive and crisis approaches, where immediate decisions and actions are called for.

29 One of the organic (adaptive) ways in which organisations can bring about change is by means of an organisation development programme, which has been described (French and Bell, 1978) as follows:

> '... organisational development is a long-range effort to improve an organisation's problem-solving and renewal processes, particularly through a more effective and collaborative management of organisation culture, with special emphasis on the culture of formal work-teams, with the assistance of a change agent ... and the use of ... applied behavioural science ...'

It is clear from this definition that organisation development is basically a strategic process, aimed as it is at long-term issues at the heart of strategic management (decision-making processes, organisation cultureand so on). What is less clear is that organisation development programmes, and the activities that underpin them, are primarily human-resource focused, since they are aimed principally at changing structures, values (culture) and individual behaviour. They also affect both the effectiveness of strategic plans, and the efficiency with which they are executed.

30. An organisation development (OD) programme is usually composed of the following steps:

1 Agree nature and scope of change programme, and allocate resources, especially the person or group acting as change agent(s).

2 Undertake required analysis of organisation and diagnose problems and issues.

3 Agree programme objectives in light of 1 and 2. (For example, establish more effective structure following an acquisition, introduce IT-based management information system, etc.).

4 Plan actions (nature of interventions, sequence, people) and allocate authority.

5 Evaluate and review progress and outcomes.

6 Revise as necessary.

7 Implement required changes.

The above steps may give the impression that OD programmes are neatly devised, perhaps even slightly bureaucratic, and certainly able to accomplish what they set out to achieve in a relatively short space of time. The truth is that such programmes are as good as the ideas and planning that go into them. Much of what they contain is already part and parcel of the strategic implementation process in adaptive organisations, as they strive to meet the demands of the strategic management cycle.

References

1. Cole, G.A. (1997), *Personnel Management – Theory and Practice* (4th edn.), Letts Educational.
2. Porter, M.E. (1985), *Competitive Advantage*, The Free Press.
3. Purcell, J. (1985), 'Is anyone listening to the corporate personnel department?', *Personnel Management*, September 1985.
4. Peters, T. & Waterman, R. (1982), *In Search of Excellence*, Harper Collins.
5. Mintzberg, H. & Quinn, J. (1991), *The Strategy Process – Concepts, Contexts and Cases*, Prentice Hall International.
6. Handy, C. (1993), *Understanding Organisations* (4th edn), Penguin.
7. Ansoff, H.I. & McDonnell, E.J. (1990), *Implanting Strategic Management* (2nd edn.), Prentice Hall International.
8. Lewin, K. (1951), *Field Theory in Social Science*, Harper.
9. Moss Kanter, R. (1984), *The Change Masters*, Allen & Unwin.
10. Schein E. (1964), 'The mechanisms of change'. Bennis, W.G. et al. (eds), *Interpersonal Dynamics*, Dorsey.
11. French, W. & Bell, C. (1978), *Organisation Development* (2nd edn.), Prentice Hall.

Questions for reflection/discussion

1. In what ways might top management make different demands on personnel specialists compared with line managers and other personnel staff?

2. How far are (a) **customers**, and (b) **suppliers** affected by the effectiveness and efficiency of the personnel function?

3. What contribution can personnel policies make to the establishment of an organisation's culture? What particular policies have the greatest impact on culture?

4. How might factors in an organisation's *external* environment affect the success or otherwise of personnel strategies?

5. In what ways can personnel specialists help to facilitate the process of change in an organisation?

15 Measuring strategic performance

Introduction

1. In one sense the measurement of strategic performance is primarily about assessing the extent to which a strategy has achieved its broad goals. Thus, the measurement is just as likely to be qualitative as quantitative in nature. In other words, assessing whether the organisation has done the right things (effectiveness) is just as important as doing things right (efficiency). Some of the evaluation tools used in assessing strategic performance will, therefore, be qualitative and non-financial, and some will be financial or quantitative. However, since the impact of strategic performance on the organisation is felt from top to bottom, it is also true to say that the measurement of such performance is also about assessing the extent to which operational objectives have been met. These are far more likely to be measured in some quantitative ways, and most of them will have been the subject of budgets in any case.

2. The content of this chapter, not unexpectedly, draws on material from several earlier chapters, especially the following:

   Chapter 2 (Purposes, goals and objectives) – references to real company goals, etc.

   Chapter 3 (Assessing the environment) – especially content of Figure 3.3

   Chapter 5 (Forecasting the future) – especially the definitions of financial ratios

   Chapter 6 (Formulating a strategy) – references to various strategic models

   Chapter 8 (Business plans) – reference to earlier Figure 8.1 (re-introduced here as Figure 15.1)

Strategic performance – key measures

3. In order to put strategy measurement into perspective, it will be useful to see it in terms of the model of a Strategic Business Plan introduced in Chapter 8. This is shown here in slightly modified form as Figure 15.1.

4. From the diagram in Figure 15.1, it is possible to spotlight the key areas of concern that organisations must focus on when measuring their strategic performance. These key areas are principally as follows:

   - Corporate strategy (i.e. the strategic choices made for the overall success of the business)

   - Corporate objectives (i.e. the major objectives or goals set for the business as a whole, and which govern those set by SBUs)

   - Corporate policies and review procedures

   - Strategic Business Unit (SBU) objectives (i.e. major objectives/goals in key product-market, financial, resourcing, etc. areas)

   - Efficiency in the use of resources as allocated (especially personnel and physical).

   Also, since the performance of the operating units within an SBU affects the latter's own performance, then it is likely that a strategic review will also encompass the performance against targets/budgets set for the operating units.

Figure 15.1 Strategic business plan – measuring performance

5. Taking this analysis a little further, what is it, precisely, that a company needs to measure when assessing the effectiveness of its strategy and the efficiency of its systems? Judging from the evidence obtained by researchers, such as Peters and Waterman (1982) in their search for 'excellence', and Goldsmith and Clutterbuck (1984) in their search for what constitutes 'success', there are some primary measures against which successful companies can be assessed. Some of these measures are of effectiveness, others are of efficiency. The most common measures employed by firms and business analysts were defined in Chapter 5. Peters and Waterman, by way of example, selected the following in their analysis of 'excellent' companies:

❶ Compound asset growth
❷ Compound equity growth
❸ Average Market to book value
❹ Average Return on total capital
❺ Average Return on equity
❻ Average Return on sales
❼ Long-term record of innovation.

In order to reassure themselves of the excellence of their companies in terms of long-term effectiveness, Peters and Waterman studied their results over a period of twenty years. Goldsmith and Clutterbuck, by comparison, chose the following:

❶ 'High growth in assets, turnover and profit over the past ten years …'
❷ 'A consistent reputation within the industrial sector as a leader.'

❸ 'A solid public reputation.'

6. Other measurements of organisational performance that could be selected might focus on the following:

❶ Markets and market segments (including niche markets)

❷ Product (or service) range

❸ Sales (by product (service), brand, market, etc.)

❹ Production levels/service activity

❺ Costs (of production, sales and overheads)

❻ R & D effort

❼ Investment programme

❽ Personnel (numbers, skills, training, effectiveness)

❾ Financial management.

Some of the above will be tested for their effectiveness, others for their efficiency.

7. The measures of *effectiveness* (i.e. as opposed to efficiency) selected by a company are likely to be influenced as much by the relative importance of its various stakeholders, as by their own needs for assessing the appropriateness of their chosen strategies. Some examples of stakeholders' perspectives on organisational performance, and the performance indicators likely to be of greatest interest to them, are shown in Figure 15.2. Customers' expectations have been dealt with elsewhere (see Chapter 12 paragraphs 2-6) and are therefore not included, neither are community interests. All of the indicators are outcome-oriented, and most are applied to activity over a period of time (i.e. at least over several months and often over several years).

Figure 15.2 Stakeholder perspectives on effective performance

Shareholders	Banks, etc.	Employees	Suppliers	Company management
Earnings per share Price/earnings ratio Dividend yield Market to book ratio	Gearing Cash flow Current ratio	Cash flow Turnover	Cash flow Turnover Growth	Profitability Asset growth Turnover growth Cash flow Market to book ratio

Note: Definitions of the above-mentioned ratios appear in Chapter 5

8. What the above table shows is that *shareholders* are primarily interested in (a) the profitability of the company, and (b) its rating on the stock market, thus enabling them to enjoy a satisfactory return on their investment; *banks* are interested in (a) the proportion of internal funds versus borrowings, (b) current assets vis-à-vis current liabilities, and (c) the cash flow position, thus reassuring themselves that the company is generating enough funds from its business activities, is not over-borrowing, and will eventually be able to repay its loans; *employees* are *primarily* interested in cash flow, since that is what enables their wages and salaries to be paid; of course, they also want their company to survive, so are interested indirectly in turnover growth and profitability; if employees are also shareholders, then their interests will extend to share values as well; *suppliers,*

too, want to feel reassured that their invoices will be paid, and are thus interested in the company's cash flow position; however, they are also interested in the rate of growth in sales (turnover), since that will affect their supply role. The *management* of the company are primarily interested in growth, profitability and market standing as measures of their success in positioning the company correctly in its markets.

9. For top management, in particular, there are other more general areas of accountability, which require a *qualitative* assessment of performance. These include a review of performance in terms of the company's mission statement, qualitative goals, and the conduct of its policies. In general, such areas of assessment indicate how responsibly, and, perhaps, how *ethically*, the organisation has behaved in carrying out its business goals during the period under review. Mission statements, once made, are unlikely to be changed on a regular basis. Nevertheless, it is important for all organisations to assess their adherence to their mission, which is a major aspect of their organisation's culture. Thus, financial performance can be reviewed in terms of the *spirit* of their mission statements. Leading business enterprises are usually keen to emphasise the importance of keeping to the values expressed in their mission statements. For organisations undergoing major change, of course, there is certainly a need to re-examine the basic mission statement.

10. Corporate primary goals of a qualitative nature are also unlikely to be changed regularly, but in practice will be scrutinised at least annually. London Transport, for example, which has a fundamental role in providing transport needs for the London metropolis, presently examines its major goals every three years. Its key objectives for the years 1991-4 included the following useful examples of long-term, generally-stated objectives:

   • Continue to give the highest priority to safety

   • Improve the quality and reliability of Underground services, with particular attention to combating overcrowding

   • Promote efficiency in all areas …

   • Plan and implement major developments in the rail infrastructure of London …

   • Prior to deregulation, promote the role of the bus …'

(Source: London Transport – Statement of Strategy 1991-1994)

The above goals may remain valid (i.e. serving the cause of effectiveness) for several years. Other organisations, by comparison, may have to replace theirs every two or three years. Much will depend on the nature of the external environment. If this is relatively stable, little change will be called for. If, however, it is turbulent, then considerable adaptations will be required in order to survive (if a business), or to prevent the collapse of the service (if a public service). It can be seen that most of the London Transport goals just described have to be assessed qualitatively, that is, judgements have to be made as to how far they are being achieved. Some goals, however, do lend themselves to quantitative assessment, e.g. improving reliability can be measured in terms of number of trains operating as per the timetable, number of train failures, time-keeping and so forth. The promotion of *'efficiency in all areas'*, of course, requires that standards be set beforehand, and performance judged against them (for example, for speed of issuing tickets, operation of automatic ticket barriers, escalators and lifts, and response times for clearing stations in emergencies).

11. Policies usually remain valid for long periods of time, and this is primarily because they are rules, or guidelines, of conduct, and are less susceptible to changes in the market-place or in the internal organisation structure. Policies are more likely to change in response to *external* changes of a political or social nature. Thus changes will be required following the introduction of new legislation on personnel matters, or on company law, for example. Other changes can be brought about by the actions of pressure groups, such as consumer organisations, who may cause firms to improve the labelling of their products, or widen their advice to clients when giving 'impartial' financial planning advice.

12. The previous paragraphs have pointed to a considerable number of issues raised by questions such as 'What should we measure in our strategic plan, and how should we measure it?'. It is helpful to consider the answers to these questions in terms of actual practice. The following examples (Figures. 15.3 – 15.5) are taken from a recent strategic review, published by one of the world leaders in consumer products – the Unilever Group. The review highlights several of the issues mentioned above, and exemplifies a number of key measures for assessing strategic performance at the corporate level.

Unilever – a practical example

13. The Unilever Group is made up of two parent companies – Unilever PLC (British) and Unilever NV (Dutch). The Group has two joint chairmen, who are the chairman of each parent company, and a joint Board composed of fifteen directors, drawn from the two companies. The Group is organised along divisional lines, based on product groups, regions and functions. For the purposes of this chapter, the role of Unilever's so-called 'Special Committee' is worth describing. This is a triumvirate body, composed of the two joint chairmen plus one other director, which forms a 'chief executive'. The key tasks of the committee, which reports to the full Board, are as follows:

- setting long-term overall strategies for the Group
- agreeing the objectives and strategies of the product, regional and functional groups
- monitoring performance against agreed plans
- controlling overall financial policy/strategy (i.e. allocating financial resources)
- controlling all major items of capital expenditure
- appointment of senior management staff, especially the heads of product, regional and functional groups.

Such an executive group is clearly able to exert considerable corporate power, which enables tight control over essentials, whilst delegating substantial powers to the product and other groups within the overall strategic framework. This structure illustrates the Peters and Waterman (1982) point concerning 'loose-tight' properties (see Chapter 11 paragraphs 12).

14. The following summaries of, and extracts from, the Group's 1993 Review are given to illustrate (a) the concerns and priorities felt by a large and successful company (Figure 15.3), and (b) the key financial and other measures that may be employed in these circumstances to identify relative success (Figure 15.4).

15. The next section of the Unilever review (Figure 15.4) is based on extracts rather than summaries, because it give a clear idea of the sort of issues that are important to a major global business in pursuing its principal product-market strategies.

Figure 15.3 Unilever Group – Extracts from Annual Review 1993
(Overall Strategic Situation)

1) The Chairmen's Statement referred to the following issues:

    - intensified competition in the major economies (Europe & North America)
    - need for efficiency to protect margins
    - need for restructuring as a major contribution to efficiency
    - net profit declined but underlying growth in earnings increased
    - market share sometimes had to be defended at the cost of margin (e.g. in USA)
    - continued withdrawal from activities outside the core businesses (i.e. the four product groups – Foods, Detergents, Personal Products, and Speciality Chemicals)
    - intention to concentrate strategic attention on potentially profitable growth markets outside Europe and North America.

2) Business Overview – This referred to the acquisition of selected overseas companies in the core businesses (e.g. in Italy, United States, Poland, Brazil). Also to joint ventures in Saudi Arabia and China, and an increased holding in two tea companies in India. The emphasis is clearly on market development in markets outside Europe and North America through acquisitions and joint ventures, but always in the core business groups (Foods, Detergents etc).

In the Review the part dealing with the overview of the business referred to a number of key areas which have a major effect on the successful implementation of strategy. The concerns expressed and the emphases laid down give a useful indication of the day-to-day priorities that are important to sustain mission, strategy and policies. The key areas are given in Figure 15.4.

16. The above illustrations for the Unilever Review set the scene for a more detailed examination of the Group's performance, which is set out in the Group's Financial Report for 1993. This supplies not only the consolidated Profit and Loss Account, and consolidated Balance Sheet for the year ending December 1993, but also consolidated statements over a five year period. Thus, shareholders, managers and other stakeholders can view developments in the business over a significant period of time. The key parameters employed in the Review are summarised in Figure 15.5.

The financial measures adopted for the review follow the reporting requirements for public limited companies. Most of the information available, therefore, arises from the Profit and& Loss account, the Balance Sheet, and the Cash Flow Statement. Other financial data is, however, supplied. The total picture gives information about the measures of performance shown in Figure 15.5.

Efficiency of performance

17. Measuring strategic performance is not only a question of assessing effectiveness; it is also about *efficiency*, that is the productivity of the resources that have been employed in pursuing the organisation's objectives. Efficiency is essentially a matter of managerial stewardship. Yardsticks of efficiency indicate how well the management of an enterprise have utilised the human, physical and financial resources at their disposal. Some such yardsticks are appropriate to assess overall corporate performance, and these include: Return on Total Assets (ROTA), Return on Shareholders' Capital (ROSC), Return on Capital Employed (ROCE), Profit margin on sales, and Earnings per share. These ratios

would, of course, be considered in the context of a healthy Balance Sheet, showing a growth in assets, and a profitable Profit and Loss situation.

Figure 15.4 Unilever Group – Extracts from Annual Review 1993 (Key Business Concerns)

'**Reducing costs** ... The (restructuring) programme will deliver significant annual savings ... It comprises some 60 separate projects and will lead to ... site closures and job reductions ... Opportunities will be sought to redeploy staff ... to use natural wastage ... and to offer early retirement or retraining as appropriate ...

Technology and innovation – Our investment in research and development has been steadily rising in recent years in line with sales. In 1993 it was £518 million, equivalent to just under 2% of turnover ... The budget is distributed between large central research facilities in the United Kingdom, the Netherlands and the United States, and small development laboratories in over 40 countries ...

Advertising and marketing – Competition in the sale of branded and packaged consumer products is intense. It is characterised by the substantial costs associated with the introduction of new products and the promotion of our brands ... we followed our deliberate policy [strategy] of maintaining investment in countries which are in recession.

Human resources – The skills, imagination and commitment of our employees will determine Unilever's success. It is essential that Unilever attracts, and retains, the best people at all levels ... In recruitment, Unilever operates a policy of equal opportunity ... Continuous training and development is a key priority ... essential to respond to changing work practices within most of our operations ... less hierarchical method of working will improve morale but equally impose on employees the need for greater self-reliance and self-motivation ... Expatriation ... is becoming more difficult to achieve ... it is ... part of our equal opportunity policy to seek job opportunities for partners of potential expatriates ...

Corporate responsibility – In all Unilever's operations, product safety, employee health and safety and environmental care are central elements ... in company strategy ... In 1993, there was further development of ... Life Cycle Analysis. This involves the evaluation of all aspects of manufacturing and commercial activities ... and the examination of the aggregate effect of all these on the environment ...

---

18. At the operational levels of a business, detailed plans in budget form will have been prepared and implemented. These will include targets for sales and output, which are readily measurable. They will also provide financial boundaries to help contain costs, which again can be measured against the limits set in the budget. Since budgets are plans defined in financial and quantitative terms, they are easily measured compared with wider strategic objectives. They also enable corrective action to be carried out whenever there is a wide variance between a budgeted standard and actual outcomes. This action enables the organisation to respond rapidly to unforeseen developments in business activity, and thus gives flexibility to the way plans are implemented, especially at the strategic business unit level. Variance analysis is also an important part of the planning cycle, aiding the review of the internal environment that is usually carried out prior to the revision, or introduction, of a strategic plan.

Figure 15.5 Unilever Group – Extracts from Annual Review 1993
(Key Financial Parameters)

Profit and Loss Account

1   Turnover (i.e. Total Sales)
2   Operating profit (i.e. profit before tax and interest, but after the deduction for exceptional items e.g. restructuring costs)
3   Profit on ordinary activities before taxation (i.e. after interest but pre–tax)
4   Profit on ordinary activities after taxation (i.e. post-tax)
5   Net Profit (i.e. post-tax profit less minority interests)
6   Dividends (i.e. amounts paid to shareholders)
7   Retained profit (i.e. amount left after payments to shareholders, and available for reinvestment in the business)
8   Earnings per share (i.e. for UK = pence per 5p of ordinary capital)
9   Ordinary dividends (i.e. for UK = pence per 5p of ordinary capital)

Balance Sheet

1   Total capital employed (i.e. capital and reserves, provisions etc)

Cash Flow Statement

1   Net cash inflow from operating activities
2   Net cash outflow from returns on investments and servicing of finance
3   Taxation
4   Net cash flow from investing activities (e.g. acquisitions, disposals etc)
5   Increase/(decrease) in cash and cash equivalents

Other Financial Data

1   Share prices (High/Low) per 5p ordinary share
2   Combined market capitalisation
3   Return on shareholders' equity (%)
4   Return on capital employed (%)
5   Post-tax profit as percentage of turnover (%)
6   Net gearing (%)
7   Staff costs (£ million)
8   Staff numbers (000's)

---

19.   Ratios which identify efficient use of resources may be expressed either in financial or non-financial terms. Examples of financial ratios, which test efficiency (usually in addition to measuring effectiveness) include the following:

❶   Return on total assets = $\dfrac{\text{Profit before interest and tax (\%)}}{\text{Total assets}}$

❷   Return on capital employed = $\dfrac{\text{Profit before tax (\%)}}{\text{Capital employed}}$

Ratios expressing relative efficiency in non-financial terms include the following:

❶   Sales per square foot/metre = $\dfrac{\text{Total sales of unit (£)}}{\text{Total floor space}}$

❷ Sales per employee = $\dfrac{\text{Total company sales (£)}}{\text{Average no. of employees}}$

❸ Profit per employee = $\dfrac{\text{Total profit for unit (£)}}{\text{Average no. of employees}}$

❹ Overheads to sales = $\dfrac{\text{Cost of (office/factory) overheads (\%)}}{\text{Total sales}}$

Like many other measures of efficiency, ratios need to be treated cautiously. They can be helpful for the purposes of internal comparisons within, or between, units in the same organisation, and are generally more useful when applied in conjunction with other measures.

20. These other measures could include such tests as percentage reduction in delivery times, stock levels, credit periods, accidents to personnel and a host of similar internal comparisons that help to identify improvements in, or worsening of, operating performance over a given period. (For an example of efficiency measures see Case-study 13).

PIMS programme

21. Before concluding this chapter on measuring strategic performance, it will be useful to refer to the work of Buzzell and Gale (1987), arising from their involvement with the PIMS programme, since the early 1970s. The title PIMS reflects the core focus of their interest in business strategies and business performance – Profit Impact of Market Strategy. The PIMS programme has collated detailed information about more than 2500 business 'units' (i.e. a division, or other profit centre of a company requiring a separate strategy, and similar to the concept of the strategic business unit used in this book). Like other models of strategic behaviour, the PIMS model aims to provide insights of a generic nature about strategy and performance, and thus is only concerned with those aspects of strategy that are (a) of general industrial relevance, and (b) are measurable. The resulting PIMS database now has substantial information, gleaned over a period of several years, about performance in the source companies.

22. The principal measures of performance quoted by the authors are Return on Investment and Return on Sales. The findings of the research indicate that both profitability and growth are directly affected not only by the business unit's strategy and the actions of its competitors, but also by market and industry factors, such as the following:

- the stage of the market (i.e. embryonic, growing, mature, declining)
- degree of selling price inflation
- degree of product standardisation
- extent of supplier concentration
- amount and relative importance of typical customer purchases
- extent of exports and imports in the industry.

23. In summarising the most important linkages between strategy and performance, in the light of their research, Buzzell and Gale produced the following six 'principles':

1. The most important single factor affecting business performance is the *quality of its goods and services*, in relation to its competitors.

2. *Market share* is strongly related to profitability (market share in this context refers to the market-share rank that a business holds in relation to its competitors' market shares).

3. High investment intensity adversely affects profitability.

4. With reference to the BCG Matrix, many 'dogs' and 'question mark' businesses generate cash, whilst many 'cash cows' do not!

5. Vertical integration (i.e. buying-in upstream or downstream) is only a profitable strategy for some businesses.

6. Most of the strategic factors that have the greatest impact on Return on Investment also contribute to long-term shareholder value.

24. In the final analysis, it is the customer's perception of the relative, superior quality of an enterprise's goods and services that gains a company increased market share. This in turn enables it to achieve advantages of scale, thus reducing costs, and enhancing profitability.

References

1. Peters, T. & Waterman, R. (1982), *In Search of Excellence*, Harper Collins.
2. Goldsmith, W. & Clutterbuck, D. (1984), *The Winning Streak*, Penguin.
3. Buzzell, R. & Gale, B. (1987), *The PIMS Principles – Linking Strategy to Performance*, The Free Press.

Questions for reflection/discussion

1. How would you distinguish between *'effectiveness'* and *'efficiency'* when analysing an organisation's production performance?

2. Why does cash flow performance rate so crucially with banks and suppliers?

3. How far is it possible to measure performance in relatively non-quantifiable aspects of strategic management, such as the mission statement and goals relating to ethical values?

4. What performance information is likely to be available from an examination of a company's Profit and Loss accounts?

5. What financial yardsticks are likely to demonstrate how *efficiently* a company is using its resources?

16 Strategic management: a concluding model

Introduction

1. This final chapter sets out to refine the basic model of strategic management referred to at the start of the book. The refinements, although adding to the original model, still enable a relatively uncomplicated picture of strategic management to be drawn. This, perhaps, is as it should be, since strategy is primarily about getting the basics right.

2. In Chapter 1, an initial working definition of strategic management was put forward as follows:

   'Strategic management is a process, directed by top management, to determine the fundamental aims or goals of the organisation, and to ensure a range of decisions which will allow for the achievement of those aims or goals in the long-term, whilst providing for adaptive responses in the shorter term.'

   This definition was followed by a model of strategic management shown as a cycle of key decisions, which comprised:

   ❶ definition of overall purpose or mission

   ❷ setting (or adapting) of fundamental aims or goals

   ❸ establishment (or adaptation) of mechanisms to facilitate decision-making

   ❹ assessment of internal and external environments

   ❺ agreement to, and promulgation of, key product-market and other key objectives

   ❻ implementation of the strategy via the management structure

   ❼ review of results and revision of aims/ goals as appropriate.

3. The strategic management cycle was referred to, and adapted, in subsequent chapters, including Chapter 13, in which an extended definition of strategic management in the context of marketing was proposed, as follows:

   'Strategic management is a process, directed by top management, but engaged in throughout the management structure, which is aimed at determining the fundamental aims or goals of the organisation, including those concerned with satisfying customer's legitimate needs and wants, and ensuring the attainment of those fundamental aims or goals through the adoption of adequate decision-making mechanisms and the provision of adequate resources in support of a planned direction for the organisation over a given period of time.'

   This revised version added references to customer needs/wants, the provision of adequate resources, the inclusion of every level of management in the process, and the assumption of a planned direction for the organisation.

4. These earlier definitions and models will be further developed in this short final chapter. The intention is to produce a comprehensive, and somewhat eclectic, model of strategic management based on the theory and the practice that have been described before.

A model of strategic management

5. The previous fifteen chapters have outlined theory and practice in the major aspects of the strategic management process. Essentially, those chapters have clustered around five principal features of strategic management. These will be highlighted in the following paragraphs under the headings of:

    1 The bedrock of strategic management (mission, strategic aims, etc.)

    2 The environmental review (internal and external)

    3 Strategic choices (markets, products, resourcing priorities)

    4 Operational aims and objectives (market share, personnel requirements, etc.)

    5 Implementing plans (timescales, budgets, manpower plans, etc.)

    6 Strategic review (monthly, quarterly, annually)

The bedrock of strategic management

6. The bedrock elements of strategic management, without which no strategy can succeed, are made up, essentially, of the following:

    1 a clear understanding, or vision, of what business the organisation is in and what it sees as its principal purpose in life, usually expressed nowadays as a **mission statement,** and usually defined in terms of the **'core business'**

    2 a clear statement of the **major goals or aims** that must be achieved by the core business, usually expressed in terms of the markets to be served, the services to be rendered, the quality of those services, and the financial returns expected from them

    3 a clear set of guiding policies to indicate to all managers and employees the manner in which they will be expected to conduct the organisation's business. These have the effect of strengthening the organisation's mission statement, and are a major contributor to the **organisational culture,** or shared values of the organisation.

The environmental review

7. This consists of two dimensions – the review of the organisation's external environment, and the review of its internal situation. A comprehensive **external review** is likely to focus on the following:

    1 the **business environment,** especially in terms of competitor behaviour and situation, customer needs/wants and reactions, suppliers' situation, and the state of the industry in its life-cycle

    2 the **political and economic environment,** especially government attitudes towards business, and prospects for growth in the domestic economy (including industrial development policies, interest rates, level of consumer demand, corporation tax rates, exchange rates, etc.)

    3 the **social environment,** especially the attitudes of pressure groups, people's attitudes towards the physical environment, work, unemployment and rewards

    4 the **technological environment,** especially the application of microelectronic technology to the administrative and production processes of the organisation, and including factors likely to affect prospects for research and development within the organisation

⑤ the **international dimension** of the external environment, especially the challenge presented by overseas competitors, the prospects for marketing the organisation's goods or services overseas, and the impact of supranational bodies (e.g. the European Union/GATT) on trade.

The benefits of a comprehensive review of the external environment are that potential threats and opportunities can be identified across a broad spectrum of organisational activity, thus enabling corrective or development measures to be taken in a timely fashion.

8. A similarly comprehensive review of the organisation's **internal environment** is likely to cover the following aspects of the internal life of the organisation:

- the appropriateness of the current **organisation structure** given the new strategy/changed external circumstances
- the capability of the current **systems** in use
- a review of the present **management style** given the new strategy/challenge of competitor organisations
- the numbers, categories, attitudes and performance of **current staff**
- the current profile of **skills** amongst staff
- the appropriateness of the current **culture** in the light of the new strategy/external conditions
- a review of the organisation's present policy towards (a) **direct stakeholder**s and (b) **indirect stakeholders**
- a review of the use and impact of new **technology** on the organisation's internal systems
- a review of the contribution of **support functions** (e.g. marketing, personnel, R & D)
- a **financial review**, especially to assess present efficiency in the use of assets and the generation of sufficient cash flow.

As will be noted, the above list contains more reference points than the Seven-S framework referred to in earlier chapters. That framework was designed originally as an aid to organisation analysis. Not surprisingly, for the purposes of *strategic* analysis, a wider range of organisational outcomes needs to be considered. Thus, when an examination of potential strategic strengths and weaknesses is conducted, a full repertoire of organisational activities is required for a purposeful analysis.

Strategic choices

9. Decisions about the particular strategies to be followed in an organisation have been discussed in previous chapters under the heading of strategic choice. Of course, in a major sense strategic choices have already been made earlier in the cycle of strategic management, since defining mission and formulating major strategic goals are key strategic choices. However, the term strategic choice has been applied principally to the strategic business unit level, where it has been used to describe the process of setting the key product-market aims of the organisation, and allocating funding priorities between functional and operating units. The ultimate purpose of such activities is the optimum satisfaction of the organisation's direct shareholders (customers, shareholders, employees, creditors and suppliers). The key issues and main alternatives available to

organisations (especially business organisations) are summarised in the following two paragraphs.

10. The principal product-market strategies open to business organisations are as follows:

  ① **Consolidation** of present product-market strategy (i.e. a 'no-change' strategy)

  ② **Market penetration** (i.e. aim for increased sales of present products in current markets)

  ③ **Product development** (i.e. extend range of products within current markets)

  ④ **Market development** (i.e. seeking out new markets/outlets for current products)

  ⑤ **Horizontal diversification** (i.e. expanding sideways by buying into a similar business)

  ⑥ **Vertical diversification** (i.e. expanding upstream to take over a supplier, or downstream by taking over a distributor or end-user)

  ⑦ **Conglomerate diversification** (i.e. expanding into a completely new product-market situation, usually by acquisition)

  ⑧ **Divestment/ withdrawal** (i.e. selling off a business or business unit, or closing it down)

  ⑨ **Cost/price leadership** (i.e. through effective cost-cutting to achieve price advantages over competitors, usually in a mass market; could be used to pursue market penetration and market development strategies)

  ⑩ **Differentiation** (i.e. developing unique/advantageous features of products to achieve market leadership/consolidate present market position)

  ⑪ **Focus** (i.e. concentrating on either cost leadership or differentiation advantages in a narrow market; includes **niche strategy**, where focus is on a narrow segment of a market)

  ⑫ **Growth** (i.e. expanding the business principally by means of acquisitions or joint ventures; similar to diversification, market development and product development strategies).

The prime purpose of product-market strategies is to achieve profitable growth of the business by meeting customer needs and wants in a cost-effective manner. For some companies the prime purpose is less positive, in that they merely want to survive, or at least consolidate their present position.

11. The allocation of funding, and hence of resources generally, amongst the various functions and operating units of an organisation is a major strategic task. It can only take place effectively after the major goals and product-market decisions have been made. A key aspect of **corporate-level** strategy is how to allocate support to subsidiary units, and what proportion to allocate to the headquarters' functions. Both management style and organisation culture are factors here. Organisations that are managed on the assumption of a powerful central headquarters controlling subordinate units will adopt a much more political and paternalistic approach to allocating resources than organisations that believe in decentralisation with the maximum amount of delegated authority. Most organisations demand that the subordinate units (specialist functions, HQ administration, cost centres, profit centresand so on) have to justify their funding not only in terms of their unit plans, but also in terms of their overall effectiveness and efficiency, and the contribution they can make to corporate goals. One particular funding activity – capital

expenditure planning – is always reserved to the top management, advised by their headquarters specialists. There is always strict corporate control over major capital items.

12. Even decentralised organisations need a modicum of structure at the centre. At the very least this is likely to be composed of (a) the top management (directors), (b) senior management groups, composed of directors and heads of key specialisms – marketing, finance and personnel –, and (c) a secretariat (administration staff). This minimal form of organisation allows for regular communication and discussion between the Board of the company and its key senior functional heads. If these functional heads are based at the headquarters, it is likely they will have small staffs of advisors to maintain a watch on the outside environment and report back with their findings and situation assessments. Thus the organisation can keep in touch with competitor developments, market changes and other key features of the external environment.

13. Some headquarters functions (e.g. personnel and finance) are especially focused on the internal environment, assessing the organisation's response to its product-market and other goals, and taking appropriate steps to meet needs expressed, implicitly or explicitly, in monthly/quarterly reviews and budget meetings. Thus both personnel requirements and financial needs can be met by suitable action taken by headquarters staff. For example, senior management recruitment and management development are often best handled by staff employed at the corporate level. Also, since performance assessment is a vital role for top management, it is essential to have a minimum of accountancy personnel at the centre, who are able to take a strategic view of developments and make appropriate proposals for optimising the internal use of funds, for example.

Operational aims and objectives

14. Once the basic product-market and resourcing choices have been made, the next step in the strategic management process is to establish the short-term operational aims or objectives, which will contribute to the strategic plan. These set out the detailed intentions of the organisation's principal operating units and their supporting functional units. These intentions will be expressed in quantifiable terms using measures such as:

- volume (e.g. numbers of units sold or percentage reduction in costs)
- time (i.e. a volume target to be achieved during the first three months of a budget period)
- quality (e.g. all sub-assemblies to conform to requirements every time, or customer satisfaction surveys to show at least 90% satisfaction rate with company's new service)
- costs (e.g. proportion of materials costs as element of final cost to be reduced by one third, or total wages bill not to exceed £x m. for new project)
- ratios (e.g. Return on Total Assets to be increased from 12% to 15% by the year-end, or Net Profit Margin to be increased by 2% by year-end).

15. Operating objectives will be set for all the line units (i.e. all those contributing directly to the output of the organisation, be that a manufacturing or a service organisation). Such objectives are as likely to be set for public sector organisations, such as government departments and local authority units, as they are for charities, other not-for-profit organisations, and businesses. Objectives will also be set for the principal functional and

administrative units, such as: the marketing department, the specialist personnel function, research and development, purchasing/ procurement, finance and accounting, and the headquarters administration (company secretarial, legal, corporate planning, estates, public relations and so forth).

Implementing plans

16. Achieving goals and objectives is not the same thing as intending them! Thus, for senior and middle management, in particular, the putting-into-effect of plans is an important, sometimes principal, reason for their existence. Implementation is conducted within the framework of plans and budgets, which provide timescales and targets of various kinds. However, there are two other major planks of implementation: **management systems** and **staff**. The former refers to the *co-ordination* of the organisation's operations, which is usually undertaken by means of several of the following:

- an appropriate organisation structure (jobs, responsibilities, teams, etc.)
- a production control system (or equivalent for service industry)
- a management decision-making hierarchy suitable for managing change
- a communication system for all employees (for lateral as well as vertical communication)
- a quality management system
- a grievance/ disciplinary/ negotiating system to handle conflict
- a management information system to supply accurate and early details of progress against budgets and other plans on a regular basis
- a review mechanism able to deal with progress across the organisation as well as within specific units or functions.

17. The staff aspect of implementation is critical because of the high proportion of total costs represented by employees. The management of the organisation's personnel/staff requires attention to such concerns as:

- the recruitment and selection of new employees
- handling internal promotions and career planning
- the provision of adequate reward systems to retain staff
- the provision of adequate training and development for staff
- adequate management development and succession system
- adequate leadership by managers and supervisors
- provision for 'releasing' employees (i.e. dismissals)
- the provision of adequate welfare arrangements for staff.

Strategic review

18. Reviews are conducted at a number of levels within the strategic framework, but primarily at (a) the operational level, (b) the strategic business unit level, and (c) the corporate strategic level. At the **operational** level the review process is largely dominated by the budget system, and the emphasis is on the efficient, productive and timely use of resources. Reviewing is usually conducted on a monthly basis at this level. At the **strategic business unit** level the review process is a combination of budget-led progress

reports and an examination of the goals that have been set. Thus the emphasis is as much on effectiveness as on efficiency. SBU reviews are likely to be a mixture of monthly budget reviews and quarterly strategic reviews. At the **corporate** level the process combines consolidated budget reports, management reviews of SBU progress, special projects (e.g. capital investment) and reviews of the whole corporate performance. The emphasis is usually on performance against major targets (e.g. profit margins, sales volumes, return on assets and cost ratios), and on an examination of strategic goals. So, the focus of attention is rather more on **effectiveness** than on **efficiency**. Corporate reviews are generally conducted on a quarterly basis, although some may take place at longer intervals.

Strategic management redefined

19. It is now possible to come to a fuller working definition of 'strategic management', based on the theories and practices which have been described earlier. This is proposed as follows:

> 'Strategic management is an organisational process designed to sustain, invigorate and direct the organisation's human and other resources in the profitable fulfilment of the needs of customers and other principal stakeholders. The process is guided by the organisation's value system, or culture, which is manifested not only in the organisation's mission statement, policies, and strategic goals, but also in the behaviour of top management and other key managers in the organisation. The process of strategic management involves setting goals and objectives, and assessing the organisation's prospects for attaining these in the context of its internal resources and external environment. It involves deciding which customers to serve, with which products or services, and meeting those customers' legitimate needs and wants by allocating resources in the most advantageous way. Strategic management also involves decisions about stakeholders other than customers. It is particularly concerned to meet the needs of the organisation's shareholders for an adequate return on their investment. It is concerned to treat all its employees fairly and to make reasonable efforts to ensure that they are provided with satisfying jobs. It is concerned to deal fairly, as well as cost-effectively, with all its suppliers. It is concerned to act responsibly towards its major creditors. Finally, it is concerned to act as a responsible corporate citizen in the communities within which it operates. Directing and implementing the process of strategic management is the responsibility of the organisation's board of directors, or equivalent top management. However, the process once started is an organisation-wide collaborative effort to satisfy the expectations of all its stakeholders.'

Conclusion

20. This final working definition of strategic management can be used as a benchmark for the next two parts of the book. Part II – The Workbook – provides exercises and questions designed to explore the reader's understanding of key issues arising from the theory and practice of strategic management. Part III – The Case-studies – describes examples of strategic behaviour in a range of organisations chosen for the variety of their contexts. It is hoped that readers will see many connections between the above definition and the practices described in the case-studies.

Part II The workbook

Introduction

This part of the book contains numerous exercises designed to enable students to apply their knowledge and understanding of strategic management to questions and problems arising from each of the chapters from Part I (The knowledge base). There are also some references forward to selected case-studies in Part III.

The exercises can be tackled on an individual basis, as further private study, or as homework, and some can also be used as group exercises during timetabled periods.

Each exercise has an identifier (WB1, WB2 etc.). Exercises are clustered together on a chapter-by-chapter basis, so that reference to Part I contents can be made easily when tackling the questions and problems posed.

It will be apparent from the exercises which elements consolidate understanding of the relevant chapter in Part I, and which develop understanding further. For instance, in Chapter 1 exercise WB1 on the following page, the term 'common concerns' takes the reader back to Chapter 1, whereas the references to 'retail business' and 'state railway' require further thought and application. Similarly, Chapter 1 exercise WB3 (overleaf) presents the reader with a specific case in which to apply his/her understanding to the situation presented.

For assessment purposes, some of the exercises are provided with further information, and guideline solutions, for lecturers and tutors only. Bona fide application should be made direct to the publishers in the prescribed form (see Preface).

Chapter 1 – Strategic management: the concept

WB1

❶ List what you consider to be the key strategic *concerns* that need to be addressed by strategic management, using the following enterprises as sources of ideas:

a) a manufacturing enterprise

b) a retail business

c) a state railway

d) a charitable organisation.

❷ Divide your list into two categories, one for common concerns, and the other for differing concerns, giving short explanations for each item on your list.

WB2

❶ Conduct an analysis of the likely impact of the following stakeholders on the strategic direction of either (i) a high street retail chain, or (ii) an international charity organisation:

a) customers/clients

b) competitors

c) shareholders (or their equivalent)

d) suppliers.

❷ Explain your assessment of the relative impact made by each of the selected stakeholders.

WB3

Carry out a review of the strategic *issues* that arise from your reading of Case-study CS 5 on Nuclear Electric plc. Which issues do you see as being especially important to the company at the present time, and why?

Chapter 2 – Defining purpose, goals and objectives

WB4

❶ Compare the public statements on strategy made by W H Smith plc and British Airways plc (see Chapter 2 pages 19 & 20–21) with those of the Royal Opera House (see page 19–20). What similarities do you see between them, and what differences? How do you explain these?

❷ What are the implications of your answers regarding the strategic priorities of a not-for-profit organisation, such as the Royal Opera House?

WB5

Scenario: The National Trust and the hunting lobby

The National Trust is the largest private landowner in Britain, owning more than half a million acres. The Trust's mission statement (see Part I page 18) is set out in statutory form, and can only be changed by Parliament. The Trust's strategies and supporting policies are decided by the 52-member Council, which is composed half of members elected by the whole membership (over 2 million at December 1992), and half of members appointed by learned societies and 'relevant' organisations.

Among the policies which support its strategic aims is the Trust's policy on hunting (of fox, deer and hare). The current policy allows hunting on Trust properties subject to the following:

1 where it is rooted in local tradition

2 where it does not contravene the wishes of those who gave the land to the Trust

3 where it is not harmful to nature conservation, public recreation or tenants' rights and interests.

The Trust's Council itself is neither in favour of nor against hunting. In recent years some Trust members, supported by a number of pressure groups, have sought to have hunting banned. The matter has been voted on, usually inconclusively, by the membership, and has been debated by the Council. In November 1990 at the Trust's Annual General Meeting a vote to ban deer hunting was passed by a small majority (0.3% of the total membership, of whom only 7% voted) and the Council was urged to take action. After serious consideration the Council decided that the Trust's interests would best be served by continuing the present policy.

Tasks:

1 Imagine that you are a Council Member of the Trust. You have no strong views either for or against hunting. Suggest reasons why the Council would be best advised to continue its present policy of allowing hunting on Trust property, subject to the conditions mentioned above.

2 What might be the consequences for the Trust's activities if hunting were to be banned?

In your answers consider the various stakeholders whose interests might be affected by a change in the existing policy. In addition to Trust members and employees, these should include tenant farmers on Trust property, neighbouring farmers and landowners, the rural communities in which the Trust owns land, nature conservation groups, anti-hunting groups, local authorities, National Parks authorities and Parliament itself.

[Note to Lecturers/Tutors – A full list of the Council's reasons is provided in the Lecturers' Supplement]

Chapter 3 – Assessing the environment

WB6

Carry out a BPEST analysis for one of the following organisations, and present your findings in the form of a summary report to the board of directors. Under each heading (Business, Political, etc.) show which key points you think are important, and add your comments as to (a) the nature of the environmental condition you are describing, and (b) its likely impact on the organisation. It would also be useful if you indicated briefly which aspects of the environment were not considered significant at the present time. The report should be no longer than 1000 words (i.e. about three pages of A4) and may be selected from the following:

1 a former polytechnic now turned university

2 a publicly-owned underground railway service in a capital city

3 a manufacturer of telephones, switchboards and fax machines.

WB7

Scenario: Caring for the disabled – the Leonard Cheshire Foundation

The Leonard Cheshire Foundation was founded by Group Captain (later Lord) Cheshire VC in the decade following the Second World War. From small beginnings in one 'Cheshire Home' in Hampshire, the Foundation had grown by 1993 to 85 Homes and 37 Family Support Services in the UK together with 190 Homes overseas. From its inception the Foundation has drawn much of its vision from the ideas and energy of its founder and a small band of influential people who shared his views. In July 1992 Leonard Cheshire died after a short illness.

The Foundation's Annual Report for 1992 subsequently referred to the following issues as important to the future of its work:

1 The death of the organisation's founder.

2 The uncertain effects of new legislation on community care, which places the responsibility for care on local authorities, but enables them to purchase care facilities from appropriate organisations (such as the Foundation).

3 The need to maintain the level of voluntary income (from donations, legacies, etc.).

4 The use of *voluntary* income (i.e. as opposed to *earned* income) to subsidise the running costs of homes and services.

5 The consequential reduction in the proportion of income available for new developments, education and campaigning.

6 The lack of public knowledge of the work of the Foundation.

7 Intense competition from other charities for voluntary donations by the public.

8 Rising demand for domiciliary (i.e. home-based) services over residential services at a time when local authority expenditure on these services is declining.

9 Decreased investment income and interest.

10 The need to be involved in the design and development of new buildings for care.

11 Increased pressures on volunteer workers and fundraisers.

12 The desire, at a time of great change, to continue the Foundation's policy of involving residents of the Homes, and users of other Foundation services, in decisions made on their behalf.

Task:

Your consultancy firm has offered to assist the Trustees and Chief Officers of the Foundation in their assessment of the effects of changing internal and external conditions on their future strategy. You have been asked to produce a crisp, well-argued report to the Board of Trustees based on your assessment of the most important of the twelve factors referred to in the Annual Report. Firstly, for the benefit of your senior consultant, you have to rank the items in order of their importance to the Foundation, and justify your ranking. Then you have to prepare the report, which should focus on the four or five crucial issues that are likely to emerge, and how you see them affecting the work of the Foundation. The Director General has given you a copy of the Foundation's Mission Statement, which reads as follows:

'We believe that people with disabilities should be able to achieve their full potential and enjoy the maximum opportunity to determine every aspect of their own lives.

Our Mission is to promote the care, general well-being and rehabilitation of people with physical, mental or learning disability.'

WB8

Scenario: The village shop

You have the opportunity to purchase a village shop with a sub-post office included. The village is small with no other shops, but has a public house and an ancient church. There is a major dual carriageway that skirts the village, and this brings customers to the pub and visitors to the church. There is a petrol service station with small shop about two miles down the dual carriageway in the direction of a large town. There are plans to build an out-of-town supermarket run by one of the major chains, since road access is easy given the dual carriageway. In the opposite direction to the town there is little but country cottages and isolated farmhouses. The nearest alternative post office is some eight miles away by public transport. Elderly villagers rely on the village post office for their pensions and other state benefits. Younger people are beginning to move into the village as the homes of the elderly become vacant, but there are few children, as there is no longer a village school.

Task:

The price for the shop-cum-post office is attractive. It could be a bargain for an enter-prising new owner. Nevertheless, there are risks in this situation. Conduct a SWOT analysis on the basis of both what you know, and what you suspect, about the prospects for the business in the situation just described. Then decide whether you will make an offer for the premises.

Chapter 4 – Competitive advantage

WB9

1. Consider how Porter's Five Competitive Forces (see Chapter 4, pages 43–44) might affect the following two businesses, and then consider which ones are likely to have the greatest negative impact on their prospects:

   a) a large supplier of mountain bikes by mail order?

   b) a recently-privatised, but profitable, coal-mine in the Midlands?

2. Set out your answer in chart form, indicating the five forces and their respective effects on the two types of business.

WB10

Consider the following scenarios and evaluate the chances of succeeding in a new market, taking account of Porter's seven barriers to entry:

the establishment of a private hospital for cosmetic surgery in the suburbs of a large European metropolis, where the nearest centre for cosmetic surgery is in the city centre, but where there is a large public sector general hospital in the vicinity

2 launching an all-news television station to customers with access to satellite-receiving equipment in the UK

3 opening a chain of fast-food establishments in an Eastern European city with no previous experience of such services, but where things Western appear to have an immediate appeal.

WB11

Scenario: Unilever Group

Taking into account the extracts printed below and the information supplied in Chapter 15 paragraphs 13-15, suggest where, and how, Unilever might gain some competitive advantage in a range of worldwide markets.

1. Joint Chairmen's Statement:

' ... Four consecutive years of varying degrees of recession in the major economies have intensified competition and made it imperative to operate with the highest level of efficiency in order to protect margins; ... Net profit ... declined by six percent ... however ... there is an underlying growth in earnings of seven percent, which we believe represents sound progress in very difficult trading conditions ...

Underlying volume growth overall was 1.5 percent, reflecting the sluggishness of the economies in Europe and North America, where some three quarters of our sales are located. Growth in both volume and profit remained more than satisfactory in the Rest of the World ...

... in the United States ... Market shares had to be defended, in some cases at the expense of margin ...

We continue to withdraw from activities which do not fit with the four core product groups [NB these are Foods, Detergents, Personal Products and Specialty Chemicals] ... there are more business building opportunities in hitherto closed markets [NB For example Russia, Poland, India and Pakistan] than can be managed at once ... we have sharpened our strategic planning processes in order to concentrate on those product categories and regions which offer the greatest potential for profitable growth.'

2. Business overview

'Western Europe – Profitability ... was maintained, even though most economies remained in recession ... In Italy, we announced our intention to acquire the Bertolli business, which ... will give us leadership in the branded olive oil market. In France, we moved to acquire Ortiz-Miko, an ice-cream manufacturer ...

Central and Eastern Europe – 1993 saw a continuation of our policy [i.e. strategy!] of establishing a significant presence in the region for each of our core businesses ...

North America – ... we completed the purchase of the Klondike ice cream business. This was followed ... by the acquisition of the Breyers and Sealtest business ... we are now the leading manufacturers of ice-cream in the United States.

Rest of the World – The countries outside Europe and North America contain the most rapidly growing markets for most of our products and our results ... have reflected this

... [references are then made to developments in countries such as Egypt, Saudi Arabia, Brazil, Chile, India, China, South Korea and Japan].

(Source: Extracts from Unilever Annual Review 1993)

Chapter 5 – Forecasting the future

WB12

Task:

Examine the following information, showing some key results of a consumer electronics company during the last half of the 1980s, and then make a forecast for the next year against each of the items. Each forecast should be explained in terms of the major assumptions about trading and other conditions you think important.

Background information: The company manufactures and distributes televisions, video-recorders, stereo systems and personal computers. Most of its sales are direct to high street retail chains, and the rest are distributed via wholesalers. Sales turnover has been buoyant until the present year, when it levelled out for the first time in a decade. Two further factors that are known to you are (1) respected statistical services are forecasting the beginnings of a national economic recession, and (2) the company has just purchased a direct-selling (mail order/personal caller) personal computer business for £30m. The new acquisition, which includes its former senior management team, has been combined with the company's computer manufacturing facility to form a new Computer Sales Division.

The results over a five year period between 1985 and 1989 were as follows:

	1985	1986	1987	1988	1989	1990	Assumptions
Turnover (£m)	135	305	510	625	630	?	?
Pre-tax Profit (£m)	20	75	135	160	80	?	?
Profit after tax (£m)	15	50	90	105	50	?	?
Dividends (pence per share)	25	50	95	185	185	?	?
Retained profit (£m)	12	48	90	92	45	?	?
Earnings per share (pence)	2.5	9.5	17.0	19.0	9.0	?	?
Share capital and reserves (£m)	42	90	180	255	310	?	?

WB13

Using the figures supplied for the previous question, assess the company's performance for **1989** against the following key ratios:

❶ Pre-tax profit (compared with the previous year)

❷ Pre-tax profit as percentage of total sales (compared with previous year)

❸ Return on capital employed (compared with previous year)

❹ Return on shareholders' capital (compared with the previous year).

⑤ Comparative earnings per share (over the five years 1985-89)

Conclude your assessment by commenting on the company's *underlying* performance, as judged from the information available.

[Note: Further information supplied in Lecturers' Supplement.]

Chapter 6 – Formulating a strategy

WB14

Scenario: Staying afloat when your supplier goes bankrupt

A small company – owner and two full-time employees – imports and distributes a unique range of marine buoys as part of a modest chandlery business (miscellaneous gear for boats) in the West of England. The buoys have proved to be very popular, and UK demand has increased substantially over the 18 months since they were first available. There have even been a few orders from the Mediterranean area. As a result, the company has had to employ a few part-time staff in order to cope with orders, and has had to rent extra warehouse space. The company understands from customers' comments that the success of the buoys is due to two factors – first, their quality is noticeably better than competing products, and second, the prices are relatively low.

Given this optimistic situation, the owner is suddenly dismayed to learn that the Scandinavian supplier, and sole maker, of these buoys has ceased trading. This has happened at a time when he has a large batch of outstanding orders, but with few stocks available, and has incurred extra expenditure on staff and storage space.

Task:

If you were the owner of this business, what steps would you take to retrieve the situation? Explain your decisions in each case. Some options you may wish to consider, along with any others you may think viable, include:

❶ opting out of the marine buoy segment of your business

❷ seeking a UK supplier in the short-term

❸ making the buoys yourself.

[Note: The actual solution adopted by the company is summarised in the Lecturers' Supplement.]

WB15

❶ Using Mintzberg's six differentiation strategies as a model (see Chapter 6 page 74), consider which strategies appear to have been applied to the design, manufacture and sale of the following categories of motor vehicle:

  a) medium-range saloon cars aimed at the business user (fleet) market

  b) small, high-performance saloons and hatchbacks

  c) Rolls Royce saloons

  d) Land Rovers.

❷ What changes in market conditions might cause manufacturers to consider alternative differentiation strategies?

WB16

❶ What circumstances might spur the following businesses to consider a new strategy of diversification by means of *vertical integration*:

    a) a house-building firm specialising in small, up-market residential developments?

    b) a successful family printing firm with a modest history of publishing its own local history guides?

    c) a major high street retailer of carpets and soft furnishings?

❷ Give reasons for your answers, and state what form of vertical integration is the most likely.

WB17

Examine the case study on British Biotech plc (CS8) from the point of view of how the company intends to market its novel treatments. How viable are its present strategies, in your opinion, and why? What do your findings tell you about the hazards of formulating strategy in conditions of considerable uncertainty?

Chapter 7 – Implementing strategy: an overview

There are no workbook questions or exercises for this introductory chapter.

Chapter 8 – Business plans

WB18

Argue a case for the importance of 'soft' issues, such as appropriate management style, level of individual motivation and coherence of organisation culture in the development of business plans. Suggest how these aspects of strategy implementation can both assist and hinder production routines or service efficiency. Assume, for the purposes of your argument, that adequate organisation structures, budget frameworks and personnel skills are available in the context in which you are applying your case. Base your discussion on *one* of the following contexts:

❶ a Community Health Care Trust operating in an inner-city area

❷ a newly-independent educational establishment (school, college or university)

❸ a financial services office (e.g. branch of bank, insurance company, building society, finance house, etc.)

❹ a large city-centre department store

❺ some other organisation with which you are familiar.

WB19

Scenario: Planning for market leadership

A consumer goods manufacturer has set itself the goal of achieving market leadership in the coming year. Presently, according to independent estimates, the company is in second place some way behind the leader. A SWOT analysis carried out by the company's corporate planning advisory group has revealed that:

① the company's products are well-regarded, but seen as poorer value than the market leader's, even though after-sales service is seen as second to none;

② a newcomer to the market is endeavouring to offer a low-cost range of products in order to achieve market share; the newcomer's product quality is considered as reasonably good, but the presentation lacks polish; some inroads have been made into the lower end of the market;

③ small improvements in production planning, and some additions to process control technology, can bring real benefits to the company's cost-effectiveness; there is scope for improving product packaging;

④ potential cost savings have been identified in administration through improved telecommunications facilities and the use of a new supplier of office consumables;

⑤ there are small savings to be made on staff costs in production areas, but elsewhere, due to earlier cutbacks in clerical and administrative staff, there are few opportunities for reducing staff costs;

⑥ due to the company's improved cash flow over the past year, there is scope for the early repayment of certain outstanding bank loans, thus reducing the interest burden.

Task:

Taking account of the above information, set out the *principles* on which the Board's senior advisers can prepare a Business Plan for the coming year capable of achieving the company's market share target.

WB20

Prepare a Profit and Loss forecast for 1995, together with a supporting statement, for the company, on whose recent performances the following figures are based. The business is primarily electronics, the base is in the UK, but there are major operations in Europe and the Americas. About two thirds of turnover arises from export sales.

Profit & Loss Account	1992 £million	1993 £million	1994 £million	1995 £million
1. Turnover:				
Sales (main group)	5,770	5,600	5,800	?
Share of sales of associated companies:				
Joint ventures	3,285	3,685	3,750	?
Others	375	112	158	?
Total turnover	9,430	9,397	9,708	?
2. Operating profit:				
Principal operations plus share of join ventures	700	695	685	?
Share of profits less losses of other associates	22	19	20	?
Income from loans, deposits, investments less interest	105	150	162	?

		1992 £million	1993 £million	1994 £million	1995 £million
3.	Profit on ordinary activities before taxation	830	860	865	?
4.	Profit attributable to shareholders	540	535	540	?
5.	Dividends distributed	260	280	295	?
6.	Retained profit	280	255	245	?
7.	Earnings per share (pence)	18.6p	19.7p	19.8p	?

Note: The following figures for operating costs (principal business only) are relevant.

		1992	1993	1994	1995
1.	Cost of raw materials and consumables	1,920	1,980	2,120	?
2.	Staff costs	2,000	1,850	1,840	?
3.	Depreciation	250	230	220	?
4.	Cost of plant hire	35	32	24	?
5.	Other external and operating charges	1,040	1,070	975	?
6.	Other costs	4	4	5	?

Chapter 9 – The International dimensions of strategy

WB21

Scenario: Managing an international organisation

Unilever Group operates in over 60 countries worldwide. The majority of its companies are located in some 20 countries in Europe and North America, which provide three-quarters of the Group's turnover. The Rest of the World's contribution is provided by 40 countries across the globe. In Europe and North America, the Group owns 100% of the equity capital of the companies concerned. In the Rest of the World ownership varies from about 50-100%. It is a truly international company.

With such a worldwide organisation employing nearly 300,000 in 1993, the question has to be asked 'How is such a vast organisation managed?'.

Chapter 15 paragraph 13 in Part I mentioned the senior controlling body of Unilever Group – the so-called 'Special Committee' – composed of the Chairmen of the two principal companies plus one other director. This is located in the basic overall management structure as shown in the following diagram.

Unilever sees its management structure as

'designed to derive the maximum benefit from international coordination of its activities, whilst giving individual companies responsibility for their own operations....activities of companies worldwide are coordinated by product groups and regional management groups.'

It thus has the basic characteristics of Peters' 'loose-tight' approach to corporate management.

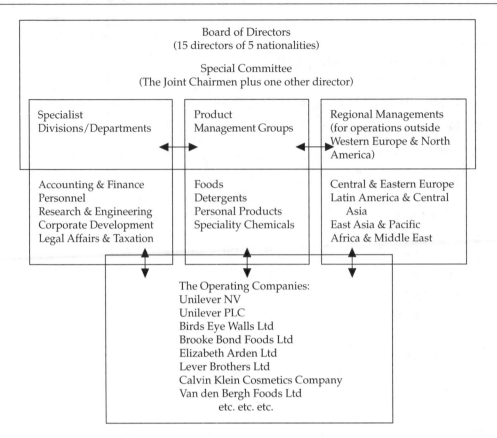

Task:

❶ Taking account of Unilever's description of its management structure, suggest key responsibilities for each of the specialist departments/divisions shown in the above diagram. These could be summarised under the four headings of:

a) advisory services

b) services provided direct

c) monitoring/review services

d) other services

❷ Explain your choices, and suggest how they could be co-ordinated with the operating companies' own activities.

[Note: Further information will be supplied in the Lecturers' Supplement.]

WB22

McDonald's fast-food restaurants serve 28 million people daily in over 70 countries. About 70 per cent of the outlets are franchised to local franchisees. In the UK, the company has opened over 500 restaurants in the last 20 years, but only 16 percent are franchised. The company has thus borne the greater part of the set-up costs of the British operations. This has included providing development centres, establishing supplier networks and manager/franchisee training centres. The company now aims to double the number of UK outlets in the next ten years, mainly by franchising.

Tasks:

❶ What advantages do companies such as McDonald's expect to gain from franchising in order to extend their operations on an international basis?

❷ How do the risks of franchising compare with those associated with *licensing* (e.g. Licences to build tractors, assemble motor vehicles etc. in foreign countries)?

Chapter 10 – Organisation culture and strategic management

WB23

How might the following organisations set about strengthening their corporate culture, and what difficulties are likely to face the senior management in each case:

❶ a family firm in the Yorkshire clothing trade that has just been taken over by a larger rival from the Midlands, but has retained its former name?

❷ a vehicle parts manufacturer in South Wales that has just lost a large order from a Japanese motor car manufacturer on the grounds that quality was not up to the required standard?

❸ a South of England building society that has recently been taken over by a much larger society based in the North of England, and has had to adopt the new company's name?

WB24

Refer back to the details of the Leonard Cheshire Foundation supplied in WB7 above, and make an assessment of the likely culture changes that will be needed in the organisation to enable the Foundation's Trustees, Officers and staff to cope with:

❶ the consequences of the death of the organisation's founder and guiding star

❷ the competitive nature of patient care under the new community care legislation

❸ the competitive pressures of other charities seeking to attract funds

❹ the relatively low level of public awareness of the Foundation and its work for the disabled.

Chapter 11 – Managing change and innovation

WB25

❶ Read through the case-study (CS6) on British Petroleum plc, and then comment on the following two issues:

a) the effects of low crude oil prices on BP's capacity to innovate

b) the relevance of joint ventures with overseas companies to the development of new oil-fields and new markets.

❷ Comment on BP's approach to innovation and change.

WB26

❶ Which factors in the *internal* environment are likely to have the greatest impact on change in *one* of the following organisations:

a) a manufacturing company that has just introduced a fully-automated production line into one of its three main production facilities?

b) an NHS district general hospital that has recently become a private health trust?

c) a fast moving consumer goods company that has just been taken over by a large conglomerate in the same marketplace?

❷ Explain your arguments in each case.

WB27

❶ Which factors in the *external* environment are likely to exert the greatest influence over changes in company policies on:

a) health and safety,

b) customer care, and

c) employee hours of work?

❷ Give full reasons for your answers, and consider them in the context **either** of a company manufacturing and supplying parts to the motor industry, **or** of a mail-order clothing company offering ordering facilities on a 24-hour basis and delivery within 3 days anywhere in the UK.

Chapter 12 – Managing quality

WB28

Scenario:

You are the Managing Director of a small, but growing, company providing packaging materials to industrial users. Your materials include plastic film, paper and cardboard, with the emphasis on the last-mentioned. One of your biggest customers – a household name in the consumer goods industry – has decided to 'go Green' in a big way, and henceforth wants you to supply packaging made up either of recycled board or paper. This is no problem for most of the customer's requirements, but does pose difficulties for the packaging of certain healthcare products. It is important that the contract should be fulfilled, since this customer alone purchases one third of the company's total output.

Task:

Taking the quality management cycle into account (see Chapter 12 Figure 12.3), describe how you would set about meeting the customer's quality requirements. In your answer indicate whether you should charge the same, more or less, for the healthcare packaging compared with the current material.

WB29

Prepare a policy statement on quality for consideration by your Board of Directors, taking account not only the firm's customers or clients, but also the training implications for employees and any additional requirements that might be asked of suppliers. Keep the statement itself to one side of A4 paper, and then add a separate discussion paper aimed at drawing directors' attention to key points, both negative and positive.

WB30

Using Porter's model of the generic value chain (see Chapter 12 Figure 12.2), assess the relative contribution to *'value'* of each of the primary activities in *two* of the following contexts:

❶ a large branch of Marks and Spencer

❷ a motorway service area company

❸ a manufacturer of mountain bikes.

Chapter 13 – The role of the marketing function in strategic management

WB31

❶ Draw up a list of the advantages and disadvantages of adopting the marketing concept in the context of the following:

a) a community health care programme for the elderly

b) an importer of video films

c) an educational publisher.

❷ What conclusions do you draw from your listings as to who benefits and who loses in this situation?

WB32

Scenario: Building Society turned Bank turned Estate Agent

In its Directors' Report and Accounts for 1993, the Abbey National plc reported an increase in pre-tax profits over the previous year by 25% to a record £704 million. The company's Cost: Income Ratio was down slightly from 44.6% to 44.5%. Earnings per share rose from 24.2 pence to 29.7 pence over the previous year. Operating expenses for 1993 were up by 8%, part of which was due to a £20 million increase in expenditure on the promotion of mortgage products. However, the main contributor to the Group's total earnings came from retail banking, even though there was an increase in market share of the UK mortgage market.

In February 1993 the company successfully entered the direct Life Assurance market through the establishment of a new subsidiary Abbey National Life, which generated £145 million of new business premiums. This contribution was in addition to that of Scottish Mutual Assurance plc, a recent acquisition, with £390m of new business. Treasury operations (i.e. active involvement in the international money markets) saw an increase over 1992 of 45% for 1993 profit levels – a developing part of upstream diversification. The Group suffered losses (£30 million) on the disposal of its estate agency business, following an unsuccessful effort to enter a *downstream* business activity. Losses on the estate agency in 1992 were £20 million, but these were reduced to £2m in 1993 before the business was sold. There were also losses due to bad debts and repossessions in the

UK, and further losses in Continental Europe amounting to £105 million (£46m in 1992). The latter were largely due to the recession in commercial property in France.

The Directors' Report commented that they expected a 10% increase in the UK mortgage market in the coming year, and with fewer arrears and repossessions, less provision needed to be made for bad debts. The position in Continental Europe seemed to be improving and the estate agency business had been sold off. Although personal financial markets are competitive (a considerable understatement!), the Group should be in a strong position to benefit from economic recovery given the 'mutually reinforcing businesses of UK Retail Banking, Life Assurance and Treasury Operations.'

Task:

Given the above situation, state where you think Abbey National's marketing effort should be directed in the coming year. In your answer give a general indication of (a) the relative **short-term** gains or losses expected from your proposals, and (b) their **longer-term** impact on the Group's business.

Chapter 14 – The role of personnel in strategic management

WB33

Scenario: Personnel strategy and competitive cost-cutting

In an effort to reduce costs and achieve savings that can be passed on to its customers in the form of lower unit prices, a medium-sized manufacturing company intends to achieve a 10% reduction in its workforce of 3000 employees. The company's business plan calls for the reduction to be completed within 12 months. Although some production workers' jobs will become redundant, the main focus of the planned reductions will be on managerial, supervisory and staff jobs. This is where roles have been changed as a direct result of organisational restructuring leading to fewer layers of supervision. The staff jobs that are no longer required are mostly in the company's headquarters, and range from catering staff, through clerical staff in the HQ support departments, to some senior office supervisors.

Task:

You are the company's Personnel Director. You have to prepare a strategic plan to ensure that the planned reductions are carried out to the maximum effect (i.e. retaining key staff, whilst dismissing those whose jobs are no longer required, and to do this within the budget agreed by the Board). The company expects you to act lawfully and fairly, and there are agreements in place with the clerical workers' union. The Board want to see a written plan setting out the objectives to be achieved, the means by which they will be achieved, the policies that will apply, and the proposed timescale. Your submission should not be more than three pages of A4 in length.

WB34

What contribution can be made by a corporate personnel department in a divisionalised company to excellence in the following aspects of strategic management:

① the production of a succinct but visionary mission statement?

② the development of a culture to support that statement?

③ the sustaining of excellent product quality throughout the company?

④ the preparation of middle and senior management for higher office?

Chapter 15 – Measuring strategic performance

WB35

① What key ratios, and other leading criteria of 'success', might be applied to the following types of organisation:

a) a heritage/conservation trust (e.g. the National Trust)?

b) a life assurance business?

c) a supermarket chain?

d) a children's charity organisation?

② How far do you think that *business* ratios are relevant to the assessment of performance in not-for-profit organisations?

WB36

Scenario: Investing wisely to support a national church

The Church Commissioners for England have a primary responsibility to manage the investments entrusted to them to maximise their financial support for the ministry of the Church of England, particularly in areas of need and opportunity. Their mission statement includes an intention 'to provide the Church, by the year 2000, with a diversified and prospering asset base...'

The 1993 Annual Report & Accounts for the Commissioners notes that:

'We have been entrusted with the management of properties and other investments worth, at the end of 1993, £2.4 billion net of borrowings. Our strategic task is to generate as much sustainable income as is consistent with the need to preserve, over the long term, the real value of the assets as a whole.'

The Annual Accounts for the year ended 31 December 1993 showed that:

① income from all sources (property, investments, loans, etc.) amounted to £154.9 million net of interest payable

② administration costs totalled £10.4 million (slightly down on previous year)

③ total expenditure (clergy stipends, pensions, housing, etc.) amounted to £146.4 m, producing a deficit on current account of £1.9 m

④ the loss was more than compensated for by the proceeds of assets realised during the year (mainly investments and investment properties) totalling £24 m

⑤ assets were revalued during the year and rose from a deficit of £156.6 m in 1992 to a gain of £296.2 m, mainly from investments, which were valued at £171.1 m, and from investment properties (£73.7 m).

Tasks:

1 Study the figures presented below, and give a written assessment of how far you think the Commissioners can achieve their strategic aims for the year 2000, given the performance of the organisation over the past decade.

2 Where, in your opinion, should the Commissioners put their emphasis over the next five years, and why? The principal options exercised to date include the following:

a) continue to invest in commercial properties (offices, shops, etc.)

b) continue to increase the proportion of residential properties in the total property assets of the organisation

c) reduce property holdings in favour of increasing the investment portfolio (fixed interest securities, equities, etc.)

d) continue proportion of growth-producing holdings vis-à-vis higher income earning investments.

The Church Commissioners – extracts from Ten-Year Financial Record

	1984	1985	1986	1987	1988	1989	1990	1991	1992	1993
Net Income (£m):										
Property:										
Commercial property	30.9	32.1	33.8	45.3	46.1	55.8	64.9	53.2	56.6	59.0
Residential	3.8	6.2	4.7	5.2	5.9	5.0	5.1	6.2	7.1	7.4
Agricultural	6.2	6.7	7.3	7.4	7.8	8.1	7.7	8.1	8.2	8.1
Total Property	**40.9**	**45.0**	**45.8**	**57.9**	**59.8**	**68.9**	**77.7**	**67.5**	**71.9**	**74.5**
Investments:										
Fixed interest	6.4	9.6	16.2	21.4	16.2	17.7	19.2	29.5	36.5	45.1
UK equities	20.2	21.0	22.5	25.9	32.7	37.9	38.6	31.8	35.9	30.4
Other equities	8.8	8.2	6.8	5.5	5.9	7.2	7.1	4.7	4.2	2.5
Other interest	7.3	9.6	9.7	9.6	15.3	19.3	33.1	48.1	28.4	15.0
Net Income before interest	**83.6**	**93.4**	**101.0**	**120.3**	**129.9**	**151.0**	**175.7**	**181.6**	**176.9**	**167.5**

	1984	1985	1986	1987	1988	1989	1990	1991	1992	1993
Assets:										
(nearest £m)										
Property (all)	921	967	1,014	1,297	1,511	1,889	1,689	1,412	1,181	1,232
Investments (nearest £m)	707	797	1,010	916	1,042	1,249	778	953	976	1,218
Other investments (nearest £m)	96	99	105	197	302	248	408	291	253	228
Gross assets (nearest £m)	1,724	1,863	2,129	2,410	2,855	3,386	2,875	2,656	2,410	2,678

Chapter 16 – Strategic management: a concluding model

WB37

Read through the final working definition of strategic management (Chapter 16 page 168) and then prepare single-page Mission Statements for two of the following organisations:

1. an international pharmaceutical company based in Britain
2. a large NHS Hospital Trust based on a district general hospital
3. an organisation representing the interests of motorists
4. a national charity for blind people
5. a local authority in a rural area.

WB38

Refer to the case-study on Nuclear Electric (CS5) in Part III, and consider the extent to which the company is concerned to act as a responsible corporate citizen. Write up your ideas in the form of a feature article for a respected local newspaper in an area where there is a nuclear power station. Aim to give a balanced view in drawing your personal conclusions, and show that you respect the feelings of those on both sides of the issue of nuclear power generation. Restrict your article to about 1000–1200 words.

Part III The case-studies

Introduction

This part of the book contains eighteen case-studies of different aspects of strategic management taken from a selection of business and 'not-for-profit' organisations. They are nearly all based in the United Kingdom, but most have operations across the globe. Not one of them could be called parochial! The information in the cases has been drawn mainly from public sources (such as annual reports and accounts) and press reports, and sometimes from internal sources in the organisation. The events they describe are grounded in real life, and it is hoped that they will provide useful illustrations of leading concepts of strategic management. The case-studies are referenced to relevant chapters in the book and (in a few cases) to a workshop exercise. The first eight cases appeared in the first edition, but have been updated and amplified for this edition. The cases are in the following order:

	Case-study Organisation	Chapter	Workbook
1	Marks and Spencer plc	1, 2, 4, 6, 10	WB30
2	British Airways plc	1, 2, 5, 9	WB4
3	The Rover Group	1, 3, 5, 6,1 0, 13	
4	Oxfam	1, 2, 13	
5	Nuclear Electric Ltd	1, 3	WB3, WB38
6	British Petroleum plc	1, 5, 6, 9	WB25
7	Hanson plc	1, 2, 5, 6, 11	
8	British Biotech plc	1, 2, 3, 4	WB17
9	Cross-channel ferries	3, 4, 13	
10	Toyota Manufacturing UK	2, 10	
11	Railtrack plc	3, 5, 15	
12	Niche airlines	4, 5, 6	
13	Universities Superannuation Scheme	1, 2, 12	
14	Ethical investment	2, 10	
15	Legal and General Assurance	7, 11, 14	
16	BAA plc	11, 13	
17	Formula One racing	4, 13	
18	The water industry	2, 12	

The questions at the end of each case-study are intended to stimulate thinking about strategic issues, and to help in relating practice to theory.

CS1: Marks and Spencer - retailing financial services

Introduction

Marks and Spencer plc is one of the most successful and profitable high street retailers in Britain. The company began as a one-man haberdashery business in 1882, where everything on sale was priced at one penny. Michael Marks, the Russian refugee who had started the business, eventually formed what was to turn out to be a historical partnership with Tom Spencer in 1894. By 1926 Marks and Spencer had became a public company. Today turnover exceeds £7 billion, and the company has become the envy of other retailers, and a model to be followed throughout the business world. Total turnover for the year ended 31 March 1997 amounted to £7.84 billion, and pre-tax profits were in excess of 1 billion pounds for the first time.

The company has always been an innovator, and has always set itself the highest standards in quality of product and pride of service. At an early stage in its history the company pioneered specification buying – purchasing direct from manufacturers to specifications supplied by the company. The company itself manufactures nothing, but collaborates with suppliers who work to detailed specifications produced by Marks and Spencer specialist buyers. The company has had for many years the kind of quality assurance systems that many companies are only just introducing today. In the 1950s the company expanded its product range from clothing to food, setting new standards for food preparation, display and hygiene. In the 1980s the company invested hundreds of millions of pounds in computer technology in order to create links across the entire supply chain from manufacturer to the point of sale, and thus pave the way for more efficient ordering and stock control.

Financial services – a new departure

In 1984 the company introduced its own Account Card under the auspices of a subsidiary: Marks and Spencer Financial Services. This was the start of further expansion of M & S Group business – the decision to extend into financial services totally unrelated to food and clothing retailing. Since its launch the Account Card has been taken up by 4.5 million customers, according to the company's report for the year ending 31 March 1997. With this innovation the company was still much in line with other major retail groups, which had also introduced their own credit cards. Marks and Spencer then decided to go one step further by offering personal loans, which took its activities beyond those of retail competitors. Unlike the company's innovations on the supply side of its operations, where the company effectively contracts out the provision of goods and foodstuffs, the introduction of financial services has been entered into directly.

Thus the company is now actively providing extra services direct to its many retail customers, and they have been taking advantage of it. Personal lending in the last financial year topped half a billion pounds – an increase of 46% on the previous year (1995/6). The establishment of a Unit Trust Management Fund in 1988 marked a new era for the company – a quantum leap in the financial services sector. The decision to offer unit trusts to the public seemed to be justified, for by 1993 the activity had already accounted for 1.5% of the market. Sales performed well in 1996/7 with the fund increasing in value by some 35%.

Moving into life assurance and pensions

In 1994 the company decided on a further substantial and significant extension of its financial services operations by moving into life assurance and pensions. The company concluded that it would be good for customers, and profitable to the company, to offer pensions and life assurance policies. Initially, the additional service was operated from six flagship stores, and customers were able to come in off the street and discuss their requirements with M & S staff. In implementing this new service, the company set up its administrative systems and staff training in conjunction with a major insurance company (Equitable Life) that has a respected place in the market, and pays no commission on the sales of its products. Research carried out by the company had suggested that customers would prefer to go to an M & S store to discuss pensions and life assurance rather than have a salesperson calling at their home. It was also noted that customers reported their confidence in the reputation of the company.

Clearly, once a powerful reputation for service and quality has been built up over the years, as with Marks and Spencer, it is easier to contemplate a move into a new market with a new product. By the year ended 31 March 1997, there had been solid progress in this area with more than 11,000 customers applying for life and pensions policies. In 1997 a telephone call centre was established at Chester, the headquarters of the Financial Services sector, enabling customers to obtain immediate life cover. The Financial Services operation currently handles nearly 3 million contacts a year, mostly by telephone. Taking all its activities into account the Financial Services sector contributed £75.7 million in operating profits to the Group – more than 7% of the total Group operating profit. Few other organisations could afford to be so confident of achieving successful entry to such a mature industry as life assurance and pensions.

In its report for the year ended 31 March 1996, it was commented that 'The M & S principles of quality, innovation, value and service are as relevant in financial services as elsewhere in our business.' Two key aspects of the company's approach to financial services in the present highly competitive market were identified as follows:

- the building of a highly-efficient and low-cost operation
- the creation of new standards of telephone-based central servicing.

Crucial decisions required here include the provision of first-class equipment and facilities, thorough training of staff in customer relations and product knowledge, and the development of adequate control systems to avoid fraud and bad debts. As in its other dealings Marks and Spencer plc intends to be nothing but professional.

Questions

1. What factors have been particularly favourable to Marks and Spencer in diversifying its retail business into financial services (lending, pensions, life, assurance etc.)?

2. Since customer service is so important to Marks and Spencer, suggest what features you would expect to see in a full-scale training programme for telephone-based customer services staff selling financial products. What are the potential benefits of such training for the company's image in the outside world?

CS2: British Airways – onwards and upwards

Introduction

The story of British Airways in the ten years since privatisation is one of phenomenal success. It has moved from being an unprofitable state-owned airline to a thriving international business in its own right. Turnover has increased by more than two and a half times since 1987, operating profits have grown from a modest £162 million to more than £600 million in each of the last three years, and earnings per share have more than doubled over the decade. The number of passengers carried has shown a steady increase, exceeding 30 million in the last four years. In recent years the company has formed a number of alliances and joint ventures with other airlines in order to provide a truly global service for its long-haul passengers, whilst at home it has franchised several feeder services to improve connections between Heathrow and Gatwick and outlying areas, such as Scotland and the west of England.

The British Airways story

The origins of British Airways can be traced back to 25 August 1919, when the world's first daily international scheduled air service took off from Hounslow Heath, West London, to Paris (Le Bourget). In 1939, the original British Airways was merged with its more famous rival, Imperial Airways, and nationalised to form British Overseas Airways Corporation (BOAC). After World War II, BOAC was allocated long-haul flights – other than those to South America, which were operated for a few years by British South American Airways before it was subsequently merged back into BOAC. European and domestic routes were to be operated by British European Airways. In 1974, BOAC and BEA were brought together to form British Airways. The new grouping resulted in many difficulties for its management, including industrial strife and heavy financial losses.

In 1979, the Government announced that it intended to privatise the company. The necessary legislation was passed a year later, and Lord King was appointed Chairman, charged by the Secretary of State to restore the Group to profitability and prepare the way for privatisation. At that stage the company was declaring losses of £544m (1981/2). King's privatisation plan included cutting back staff, suspending unprofitable routes and disposing of surplus assets. Eventually, in February 1987, shares in British Airways were floated for the first time. The offer was so successful that it was oversubscribed eleven-fold. Later that year BA acquired British Caledonian, a second-force airline composed of several small independent airlines, which in effect formed BA's charter fleet. In May 1990, only three full years after flotation, the company announced record pre-tax profits at £345 million. British Airways is now the only leading airline in Europe which is neither state-owned nor state-protected. It is also by far the most profitable.

Maintaining profitability in a competitive industry

Since its inception British Airways has continued to return profits at the end of each financial year, unlike most of its competitors. The secret of its success is based on a number of strategic management decisions taken over the past five years, including:

- maintaining a sustained marketing campaign focusing on customer care and the airline's truly global connections

- focusing on the requirements and preferences of *business customers*. This has resulted in the development of 'brands' to differentiate between levels of service (such as Concorde, First Class, Club Europe, Club World etc). By developing links and partnerships with foreign airlines carrying business people, the company has been able to offer better service to those having to change flights in order to get to a non-capital city destination. Check-in arrangements have been streamlined for business passengers to reduce waiting times

- focusing on the needs of *private passengers* and *tourists*. This has resulted in extra cabin services, special arrangements for children and young families, and improved check-in arrangements

- providing holiday bookings direct through British Airways Holidays. The travel agency wing of the company attracts tourists onto scheduled flights by means of branded services such as City Breaks, Euro Disney, Canada Fly Drive, and Florida and America

- marketing the excellent reputation of British Airways Engineering. Aircraft maintenance is a vital aspect of any airline's operations, since the safety and security of passengers is paramount. First-class maintenance is also critical since individual aircraft are being called upon to fly more air miles as part of the company's efficiency drive. Retaining fleet maintenance and repair in-house enables the company to keep a tight control on quality, safety and efficiency. More than this, other airlines are seeking to use BA's facilities because of their reputation, and because they realise that by contracting out to BA they can achieve a better cost-effectiveness ratio on aircraft maintenance

- building on its own developments in information technology, especially in the field of passenger reservations and services systems, the company has been able to sell its technology services, brand name Speedwing, to other countries. Revenue from such consulting activities not only provides a contribution to profits, but also enables further reinvestment in technology

- purchasing or leasing the optimum type of aircraft for the particular route or market conditions. British Airways' mainline fleet at the end of March 1995 totalled 256 aircraft, composed of long, short and medium-haul jet-liners with a small number of turbo-prop aircraft. The dominant supplier was Boeing, but others included Airbus Industries, McDonnell Douglas and British Aerospace. The average age of the fleet is about 10 years, but some jumbo jets (Boeing 747s) have been flying for more than 20 years

- aiming for cost-effective purchasing/ leasing arrangements. Key issues here include aircraft safety, reliability, economy of operation, seating capacity and price (or leasing terms). Recent acquisitions by the company include the purchase of Airbus long-range aircraft for the first time, matching Singapore Airlines introduction of long-range Airbus 340s. The latter is currently the world's most profitable airline with BA in second place. BA is also about to add the new Boeing 777 to its fleet. The major cost of purchasing or leasing aircraft is spread over many years, and new aircraft orders are usually scheduled on a quarterly basis

- developing its cargo operations through British Airways Cargo. This is another way of contributing to overall Group profitability, since most of the cargo is carried in the holds of passenger aircraft. A key strength of the cargo business is that more than 80% of its revenue is earned in foreign currency. The handling of cargo calls for effective computer technology, and the company has invested considerably in systems designed to speed up documentation and tracking

- promoting an extensive programme of staff training to ensure that the company's employees are efficient, productive and aware of the importance of the customer. Training programmes are labelled to reflect their intention ('Putting People First', 'Winners' and so on). The company's airline training establishment near Heathrow is one of the largest in the world, and its flight crew facility alone includes 18 simulators, each worth about £10m

- by undertaking a profit improvement programme. This is aimed at reducing costs while improving service quality. Savings have come primarily from:
  - changes in working practices, especially in passenger handling and engineering
  - improved aircraft utilisation and fuel saving techniques
  - reducing the number of external suppliers (from 10,000 to 3,500)
  - outsourcing of certain non-core facilities (e.g. vehicle management)
  - use of information technology to speed up the supply chain, reduce stock levels and minimise errors
  - a reduction in the workforce (which had been growing)
  - a 2-year pay freeze in certain sections (e.g. baggage handling and cargo operations)
  - disposal of assets which are not part of the core business (such as divestment of charter business through sale of British Caledonian)
  - development of franchise operations for feeder flights within UK previously operated by the company (franchisees include LoganAir, Brymon and so on).

Towards the millennium

The Chief Executive of the company reported in the 1995/6 annual report that '*As deregulation removes traditional barriers to market entry, it is customer preference, driven by quality and value of service, which will determine the winners in a global competitive market.*' In 1997 the company issued a new mission to take it into the new millennium – 'To be the undisputed leader in world travel'. New goals and values were published at the same time. The new goals, more slogans than statements, are:

1. to be the 'Customers' Choice'
2. to have 'Inspired People'
3. to have 'Strong Profitability'
4. to be 'Truly Global'.

The new values that accompany the new goals are described equally succinctly as:

1 to be 'Safe and Secure'

2 to be 'Honest and Responsible'

3 to be 'Innovative and Team-spirited'

4 to be 'Global and Caring'

5 to be a 'Good Neighbour'.

Implementation of the new mission has already started (1997) with the disposal of unprofitable parts of the business, an organisational restructuring involving the outsourcing of certain functions and the offer of voluntary redundancy to 5000 employees. A proposal for a major alliance with American Airlines is currently before the authorities in both countries, but is being strongly disputed by rival airlines on both sides of the Atlantic. The company has also introduced a new livery representing a range of different world cultures, which has replaced the former BA logo which incorporated the Union Jack. The message is that BA is no longer a British company but a global company. The company has also begun to extend the use of its own brand name to retail products, such as cameras and credit cards.

In early summer 1997, the company experienced strikes and other industrial action by several groups of staff, including cabin crews and pilots. Renewal does not come easily even for successful companies.

Performance Summary

The success of British Airways since privatisation is reflected in the following results:

	1987	1990	1995	1996	1997
Turnover (£m)	3,263	4,838	7,177	7,760	8,359
Operating profit (£m)	173	384	618	728	546
Pre-tax profit (£m)	162	345	327	585	640
Earnings per share (p)	20.5	34.1	26.2	49.4	55.7
Passengers carried (m)	n/a	n/a	35,643	36,061	38,180
Cargo carried (000 tonnes)	n/a	n/a	666	672	721

Questions

1. Examine BA's strategic decisions over the past five years and state what you consider to be the most crucial for the next five years. Give your reasons.

2. What are the practical implications of meeting the new goals set by the company for the millennium? How far might they help BA to become a 'winner' in the global competitive market?

3. Suggest some forecasts for British Airways' performance in 1999 and 2001, using the headings shown in the performance summary above. Justify your forecasts.

CS3: The Rover Group - a new future for the millennium?

Introduction

The Rover marque has always been an important part of the British motoring scene, firmly middle of the range, yet up-market too. However, during the 1960s and 1970s it fell victim to the industrial relations troubles that were tearing large portions of British industry apart. As a result costs escalated, reliability deteriorated, sales dropped and severe financial losses were incurred. In the late 1970s the company was bought out in a salvage operation by British Aerospace, and the company fought to regain its former prominence and reputation. Although many of its models were unsuccessful, Rover had a winner in the Land Rover, and its luxury version, the Range Rover. The Mini was also still selling well. Additionally, at Longbridge, near Birmingham, and Cowley, near Oxford, the company had two important factories with skilled labour available.

In 1979, in an attempt to boost Rover's fortunes, British Aerospace, the parent company, negotiated an agreement with Honda, the Japanese car and motorcycle manufacturer, in which the latter took out a 20% share of Rover's equity and agreed to collaborate in building motorcars. Among other things Honda was to supply engines for a range of Rover models, whilst Rover took out a 20% stake in Honda UK and agreed to assemble one of the Honda range at its Birmingham works. The agreement also covered collaboration on the design of future models. As a result of the agreement Honda, one of the smaller Japanese car-makers, gained a valuable entry to a major market (Britain and subsequently the EU). Rover, in its turn, benefited from Honda's design and production expertise, together with its image of medium-range, up-market style and reliability.

Sold to BMW

Despite successful sales over the next few years, Rover was still making losses. In 1993, for example, the company reported a pre-tax loss of £9 million after interest charges of £65 million. Unfortunately, by the 1990s British Aerospace itself was entering a difficult phase, due partly to world recession in the airline business and partly to the reduced demand for military aircraft and hardware following the collapse of the former Soviet Union. British Aerospace took a strategic decision to concentrate on its core business, and accordingly sought a buyer for Rover. Honda offered to extend its share of Rover's equity from 20% to 47.5%, but was upstaged by BMW, the prestigious German company, which agreed to purchase the full 80% owned by British Aerospace.

The German company had been looking for some time at the possibility of investing in Rover, and was particularly interested in the highly sought-after Land Rover and Range Rover models. BMW had no four-wheel drive, off-road designs of its own. Rover was also attractive because it had much lower production costs than BMW, and as producer of the famous Mini, as well as the middle-of-the-range Rover series of saloons, was well worth considering. Honda, needless to say, were somewhat dismayed by this turn of events, especially as BMW, a competitor, had now acquired a 20% stake in its UK operations! By May 1994, however, the two original partners had agreed to terminate their cross shareholdings, whilst maintaining their existing collaborative projects for the time being. Honda relinquished its stake in Rover, and Rover returned its stake in Honda UK.

Honda's situation

Compared with their larger Japanese rivals, Nissan and Toyota, who had pursued independent investment in the UK, Honda's strategy of joint ventures and collaboration has proved insufficient to enable it to expand in Europe by co-operating with competitors. Nevertheless, by agreement between BMW, Rover and Honda, the Japanese company's car production and parts supplies will be protected for some time to come. Whether this tripartite co-operation will continue into the next century is uncertain, but certainly not impossible. In the meantime, the Honda parent company decided to increase its investment in Britain by some £330 million, enabling Honda UK to construct a pressed parts facility of its own, instead of relying on Rover for bodywork panels and the like. The company also decided to increase the capacity of its Swindon assembly plant, which by 1996 was producing some 100,000 vehicles a year. As a further step in securing its position in Europe, the company in mid-1996 entered into a joint venture agreement with Unipart, the automotive parts company, to build a £35 million factory in Coventry and to expand two existing Unipart sites, in order to supply components for Honda's UK and European vehicle production. Honda, like its colleagues at Nissan and Toyota, clearly sees Europe as an attractive and growing market. All three pose a considerable competitive threat to the newly-owned Rover Group, since most of their leading marques are in direct competition with existing Rover models.

What future now for Rover?

In August 1994 the company, now owned by BMW, which had purchased the business for some £800 million, announced plans to accelerate investment in new developments and improvements at its main production plants at Cowley and Solihull. The sum of £1.5 billion has been earmarked for regeneration over the next five years. The development cost of the new Range Rover alone is put at £300 million, the biggest single investment yet made by Land Rover. Rover group sales rose by 16% in the first half of 1994, and expectations of increased sales in Germany are higher than ever since the take-over by BMW.

The present (1997) Rover series comprise the Rover 100 (Mini), 200, 300 and 400 (middle-range saloons), and the 600 and 800 larger saloons. It seems likely, according to the pundits, that BMW will seek to phase out this system of numbering in favour of a branding approach based on some of the famous marques of the past. The Mini brand-name is almost certain to return, and there are strong possibilities that such marques as MG, Austin-Healey and even Triumph will also return. The Rover brand itself is likely to be kept for an up-market range of saloons that will be cheaper than a standard Jaguar, for example. Clearly, any new models will need to complement rather than compete directly with BMW's own models. One thing is certain – however many brand-names are employed, they will all have an underlying production platform to supply chassis, engines, gearboxes and electronics. In this way lower British costs combined with more standardised production procedures should lead to cost-effective manufacturing. If designs are attractive to customers in the major markets, and quality comparable with competitors, then there is no reason why the new-look Rover and its brands should not sell large numbers of cars in the last years of this century. Taking everything into account, it seems as if the future for Rover is bright.

Questions

1. To what extent does the above case-study suggest that the way ahead for any major car manufacturer depends more on strategic alliances with other manufacturers than by developing niche markets with particular groups of customers?

2. Given that in the past there were almost too many different models of car produced in Britain, why should branding of vehicle models be considered seriously for the future?

3. If you were the marketing director of BMW, what would you see as the threats and opportunities offered by a renewed Rover company with leading name brands?

CS4: Oxfam Ltd – charity and business in the relief of suffering

Introduction

The principal objective of Oxfam (Oxford Committee for Famine Relief) is

'the relief of poverty, distress and suffering in any part of the world ... and primarily when arising from any public calamity ... or ... of want of natural or artificial resources or the means to develop them ...'.

To this end the company (it is a company limited by guarantee) aims to raise money to fund aid and disaster projects in a variety of locations all over the world. In recent years it has raised more than £70 million in each of the years ending 30 April 1992 and 1993, and by the same period in 1995 had raised almost £100 million. As a general rule the company aims to spend 84% of its income on its Overseas Aid Programme, 6% on public affairs and campaigning, and 10% on fundraising and administration. Any surplus at a year end is put into reserves, which are called upon if there is a sudden and unexpected crisis (for example, as in Rwanda in 1995).

How does a charitable organisation like Oxfam raise such large sums for the poor and the needy, and how does it distribute them? In general terms, as the figures below indicate, Oxfam does so by spending several million pounds on campaigning, fund-raising, educational activities, and administration. This is the degree of investment that Oxfam requires in order to obtain revenues of the order of £75–100 million every year. As the Finance Director put it in the organisation's report for 1992/3:

'There is always a dilemma between maximising income and keeping fundraising costs to the necessary minimum. It is therefore pleasing to be able to report that fundraising costs increased more slowly than total income in 1992/3.'

Unlike a typical business organisation, for it is also a Registered Charity, Oxfam achieves many of its objectives through the generosity of volunteers, who give their time freely. In the year 1992/3 Oxfam could count on the services of about 30,000 such voluntary workers, compared with the total of 1028 full-time UK-based salaried staff. There were also 764 staff based overseas on local contracts.

Oxfam's income – how much and where from

The picture to be drawn of Oxfam's revenue-earning activities from reading the company's Annual Report and Accounts for recent years is as follows (all figures are rounded to nearest million):

	1995 £m	1993 £m	1992 £m
Donations	38	32	29
Shops and Trading	19	23	23
Contributions from other agencies (e.g. UN)	15	5	3
Contributions from UK Govt. and EU	19	13	13
Miscellaneous	9	6	5
TOTAL	100	79	73

Donations have continued to increase over the years as a result of fundraising activities and the award of legacies from those who have died. Income from shops and trading has, conversely, shown a downward trend, which may reflect the competition resulting from the growth of charity shops in the average British high street. Contributions from UN agencies and others are usually related to a specific disaster or special UN-funded projects, and are less predictable than other sources of income. Government and official sources of income (including the European Union) tend to be known in advance and can thus be incorporated into annual budget planning. Miscellaneous sources include the proceeds of non-monetary gifts (such as property), and bank deposit interest. This source has shown a tendency to increase. The total receipts of nearly £100 million in 1995 are a far cry from the £3.3 million raised in 1970/1, and show how Oxfam has developed over 25 years.

Expenditure and allocations

The Accounts for recent years show expenditure allocated between aid, campaigning, fund-raising and administration as follows (all figures rounded to nearest million):

	1995 £m	1993 £m	1992 £m
Overseas Aid Programme	84	57	52
Public affairs, information, campaigning, etc.	6	4	4
Total allocations	90	61	56
Fundraising	8	13	12
Administration	2	4	4
Total allocations and expenditure	100	78	72
Surplus of income over expenditure	0	1	1

As the figures show, the bulk of Oxfam's funds go into supporting its Overseas Aid Programme, which is comprised mostly of relatively small-scale overseas projects in the

Third World. Most of the projects are run by local people whose knowledge and contacts ensure that money and time are used as effectively as possible. As well as providing direct aid, Oxfam aims to help local people to claim their basic rights to employment, shelter, food, health and education. It is also concerned to raise the status of women, which it sees as central to any real breakthrough in the cycle of poverty and deprivation experienced by so many Third World citizens.

In pursuing its projects, Oxfam adopts an approach called 'sustainable development', which seeks explicitly to nurture, or at least to protect, the physical environment. Since most Third World countries are producers of primary products, such as timber, mineral products, tea and coffee, there is a real danger of supporting projects which are capable of destroying the environment rapidly. Oxfam acknowledges that the rich nations of the world have a part to play in preventing this destruction, since they control world prices of such primary products. Part of the organisation's lobbying role is to persuade its own Government and other rich nations to do more to assist poor countries, and do less to harm their people and their environments. The organisation has been an active supporter and collaborator in ethical trading developments in recent years (see also Case-study 14 below), and has helped to ensure that leading whole-salers and super-market chains are stocking Fairtrade products, such as tea and coffee, on their shelves.

More than a third of overseas grants in the year 1992/3 was devoted to emergency relief. In this situation Oxfam responds on a reactive basis after official requests for help, and following an on-the-ground assessment by local staff. Unlike other aid work, which is planned and thus has funding allocated to it, emergency relief has to come out of general funds, unless any specific funding becomes available. The organisation's strategy is to provide help using local people, their agencies and governments. The object is to enable them to recover from the disaster primarily by using their own efforts. Increasingly, however, emergency situations arise from warfare rather than natural disasters and involve millions of displaced people (such as in Zaire), producing conditions in which the United Nations Refugee Relief organisation is likely to become involved. In these cases it is more likely that UN grants will be made to the relief organisations to enable them to play their part.

When assessing the aid problems of many Third World countries, Oxfam is as much concerned with bringing about changes in society as it is in giving relief to the poor and the suffering. This concern for social justice is a central theme in Oxfam's work, and adds an extra challenge to the way it manages its efforts on behalf of many of the world's poorest people.

The organisation is aware of the need to keep fundraising costs and administration as low as possible, and has succeeded in reducing the proportion of such costs from nearly 22% of total income in 1992 to 10% in 1995. The latter figure is now established as the target to be achieved for these costs. It has to be recognised, however, that the organisation depends for its success on the effectiveness of its key personnel, and these have to be paid proper salaries and given adequate administrative support. Raising money and supplying aid to the world's unfortunates is never easy and does not come cheaply either.

Questions

1. Argue a case for the proposal that it just is not possible to run a charity like Oxfam on a truly business-like basis.

2. What cultural messages about Oxfam's way of doing things do you sense from reading this case-study?

CS5: Nuclear Electric Ltd – nuclear power, safety and the public

Introduction

Nuclear Electric Ltd is one of two subsidiary companies of British Energy plc, the holding company of the nuclear power generating industry privatised by the UK government in July 1996. Nuclear Electric operates five advanced gas cooled reactor stations (AGRs) and one pressurised water reactor station (PWR) in England and Wales. Between them these stations contributed about 17% of electricity sales in the area during the financial year ended 31 March 1997. Scotland has its own company, Scottish Nuclear – part of British Energy – which supplies about 52% of the Scottish market.

The two subsidiaries operate in different kinds of market. Nuclear Electric generates and sells electricity into a competitive market known as 'the pool', which organises the bulk sale and purchase of electricity throughout England and Wales. The other main generators in the area are National Power and Powergen, whose market share of the generation market is about 24% and 23% respectively. Electricity is transmitted by the National Grid Group plc through a high voltage transmission system known as the 'grid'. This is then distributed across low voltage systems and supplied to customers by the 12 regional electricity companies (RECs), who are now in competition with each other. The 'pool' is administered by National Grid on behalf of all the bulk sellers and buyers in the market.

In its Report and Accounts for 1996/7, the first since privatisation, Nuclear Electric's parent company showed a profit for the first time (£61 million) compared with a loss of £155 million the previous year. This improvement resulted from three main factors: an increase of 10% in electricity output, an 11% fall in unit operating costs, and a reduction of £39 million in financing costs. The parent company's concern for the development of the business is, not surprisingly, one of its major corporate values. What is more unusual is that its first concern is safety, which 'is, and always will be, British Energy's top priority.' (Annual Review, 1996/7) During the year there was no incident above the lowest level on the International Nuclear Event Scale. All the company's power stations operate quality management systems to BS 5882 (Nuclear Quality Assurance), and the Hinkley Point AGR station in England, which is one of the oldest nuclear installations, was cleared by the independent Nuclear Installations Inspectorate to operate for a further 10 years.

Public anxiety about nuclear energy

One of the key issues that has to be faced by nuclear power companies is to convince the public that not only is their product (electricity) safe, but also that the process by which it is produced (nuclear fission) is safe. The companies have tackled this issue in several ways. Firstly, they have pointed out that there is radiation everywhere. It isn't something that has been 'invented' by nuclear power stations. In fact 87% of the radiation we receive comes from our normal surroundings – earth, air, food and drink. The remainder comes from man-made sources, such as medical X-rays, and less than one percent arises from the presence of nuclear power stations.

Secondly, they have emphasised the excellent safety record of nuclear power in the UK, where there has not been a hazardous accident in nuclear plants since they first started operating in 1962. They stress that accidents like the one at Chernobyl could not happen in Britain because the Chernobyl plant, which did not meet UK safety standards, was designed and operated with inherent flaws.

Thirdly, they point to the existence of statutory and other safety standards designed to prevent escapes of nuclear gases, materials and waste products. These are backed up by the Nuclear Installations Inspectorate, who may visit any power station at any time without warning to inspect plant and processes. The reactors themselves are monitored continuously by their own independent safety systems, and are closed down automatically if safety limits are exceeded. The latter are set at conservative levels to err on the side of taking no chances. The training of the engineers and other staff at nuclear power stations is rigorous. The engineers who operate the reactors are trained on highly detailed simulators, much like the training of airline pilots.

Employee health is monitored constantly, and exposure to radiation is logged under stringent reporting systems. The average radiation dose to each worker in 1992/3 was less than 0.4 on a scale that would rate average doses for the public at 2.2 (for the UK as a whole), and 7.5 for people living in Cornwall, where the granite level produces naturally higher radiation.

Finally, they point out that nuclear waste is treated, and transported, in conditions of highest concern for safety. In 30 years British Energy, Nuclear Electric and their predecessors have moved nuclear waste over 6 million miles by road and rail without a single accident involving the release of radioactivity. In a well-publicised safety demonstration, Nuclear Electric once arranged a special test with British Rail, in which a 140-ton locomotive pulling three 35-ton carriages was deliberately crashed head-on into a Magnox flask containing nuclear waste. The crash took place at 100 miles per hour. The result was described as 'spectacular' in more senses than one – the locomotive was a total write-off, but the flask had no more than a few dents and scratches, and was fully intact.

High-level waste (that is, the radioactive spent fuel rods from the core of a reactor) is held at the Sellafield plant of British Nuclear Fuels (BNFL) under strict safety conditions. The amount of such waste produced to date (over 30 years) would just about fit into two medium-sized semi-detached houses. The companies have fixed-price contracts with BNFL for the storage and reprocessing of spent AGR fuel, and British Energy is obliged to set aside a sum each year (£16m in 1996/7) into a special decommissioning fund to meet the long-term costs of decommissioning power stations.

Selling the benefits of nuclear power

Apart from persuading the public that nuclear power generation is safe, which is essentially a defensive strategy, the companies spend considerable effort in promoting the positive aspects of nuclear power. They point out that electricity can be generated in three ways: by burning fossil fuels, such as coal, gas or oil; by utilising renewable energy/natural sources, such as the wind, sun or water; or by generating heat through nuclear fission. Fossil fuels currently account for about 78% of electricity generation in Britain, renewable sources account for 2% (and are likely to contribute no more than 10% even at the most optimistic forecast), and nuclear energy accounts for about 20% to date.

Nuclear power, it is argued, is not only more efficient than other sources, but is cleaner and less damaging to the environment. Nuclear power stations neither produce carbon dioxide – a major cause of global warming – nor do they produce gases such as sulphur dioxide and nitrogen oxide, which contribute to acid rain. More than this, nuclear fuel is extremely efficient. For example, two uranium pellets the size of sugar cubes can meet the electricity needs of one person for an entire year! A single ton of uranium can provide the same amount of power as 20,000 tons of coal, and into the bargain can be reprocessed and used again, unlike coal. It is recognised, however, that reprocessing, waste management and, above all, eventual decommissioning of power stations is a complex and costly business.

A further advantage of nuclear fuel is that it is an economically-secure form of energy, so far unaffected by fluctuating world markets or supply crises caused by war or embargoes.

Britain's nuclear power producers aim to earn public confidence in nuclear power as a safe, clean and economic form of power-generation, which has a major role in electricity supply both now and in the future. It is a challenge the companies are willing to accept, and as the effects of pollution by other forms of fuel become more evident, it is likely they will succeed in their aim.

Questions

1. In what ways might the nuclear power generating companies be considered at a disadvantage in the marketplace compared with their fossil fuel rivals? Give your reasons.

2. How far is it true that whilst attention to safety in the nuclear power industry may not hinder opportunities for increased output, it will certainly increase operating costs and thus reduce profits?

3. What facts would you want to bring before the public if you were responsible for public relations in a region containing an AGR nuclear power station? Justify your choice in each case.

CS6: BP – five years in the life of an international oil company

Introduction

The British Petroleum Company plc is one of the largest companies in Europe and the third largest oil company in the world. Its total turnover in each of the last five years has been in excess of £30 billion with a total capital employed in excess of £17 billion. At the year ending 31 December 1996 it employed 53,150 employees worldwide. The BP Group is composed of three core businesses as follows:

❶ **BP Exploration**, the upstream part of the business, which is responsible for the exploration and production of oil and gas; it operates all over the world – in the North Sea, off the Shetland Islands, off the coasts of Venezuela and West Africa, and in Azerbaijan to name but a few of its drilling and exploration sites.

❷ **BP Oil**, the downstream part of the business, responsible for the refining, marketing and supply of petroleum products.

❸ **BP Chemicals**, which manufactures and markets a wide range of petro-chemical products.

Progress and change in recent years

In the company's Annual Report for 1993 BP's Chief Executive noted that the targets set in 1992 had not been fully achieved, due to slower than forecast economic growth in the Group's two main markets – Europe and the USA – combined with a steep fall in crude oil prices during the year. The Group's revenues were thus lower than expected. The unsettled nature of the external market had led the Group to focus increased attention on improving productivity primarily through better use of technology and by changes in the organisation structure. Also contributing to improvements in the core businesses had been the sale of non-core assets. During the year five of the nine business segments of BP Nutrition had been sold, and the main task for 1994 was seen as divesting the four remaining businesses, which eventually happened. The organisational changes had led to some drastic reductions in staff (10,000 employees in one year), and this cut-back was continued. Whereas staff numbers in 1992 were about 100,000, the figure was almost halved by the end of 1996.

The most successful part of the Group during 1993 was BP Exploration, where despite falling crude oil prices, profits exceeded the previous year by some £240 million. This situation had been helped by improved productivity, cost savings, a stronger dollar and a reduction in petroleum tax in the UK. The downstream business, BP Oil, had also produced better figures than the previous year with operating profits up from £506 million to £810 million. The retail sector alone had some 18,000 service stations, the shipping fleet comprised 27 crude oil and product carriers, the aviation fuels business (Air BP) serviced more than 400 airline customers, and BP Marine, the marine fuels and lubricants business, was one of the world's leading suppliers.

The other core business did not fare so well during 1993. BP Chemicals had turned in a loss of £68 million, due mainly to the exceptionally low margins in its ethylene and derivatives markets in Europe. Some restructuring (that is, 'pruning') had taken place, and one casualty was the ethylene cracker plant in Wales, which was closed down. There were opportunities elsewhere, however, as suppliers of advanced materials for use in the aerospace, automotive, electronic and marine industries. The group was plannning for selected divestments, closures and investments in order to get a better balance in its asset structure.

Three years on

The situation has changed considerably for the better over the last four years, as the financial summary indicates (see below). In particular, 1996 was 'an outstanding year' for BP. As before, the upstream part of the business – BP Exploration – performed well. Thanks to higher crude oil prices operating profits rose by 40% over the previous year. The overall situation was helped by the improved production of natural gas in the UK, which exceeded previous records. Prospects for the future were also buoyed by the substantial new finds of oil and gas in Venezuela, West Africa and Azerbaijan.

The downstream business – BP Oil – also produced a better operating profit than the previous year, up from £406 million to £679 million. Improved refinery performance plus a range of cost savings helped to offset lower margins in the retail sector, notably in Britain. Nevertheless, in Eastern Europe 100 new retail sites were opened during 1996, and 300 more are planned. In the UK a joint venture with the Safeway supermarket chain will produce 100 jointly owned outlets providing food and fuel in prime locations. Another major change took place during 1996 when the company agreed a joint venture in its petroleum refining and marketing operations with the Mobil company. Against a background of rising costs and falling profits in a highly competitive market, with supermarkets taking a substantial market share of retail sales, it was decided that combining the operations of the two companies would eliminate duplication, reduce costs and achieve valuable synergies in procurement.

The agreement has led to a dominant role for BP in retail petrol sales (70% share of the partnership) and for Mobil in lubricants (51% share). Taking the European market as a whole (that is, including Eastern Europe and parts of the Mediterranean), the BP-Mobil link will have a 12% share of the total fuels business, and an 18% of the market for lubricants. It is expected that the merger will enable the partners to compete more effectively in mature markets (such as in the European Union) whilst offering a concentration of brands in new markets in Eastern Europe. The present (1997) situation is that supply is still ahead of demand for refined products, despite refinery closures. This has led to a fall in the wholesale prices of petroleum products and a cut-throat price-war at the downstream (retail) end of the business.

The remaining core business – BP Chemicals – also had a good year in 1996, turning in an operating profit of £476 million, thanks to a number of new developments in areas ranging from Scotland, USA (Texas), Korea, Philippines, China, India and Egypt. As the economies of Asia and Latin America gradually improve, so the demand for petrochemical products in those areas increases. In the meantime the central theme in BP Chemicals product strategy is to develop and apply process technologies in those products where it is strong – polyethylene, acetic acid and acrylonitrile.

Future prospects – towards the millennium

The future prospects for the Group appear encouraging, as the major world economies emerge from recession and demand for BP's products increases among the developing economies of Asia, Latin America and Eastern Europe. The company forecasts that oil, gas and petrochemicals will be growth industries as populations increase, and as prosperity comes to developing nations. Two thirds of the world's energy growth in the next few years is forecast to come from Asia and Latin America, as populations seek to meet their basic needs for warmth, light and transport. Eastern Europe too is a potential growth area now that its markets are open to competition following the fall of the Soviet Union. Recent substantial finds of gas and oil in quite different geographical regions can provide both long-term production potential and cost advantages to the company. In the downstream markets, where competition is fierce and margins tight, the company aims to hold its place by building and maintaining its commercial and industrial customer base as well as the private motorist sector. Alliances will be made where appropriate, as with Mobil, for example, which collaboration alone is expected to achieve savings of $500 million within three years.

The core elements of the company's strategy as it moves towards the millennium can thus be summarised as follows:

- Develop world-class and world-wide assets.
- Secure access to rapidly growing markets.
- Sustain present leadership in production technologies.
- Maintain good quality relationships with customers, joint venture partners, suppliers, communities and governments.
- Motivate employees to make their best contribution to the business and to share their know-how within the organisation.

Financial Summary – Progress 1993–1996

	1993	1994	1995	1996
Turnover (£billion)	34.95	33.12	36.11	44.73
Pre-tax profits (£billion)	1.30	2.28	1.95	3.67
Earnings per share (p)	11.3	28.8	20.2	45.5
Capital employed (£billion)*	18.23	17.91	17.42	17.44
Return on capital employed (ROCE)	9.4%	11.3%	14.3%	17.5%

* The reduction in capital employed has been achieved exclusively by reducing debt and increasing shareholder equity.

Questions

1. Taking Ansoff's product-market model as your guide, what would you suggest as the recommended future strategy for BP Oil over the next 2–3 years? Explain and justify your reasons.

2. Conduct a BPEST analysis of BP Group's external environment and then summarise what you see as its prospects in the short-term, giving your reasons.

CS7: The Hanson empire – change in a conglomerate organisation

Introduction

The Hanson Group built up its reputation as an Anglo-American conglomerate with interests in a variety of businesses, ranging from tobacco and foodstuffs to quarrying, coal-mining, brick-making and house-building. Until recently the Group's UK arm has been Hanson plc, and the US arm was Hanson Industries. Each operated through a number of subsidiary companies, which between them employed some 70,000 people. The Group's turnover in 1994/5 was almost equally shared between the UK and the USA. In the 1980s Hanson's had established something of a reputation for asset-stripping, that is, buying up ailing groups cheaply, pruning them drastically, and selling off a proportion of their best assets at a much higher price. This approach relied on high levels of borrowing to fund purchases and was always a risk.

As the company moved towards the nineties, and economic recession was hitting both Europe and the USA, it began to consolidate its businesses. In the UK it clustered its subsidiaries into seven divisions, whose attributes and performance are outlined below. However, during 1994/5 Hanson's decided to adopt a strategy of devolved ownership by demerger, and in the period 1994 to 1997 a considerable number of changes were made in the ownership and structure of the Group. This case-study describes the leading changes that took place in Hanson plc, the UK arm, between the period 1992–1997.

Hanson plc – Organisation in 1992/3

The UK holding company – Hanson plc – at this stage comprised a number of separate operating companies organised on a divisional basis, as follows:

Imperial Tobacco	Manufacturing and marketing cigarettes, pipe tobacco, etc. (acquired by Hanson in 1986).
ARC	Originally known as Amalgamated Roadstone Corporation. Extracts and supplies aggregates for the building and construction industries (acquired by Hanson in 1989).
Hanson Building	Beazer Homes (fourth largest UK house-builder); two Brick Division companies (Butterley Brick acquired in 1968; London Brick in 1984).
Hanson Industrial	Smith Meters Ltd (gas meters – acquired in 1982); Rollalong (prefabricated buildings); Crabtree, Volex and Marbourne (electrical products); Seven Seas (health and animal products).
ERSA	Eveready South Africa (battery manufacturer – acquired in 1981).
Hanson Properties	Management and disposal of properties owned by Hanson – some for investment, others acquired following new business acquisitions.

The UK business at that time also included a waste disposal company (Greenways), a banking operation (Hanson Bank Ltd – established in 1975; based in Guernsey), and an aviation service (Air Hanson) supplying services to the corporate aviation industry (business jets, helicopters) since 1967.

Financial Situation 1992/3

The following figures, taken from the Group's Consolidated Profit and Loss Accounts for the years ending 30 September 1993/ 1994, give an idea of the scale of the Group (i.e. both UK and US operations) at that time:

	1993	1992
Sales turnover (£m)	9,760	8,798
Operating profit (£m)	978	1,068
Earnings per share (p)	15.2	22.6

The breakdown of turnover between the major activities was as follows:

	1993	1992	Notes
Industrial (coal mining, chemicals, etc.)	2,700	2,504	Coal-mining is US-based
Consumer (tobacco, etc.)	4,056	3,709	Also included foods
Building products (aggregates, timber, etc.)	2,912	2,279	Included house-building
Sales from discontinued operations	92	306	Divestments during year

Total assets less current liabilities, as shown in the Group's Consolidated Balance Sheet, were as follows:

1993	1992
£16,992m	£14,155m

Managing conglomerate diversity

Whereas most large business organisations are keen to focus on their core business, conglomerates like the Hanson Group focus on developing (including divesting) a wide range of businesses. The key skills according to Hanson are as follows:

- knowing what components make sensible clusters within the groups of activities
- setting clear financial targets for each individual business
- allowing subsidiaries' managers a high degree of autonomy within their targets
- sensing where a business can reward capital or other investment
- having the strength of purpose to sell off businesses, or business activities, that are not performing to target, or no longer fit in.

Not surprisingly, in this context, Hanson clearly sees its principal stakeholders as firstly shareholders, and secondly customers. When in the business of buying and selling businesses, it is important to maintain each business as an attractive proposition, either to existing shareholders, or to potential buyers. Thus, it is possible for Hanson to acquire a business that has performed poorly in the past, knock it into shape, and then sell at a profit at a later date. This, of course, is a risky business, and calls for a real aptitude for sizing up a potentially profitable business, and knowing where best to improve its performance – a truly entrepreneurial task!

The Hanson philosophy, as stated in 1993, comes as no surprise in the light of the above commentary:

> 'Our philosophy is to develop, promote and delegate real authority to managers of the highest quality. They are trained in our proven system of financial controls, which concentrate on profit and return on capital employed...the success of that philosophy rests on channelling capital investment where it will be most profitable; on serving our customers and on caring for our workforce, the community and the environment; on product development and increased efficiency. Over the next decade Hanson aims to enhance shareholder value by increasing earnings per share and dividends, generated through profitable internal growth and selective acquisitions.'

In the light of the above philosophy, it is interesting to see what changes have been made in Hanson plc in the years that followed up to the present (1997).

Hanson plc – organisation structure 1996

The year ending 30 September 1996 was dominated, according to company Chairman Lord Hanson by 'the implementation of our plan to continue the demerger of Hanson's five divisions into separately quoted companies'. The Annual Report for the year indicated that Hanson plc's wholly-owned businesses were now confined to just two divisions: Building Materials & Equipment, and Energy, made up as follows:

Building Materials & Equipment:
- **ARC Ltd**
- **Hanson Brick Ltd**
  Butterley and London Brick
- **Hanson Industrial Services**
  Crabtree, Volex Accessories, Marbo,
  Wylex, Dorman Smith (electrical)
  UGI Meters (gas meters)

Energy:
- **Eastern Group plc**
  Electricity generating and supply;
  Gas supply; acquired September 1995;
  Eastern Electricity is the largest
  regional electricity company in Britain.

The major players missing from earlier years were **Imperial Tobacco**, which was demerged with effect from 1 October 1996, **ERSA** (sold in 1995/6), **Beazer Homes** (sold in 1994) and **Seven Seas** (also sold off in 95/96). Plans were well ahead for the demerger of **Eastern Group** in early 1997.

The resulting structure which will be in place by the year ending 1 October 1997 will see the Group in four principal businesses: Chemicals (all US-based, but with some UK plants), Tobacco (cigarettes and tobacco, UK-based but global), Energy (UK-based but incorporating US coal-mining and Australian mining) and Building Materials & Equipment (the sole surviving grouping under the Hanson name). The four businesses will be established as separate companies as follows:

Chemicals	**Millennium Chemicals Inc (USA)**
Tobacco	**Imperial Tobacco Group plc**
Energy	**The Energy Group plc**
Building Materials & Equipment	Hanson plc

The financial performance of the newly established companies appeared to be sound. Figures published for the year ended 1 October 1996 showed the following:

Activity or group	1996 Turnover (£m)	Operating profit (£m)
Building Materials & Equipment	2,453	231
Energy	3,737	458
Millennium Chemicals	1,910	373
Imperial Tobacco	3,820	311

Total operating profit in the consolidated Profit & Loss Account was £1,526, and earnings per share were 25.6p. What these figures do not show is the high level of gearing (debt to equity) due to the borrowings made to purchase the Eastern Group. At the end of the year net debt stood at £1,286 million.

In his introduction to the Annual Report to shareholders for the year ending 1 October 1996, the Chairman ended on an optimistic note:

> 'We are convinced that the merits of this radical reorganisation will be proved when the performance of these companies on their own is measured. They all have first class management, very good prospects and have produced excellent profit in the past as part of Hanson plc. There is every reason to believe they will improve on that in the future.'

Whether this optimism is justified remains to be seen, but the future could be bright if the changes have gone far enough.

Questions

1. What do you see as the strengths and weaknesses of the new structure in the UK? Indicate what else might be done to improve it.

2. The Hanson Group have been accused by some commentators of buying and selling companies merely to make a quick profit for shareholders rather than to see them grow to the benefit of a range of stakeholders. How far do you think this criticism is justified from your reading of this case-study?

CS8: British Biotech plc – a budding success story?

Introduction

British Biotech plc, formerly the British Bio-technology Group plc, is a young pharmaceutical company, founded in 1986, for the launch of *'new and better drugs for the treatment of important human diseases – particularly diseases for which current therapy is inadequate'*. The company was formed on the basis of research into potential 'breakthrough' drugs directed at key diseases such as cancer, bacterial sepsis, asthma, multiple sclerosis and arthritis. From the very beginning the company set itself the challenge of finding niche markets in clinical areas of greatest human need and least currently effective treatments.

The company has grown substantially in the decade since it was founded. From an initial team of 12 people, it now employs 350 permanent staff. The company's vision, as stated by the Chief Executive in 1996, remained the same:

'to build a new international pharmaceutical company competing effectively in today's rapidly evolving pharmaceutical market ... the route to success ... is to provide patients with new and better medicines for diseases which are inadequately treated today. Such breakthroughs can only come from high quality research and innovation'.

The company's strategy, whilst clearly research-based, is now about to widen its scope so as to provide for the commercial development of its products. As the figures below indicate, the company's sales revenue (turnover) is currently far too small to fund its research and development programme, which has to be supported from equity (i.e. shareholders' funds). The company's reputation in the financial markets has proved to be sufficiently high for it to raise two rights issues in the last three years. With these successful flotations behind it, the company had a very strong balance sheet with cash reserves in excess of £200 million at the year end 1996/7.

Financial situation

Given the size of the annual losses of the company since its inception, many investors would consider British Biotech as a risky investment and certainly not likely to produce profits for some time. Others looking at the company's performance might judge that the company has great prospects of profitability in the long-term, and will be willing to invest their money. Major investors in the past two years include insurance companies and pensions institutions, generally long-term and conservative in their approach to investment. The following figures for the year ended 30 April 1997, compared with those from the previous four years' Annual Report and Accounts, give an interesting picture of the financial state of the company:

	1997 (£000)	1996 (£000)	1995 (£000)	1994 (£000)	1993 (£000)
Turnover	10,087	8,462	3,191	3,986	7,847
Operating loss	37,853	27,419	29,052	23,043	17,302
R&D expenditure	36,277	29,146	26,210	20,650	16,748
Shareholders' funds	200,725	82,993	59,087	39,399	60,881

The figures show that turnover is gradually increasing. Turnover represents income from collaborative agreeements (for example, with Glaxo Wellcome), revenue grants (such as from funded research projects) and other company business (supplying goods and services). As the company expands from its existing research-based strategy to one based on the commercial exploitation of first-class research, so turnover should increase substantially. The key to immediate progress is success in product trials. If a product meets its aims, produces no difficult side-effects and is cleared by the authorities, then marketing can begin. Until then little progress can be made on the commercial front. Without a major boost in turnover operating losses will continue, especially if new infra-structure developments (for example, new laboratories) have to be implemented in order to maintain the pace and quality of the development of drugs which are almost at the point of acceptance. Expenditure on research and development will always play a major role in the costs of operating the company but should begin to form a smaller proportion of the company's profit and loss account as commercial products come on stream.

Key products and key markets

The company's key products at present are lexipafant for the treatment of acute pancreatitis, and marimastat for the control of malignant cancer. Other drugs that are important are those directed at arthritis, asthma and multiple sclerosis. The potential markets for all these treatments is vast – there are up to 10 million patients diagnosed with cancer in Europe and North America alone; cases of acute pancreatitis amount to over a third of a million in these two areas; the number of multiple sclerosis sufferers is more than half a million taking the USA and Europe together; and the number of asthma sufferers in both areas total several millions. The lexipafant product is the first to be branded, given the name Zacutex. As the Chief Executive commented in the 1996/7 Annual Report, the company *'is undergoing significant change, from a business focused on research and development to one preparing itself for commercial success.'* As yet final trialling and approval of the two leading products has not been completed, but the company is now at the threshold of its first commercial breakthrough.

Business strategy

During 1996/7 the company appointed a Commercial Director to head up its sales and marketing operations. In conducting a review of its business strategy in the light of the changing situation, the company has adopted the following approach:

❶ to base the business on research and development

❷ to concentrate on developing drugs that address unmet needs

❸ to market new products directly in Europe and North America provided they are prescribed primarily by medical specialists

❹ to market other products that are more suited for primary care via general practitioners by means of licensing agreements with pharmaceutical companies.

The marketing structure being established by the company will result in core marketing tasks (marketing strategy, branding, market research, pricing, product training and so forth) being undertaken at a central marketing team based at headquarters in Oxford. *Specialist care products* will be marketed and supplied directly by means of regional subsidiaries in six European countries, and in North America, where the company already has a physical presence – British Biotech Inc.– which co-ordinate and manages the US clinical trials of company products, especially cancer treatments. Each of these subsidiaries will be composed of a small number of key sales and medical staff under the direction of a regional managing director. Outside Europe and North America the company is proceeding to find partners willing to take up licences to develop and market its products. The licensing approach will be adopted in all areas for the development of the company's *primary care products* (such as for arthritis).

Up-to-date product information will be required both for doctors and for sales staff, so that all concerned are aware of the nature and effects of company products and the diseases they are designed to treat. This core information is to be developed centrally to ensure consistency and cost-effectiveness in each market.

The company has decided that it will neither manufacture nor distribute its drugs directly. Thus once its drugs are ready to be produced on a commercial scale the company will license production and distribution to external manufacturers. Potential licensees will be assessed on grounds of quality, reliability and flexibility as well as on scale and costs. A business development team has been established at headquarters to analyse the needs of the business, monitor industry trends and identify new business oppportunities.

It looks as if success as a commercial venture for British Biotech is just around the corner. There is always a long lead time to research, develop, trial, register and eventually market new drugs. However, the company's research skills are of the highest order, and the new strategic plan is now able to address commercial issues strongly. The marketing arm of the company is about to swing into action, and the future is beginning to look encouraging. The long-term situation could be extremely prosperous.

Questions

1. If you were advising a pension fund, or other large investor, about the prospects for British Biotech over the next 10 years, what would you point out to them concerning the company's strengths and weaknesses as a commercial enterprise? Include qualitative judgements as well as an assessment of the financial situation in your answer.

2. You have been appointed to head up the business development team. Sketch out an initial scenario of how you see the immediate priorities facing the team, and what actions you may need to take. In particular you should be prepared to establish what are the key questions that the team should be asking itself.

CS9: Cross-Channel ferries: study in competition

Background

Cross-Channel ferry routes between England, France and Belgium have been the scene of intense competition over the past decade. Passenger and vehicle carrying capacity has increased substantially, but the number of customers carried has increased only moderately. This over-capacity has led to intense price-cutting and other customer inducements in order to retain market share. The competition between providers is at its most intense on the so-called short-sea route between Dover or Folkestone and Calais, which accounts for 80% of all cross-Channel travel. Last season (1996) the two largest ferry companies – P & O European Ferries and Stena – by dint of aggressive marketing saw bookings increase. However, they both experienced a decrease in their profits due partly to the fierce price-cutting forced on them by competition, and partly to the high costs of maintaining more ships and facilities than required by the volume of traffic. P & O, for example, saw the profits from its European operations drop from £114m in 1994 to only £75m in 1995.

The ferry companies' difficult trading situation has been worsened by competition from another source – the Channel Tunnel. The opening of the tunnel in spring 1994 brought two newcomers to the cross-channel transport market: Le Shuttle (cars and lorries with occupants) and Eurostar (foot passengers only). The annual car carrying capacity of Le Shuttle is estimated to be about 750,000 vehicles per annum at present, based on the demand during the first three quarters of 1996. Put into perspective, this figure has to be seen against the 3.2m passengers carried on the Dover–Calais sea route alone in 1994, when passenger levels were lower than in 1996. Car traffic on this route has in fact doubled since 1990.

In the meantime Eurostar has gradually improved its sales, and in July 1996 carried a record 122,000 passengers in one week. The closure of the Tunnel in October 1996 due to a disastrous lorry fire near the French end of the tunnel brought only temporary relief to the beleaguered ferry operators. The tunnel reopened in May 1997 with limited services, but was operating normally by the time of the summer holiday season. A massive advertising campaign on television and radio in the UK, France and Belgium ensured that holiday and business travellers were aware that the tunnel was back in business. The outlook for ferry firms in the short-term, therefore, is likely to be a difficult one, and will require some important strategic decisions.

The key players in the market

The two leading players are P & O European Ferries with about 40% of the cross-Channel ferry market, and Stena with about 30%. The others with 10% or less each are: Brittany Ferries, Sally Line and Hoverspeed. The latest entry into the market is Sea France, the result of a breakaway from Stena. Sea France commenced operations in 1996 on the Dover–Calais route. Its estimated market share of the short-sea route in 1996 was about 15–20%. The other major competition is provided by Le Shuttle and Eurostar, although it must be recognised that airline routes between England and France are also a factor. The table below summarises the key features of these competing companies:

Operator	Key features
P & O European Ferries	Major player, has 24 ships on 8 routes. Cross-Channel ferries can carry 2000 passengers and 500–600 cars each. On the short-sea route the Dover–Calais service offers 20 sailings a day in a crossing time of about 75 minutes with 4 ferries.
Stena	Major player. On short-sea route operates 2 superferries with capacities ranging from 1800 passengers and 600 cars, making the crossing from Dover–Calais in about 90 minutes. Also operates large, very fast catamarans on other routes (such as Newhaven–Dieppe).
Hoverspeed	Operates 3 large hovercraft. The Dover–Calais service can carry 400 passengers and 55 cars 7 times a day. Journey times are considerably faster than those achieved by conventional ferries. The company also operates a Folkestone–Boulogne service. In 1994 Hoverspeed carried almost one million passengers.
Sea France	French-owned company. Operates 3 large ferries. On short-sea route offers 5 return trips each day. Capacity averages 1600 passengers and up to 400 cars.
Le Shuttle	Railway service under the Channel from Folkestone to Calais via the tunnel. Carries cars and lorries with their passengers on

special vehicle transporters. Before the tunnel fire (October 1996) the service was estimated to hold about 50% share of short-sea route; by the summer 1997 expects to have recovered to about 38% of the market.

Crossing time is about 20 minutes and access to variety of roads and motorways at both ends is simple.

Eurostar

Comfortable high speed passenger trains from London (Waterloo) or Ashford (Kent) to Paris (3 hrs), Lille or Brussels (3hrs 15 mins) via the tunnel. In 1996 carried 4.9 million passengers compared with 2.9 million the previous year. Already it is estimated that Eurostar has taken more than 25% of the air market to Paris. Initial problems with train reliability appear to have been overcome. The service is slowest at the UK end, where existing track and routes have to be used until a new route is constructed.

Present marketing tactics – short-sea route

Against intense competition for the available custom, the ferry companies and their railway rivals struggled to find some competitive advantage during the 1996 season. The situation is much the same in 1997. Price-cutting has been employed to gain short-term advantages over competitors, but is usually not economically viable for long periods. Price wars between the ferry operators led to a considerable drop in average return fares between 1996 and 1997 from about £320 to £200 (high season fares). For example, P & O's current fares for summer 1997 range from £90–£190 for one car plus driver, compared with Stena's £78–£188. Other price reductions are usually wrapped up in the form of special offers for specific weekends or events (for example, school holiday weeks, bank holidays, etc.).

All the ferry companies have sought an appropriate marketing mix to attract customers at the expense of their rivals. Typical elements offered include the following:

- simplified check-in procedures (20 minutes seen as the standard to achieve)
- extensive duty free on-board shopping facilities
- improved restaurant and other eating facilities
- Club class supplements (£5–£7) for extra facilities at departure and on-board
- on-board entertainments for children and teenagers
- space to relax in
- the refreshing experience of a sea crossing – enjoyable in its own right
- good road/rail access to departure points at Dover and Folkestone, and onwards at Calais
- car-carrying capacity.

The extension and improvement of on-board services has become more prominent because of the entry of the rail services, which cross under the Channel in about 25 minutes. The ferries have to offer a *total experience*, something that is part of the holiday rather than just a means of transportation across the Channel.

The tunnel competition

In early 1997 Le Shuttle announced that it was to slash its standard return prices for a car and up to nine passengers from £268 to £169. Peak fares will drop from £328 to £199 in an effort to recapture customers lost during the repairs to the tunnel. Prices are for vehicle and occupants together. Eurostar prices are higher than the ferries, as is to be expected given the total length of journey (i.e. London to Paris or Brussels). Average return fares range from Normal/Standard at £169 per person to Premium First at £370 per person, and thus reflect *airline* prices rather than ferry prices, since it is primarily with air travel that Eurostar is competing. Premium class offers an inclusive lunch or dinner with champagne plus other benefits such as faster check-in and business facilities at the terminal.

Ferries versus trains – the disadvantages

The disadvantages of the ferries compared with the tunnel options are primarily as follows:

- they take longer to make the Channel crossing
- they are less direct compared with Eurostar, which can speed passengers from London into the centre of both Paris and Brussels
- they may be cancelled due to adverse weather conditions
- they can be unpleasant if the trip encounters bad weather
- they have less appeal for the business traveller.

The disadvantages of the train services are mainly:

- the boring and, for some, the claustrophobic nature of the sub-Channel journey, especially for those travelling on Le Shuttle, where they remain seated in the vehicle
- the lack of on-board services on Le Shuttle
- Le Shuttle takes passengers and vehicles only to Calais at present, leaving a long drive even to Paris
- limited on-board services on Eurostar compared with ferries (except for First and Premium First class passengers)
- current Eurostar prices are unattractive to day trippers
- doubts about tunnel safety and train reliability are likely to concern some travellers.

The present situation poses a considerable challenge to the ferry and rail-tunnel operators. There are both risks and opportunities. Those that make the optimum choices will flourish. Those that do not will fail.

Questions

1. Consider what strategic options are available to the ferry operators, and draw up a list of the relative strengths and weaknesses of these choices in respect of *ferry operations* on the short-sea route.

2. What marketing tactics would you suggest are the most important for the *ferry operators* in (a) developing their service strengths, and (b) taking advantage of the weaknesses in the services currently offered by Le Shuttle and Eurostar? Give your reasons.

3. What responses could be made by the Tunnel services to counter ferry competitors' improvements? Consider first Le Shuttle and then Eurostar, taking into account the present rail links between London, Paris and Brussels.

CS10: Concern for the environment at Toyota UK

Background

When the Toyota Motor Corporation took the decision in 1989 to build its first European motor vehicle assembly plant in the UK, it chose a large 'greenfield' site in Derbyshire, England – Burnaston. Reasons for choosing Burnaston included:

*   the availability of a large site capable of allowing further expansion if needed
*   a supportive approach to inward investors by both the national and local government authorities
*   excellent transport links both within the UK and to the Continent of Europe
*   a local workforce experienced in vehicle manufacturing and engineering
*   presence of an effective labour market with relatively cheap labour costs
*   availability of potential local suppliers of parts and raw materials
*   a large domestic market for motor vehicles
*   the huge potential of the European Union (estimated to be the world's largest market for motor vehicles with annual sales in the year 2000 estimated at 15 million).

Burnaston development represented a major investment into the UK economy of some £700m, supplemented by the construction of an engine plant in Deeside, North Wales, at a further cost of some £140m. At the time this total inward investment of £840 million was the largest such investment in the UK, and has rarely been exceeded since. Construction of both plants began in 1990, and was completed for the start of production in 1992 – September for engines at the Deeside plant and December for cars at Burnaston. Hiring and training began as early as 1990 with the recruitment of about 1000 staff for the start of production. A second wave of recruitment took place subsequently to provide for a second shift, which began in February 1994. Further recruitment brought the total number recruited and trained to more than 2000 over a period of five years.

Production of a new model – the Carina E – began in earnest in late 1992, working towards an initial target of 100,000 vehicles per annum. By 1995 production reached 90,000 units despite the weak demand in many European economies. The success of the Carina line encouraged the company to commence construction of a second assembly plant at Burnaston, where the smaller Corolla vehicles will be produced. Recruitment for this Phase II development commenced in mid-1997, absorbing up to 1000 additional employees. An advantage of the 'greenfield' conditions meant that the company was able to site the new production line in an optimum location adjacent to the existing Carina line.

The company's combined investment at Deeside and Burnaston will have exceeded £1 billion by the time the Corolla line is completed. Such an investment has a great impact on the local environment where the manufacturing units are located. For example, during the construction or development of a site there are major groundworks that have to be carried out to level or landscape the area and provide for all the necessary services such as electricity, gas and water. These usually involve a high level of noise and dirt in the form of dust or mud, as the contractors go about their work. Then there is the sheer size and appearance of the main factory buildings in what was once a semi-rural locality. All such developments have a major effect on local road and transport systems. New feeder roads have to be constructed, parking areas have to be laid out for employees and visitors, and delivery areas have to be designed for a range of heavy goods vehicles and other commercial traffic. For safety and security reasons the whole vicinity of the manufacturing area has to be well-lit and signposted. Thus, a large factory can be as obvious at night as it is during the day. Bearing these points in mind, Toyota have developed a global policy on environmental issues as an integral part of their aim of being 'good corporate citizens' wherever they are located. Such is the reasoning behind Toyota's 'Earth Charter'.

The 'Earth Charter' : Toyota and the environment

In 1992 Toyota Motor Corporation, parent company of Toyota Motor Manufacturing UK, issued a global policy on the environment founded on three core features:

❶ A comprehensive approach to environmental issues – by developing technologies that minimise the environmental impact of vehicles and their manufacture, and by implementing environmental programmes throughout Toyota's production and marketing operations world-wide, including, significantly, the involvement of suppliers and distributors.

❷ Preventative measures – evaluating and minimising at source the environmental impact of every stage of the development, design, production, marketing and distribution of the company's products.

❸ Social contribution to environmental issues – for example, by supporting and participating in wider environmental activities in the external community.

At the UK sites this environmental policy is being implemented through the following:

• the control of waste

• the careful selection of materials

• site landscaping

• sound insulation of the manufacturing areas

• nature protection on the site.

The policy towards waste in the production process is led by a so-called 5Rs philosophy:

❶ **Refine** (e.g. build in environmental considerations in selecting and labelling materials)

❷ **Reduce** (minimise waste at source)

❸ **Re-use** (e.g. re-use packaging materials, use recycled materials in bumpers)

❹ **Recycle** (e.g. materials that cannot be re-used in the same process)

❺ **Retrieve energy** (e.g. process exhaust gases are used to pre-heat other processes)

Site targets for environmental performance are set and monitored by an Environmental Steering Committee set up by the company to supervise this aspect of company business.

In respect of external emissions, the company's UK factories operate boilers using natural gas, which reduces harmful sulphur dioxide fumes to almost nil. In the paint department emissions are well within UK limits, and the company avoids the use of chlorinated solvents and CFCs in the production process. There is constant monitoring of site emissions. All trade effluent and water used during the production process is treated in a separate waste water plant before being released into the main sewers. There is no disposal of waste on site at any of the UK factories.

Noise levels at the factories are contained by various insulation measures incorporated during the design and construction of each plant. The overall colour of the factory at Burnaston, for example, was made to fit in with the natural surroundings before the whole area was landscaped, using over a quarter of a million trees and shrubs. As part of its policy on community relations, the company has established a Community Liaison Committee which meets regularly with local parish council representatives to discuss environmental issues, among other topics raised by either party.

Finally, in terms of its products, the company's vehicles are designed to be more environmentally-friendly by the use of efficient lean-burn engines and the development of more effective catalyst systems to reduce harmful exhaust emissions.

Questions

1. What are the possible benefits to Toyota UK of pursuing its present environmental policy? On what grounds would you justify the extra costs involved in implementing such a policy?

2. Draw up a list of the benefits and disadvantages to a local community arising from the creation of a large manufacturing unit in a hitherto rural area. At what stage might the benefits outweigh the disadvantages?

3. What do you see as the principal benefits of a 'greenfield site' to a manufacturing organisation? What are the disadvantages of such a site?

CS11: Railtrack – keeping private investment on the rails

Introduction

In privatising Britain's national rail network in 1996, the government of the day retained the core infrastructure of the network as one separate company – Railtrack Group plc. Other sections of the original network, such as train operations, rolling stock manufacture, and maintenance were formed into separate companies. In order to provide competition within the service side of the network, the government divided up the national passenger railway system into a number of separate routes, which were put out to tender under a franchise arrangement. Thus passenger train operations are now provided by twenty-five train operating companies (TOCs), including Stagecoach, a major bus operator, Connex, a subsidiary of a French company, and Virgin, the independent airline and leisure company. Under the agreement between Railtrack and the train operators, the latter have to meet a number of stringent targets, which are supervised by an independent Rail Regulator, who is empowered to levy fines and other sanctions if targets are not met. Railtrack itself, of course, has clear obligations to the operators to provide access to the rail network in a safe and efficient manner.

Organisation

As can be seen from the chart below, Railtrack plays a central role in the privatised railway industry. This, as currently organised, requires considerable collaboration between the principal players and a deft interaction between them and the official Rail Regulator. The position of the company in relation to its customers (the train operators, their passengers and industrial users), key suppliers and other stakeholders is shown in the following diagram:

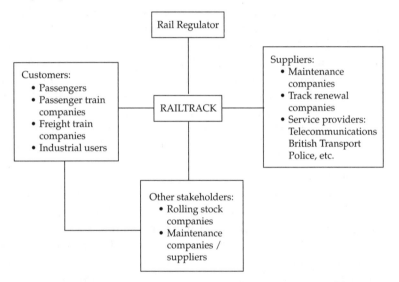

Railtrack is responsible for maintaining, improving and, where appropriate, extending the tracks on which all trains run, and for providing adequate access facilities. There are about 20,000 miles of track in Britain together with some 2,500 stations, 750 tunnels, 9,000 level crossings and over 40,000 bridges and viaducts. All of these assets, together with the responsibility for electrification, signalling and the production of timetables, fall within the remit of Railtrack. The train operating companies are responsible for developing the train services in their franchise area. The train operators are Railtrack's front-line customers together with their customers – the passengers or industrial concerns using the rolling stock. Railtrack's main suppliers are the track renewal and maintenance companies, who are helping to spearhead the infrastructure investment programme, and the service organisations, such as providers of tele-communications and the policing of Railtrack properties and stations. Other key stakeholders include the rolling stock manufacturers, who lease trains to the operators, and the companies that supply maintenance and other services direct to the operators. The role of the Regulator is to ensure fair play within the system in order to ensure that monopoly situations, such as that enjoyed by Railtrack, are not abused by those concerned. The Regulator also sets down performance standards for the various parts of the industry, and agrees the framework of inter-company charges that are made between the constituents.

Investment programme at Railtrack

The company plans to spend over £1 billion each year over the next 10 years in order to improve the safety, efficiency and economy of the network and *'to reverse the trend of under investment which has bedevilled the railway industry for decades.'* (Interim Report, September 1996). Over £6 billion is to be spent on track renewal, signalling modernisation, and improvements to stations and other structures. Whilst most stations are leased to the operating companies, Railtrack does have fourteen stations under its direct control. These are mostly mainline termini, and include Paddington, where a £50 million upgrading programme is underway linked to the development of the Heathrow Express service to be operated by BAA plc, – the former British Airports Authority.

The company's investment strategy *'is simple: by renewing the infrastructure we will seek to drive down our day-to-day maintenance costs and the resulting regenerated railway will provide enhanced returns to all our stakeholders through improved performance.'* (Annual Report & Accounts, 1996/7, p.5). The issue of maintenance costs is substantial, for despite the level of renewal investment referred to earlier, day-to-day maintenance of the system is still forecast to exceed £5 billion over the next ten years. In undertaking its maintenance, Railtrack aims to minimise the disruption to services. The result is that major engineering works have to be conducted at night or at weekends, when the level of traffic is low. The company is currently developing regional databases of infrastructure assets so as to focus maintenance on condition-based criteria rather than time-based factors.

Performance standards

During its first year of operation as a privatised business, Railtrack has pursued three major aims. Firstly, it has set out to achieve an immediate improvement in the quality of service provided to customers. This aim has been achieved, as delays to passenger services attributable to Railtrack during the year were reduced by 38%. The second aim has been to establish a major investment programme, and as noted above this multi-billion pound programme is already under way.The third aim has been to achieve the necessary cultural change required to move from the public to the private sector. Efforts have commenced to assist staff at all levels to meet the challenge of the new business environment. Former colleagues are now suppliers of major services, which have to be negotiated profitably and with attention to performance standards. Existing staff are the focus of wide-ranging training and development opportunities together with performance assessment programmes. The overall development programme is summed up by the company's acronym STEP – safety, teamwork, excellence and profitability. The fact that some 90% of the staff took up the opportunity to become shareholders in the company is seen as 'heartening' by the Chief Executive (Annual Report 1996/7).

Under its charter Railtrack is obliged to meet demanding performance standards for service and safety. Service especially refers to track and signalling reliability, since the TOCs rely absolutely on routes being open at the times their trains are running. Another aspect of service is the insertion of new or occasional services into the main operating schedules, since only Railtrack can control the timetabling of train operations. Safety applies not only to the track and signalling, but to all the trackside features owned by the company. Thus, the company is concerned with the safety of travellers and members of the public on its stations, at level crossings, under its bridges and along its tracks. Here collaboration with British Transport Police is important to minimise trespass, vandalism, disregard of level crossings and other offences which may lead to personal injury. Railtrack is also responsible for overseeing the safety standards of the operating companies, and for this purpose has established a Safety & Standards Directorate which is independent of the operational management of the company, reporting direct to the chairman.

Financial results from operations, 1996/7

In its first full year of operation as a private sector company Railtrack returned an operating profit of £339 million on a turnover of £2.4 billion. In summary the year's results were as follows:

Turnover (£m)	1997	(1996)
Passenger franchise revenue	2119	(2003)
Freight revenue	159	(158)
Property rental income	120	(112)
Other income (Eurostar, etc.)	39	(27)
Total	**2437**	**(2300)**

Costs (£m)	1997	(1996)
Production/management costs (signalling, major stations, computing, policing, etc.)	507	(457)
Joint industry costs (Industry-wide electricity costs, rates, etc.)	220	(12)
Infrastructure maintenance (on-going maintenance of track, signalling equipment, etc.)	732	(725)
Asset maintenance (repairs/renewals of track, stations, etc.)	515	(503)
Depreciation	124	(107)
Total	**2098**	**(2004)**

At the end of the year the sum of £181 million was retained from profits after tax (£54m) and dividend payments (£111m), and the company's Balance Sheet showed a growth in equity shareholders' funds of £183 million from the previous year to total £2.67 billion. The company's borrowings totalled £522 million, of which just over half is due within five years. Reserves stood at £2.54 billion and gearing (that is, debt to equity ratio) was at 16% (20% 1996). Average staff numbers employed over the year were 11,298 and the total staff costs, including directors, were £275 million.

In his review of the year the company's Finance Director (Annual Report & Accounts 1996/7, p. 22) noted that:

'Opportunities for significant revenue increases in the short to medium term are restricted ... some opportunities do exist for increasing revenue from freight ... Railtrack's financial performance to the end of the century will, however, depend largely on reducing costs through efficient management, increased investment to improve performance and lower on-going maintenance costs, re-negotiation of maintenance contracts, increased competitive tendering and new technology.'

Questions

1. How would you assess the current health of Railtrack as a going concern? Illustrate your answer by commenting on what you see as the company's principal strengths and weaknesses.

2. Discuss what steps the company could take to greatly expand its freight operations over the next five years. What are the implications for the rest of the network?

3. Discuss how far it is possible for Railtrack's staff to sustain the concept of *profitability* in the context of the STEP programme of staff development.

CS12: Flying high and flying cheap: niche airlines take off

Introduction

Air travel is on the increase, as the figures from the major world airports indicate. The major world airlines, however, are nevertheless in a highly competitive trading situation. Whilst travellers are many, airline seats are even more plentiful. Much airline company effort, therefore, is put into finding some competitive advantage over one's nearest competitors. Advantages may accrue from more comfortable seating, especially on long-haul flights, the provision of on-board haute cuisine, in-flight entertainment and extra facilities for business travellers. Because of the sheer costs involved in leasing, maintaining, fuelling, crewing and operating a large modern jet-liner, it is not generally considered sensible for the major companies to offer substantially discounted prices in order to gain an advantage, even on relatively short-haul journeys. However, there are exceptions to every rule, and a small number of independent niche operators have appeared over the years.

Laker Airways was the first notable niche player, offering discounted flights to the USA in the late 1960s. Laker was eventually forced out of business by his larger rivals at a time when route licensing was much tighter than today. In more recent times Richard Branson's Virgin Company set up Virgin Atlantic, which has succeeded in obtaining a sound foothold in the trans-Atlantic market, and is set for expansion on other long-haul routes. It is only in the last two years that *short-haul* operators have been prepared to offer cheap flights, indeed substantially cheaper than their scheduled rivals. They have been considerably aided by Europe's 'open skies' policy, which opens up previously regulated routes to open competition. This case-study outlines the services offered by two such independent operators – easyJet and Debonair.

The easyJet story

The inspiration for a niche airline offering cheap, 'no-frills' flights on short-haul routes came to Stelios Haji-Ioannou, son of a Greek shipping magnate, following an abortive business deal with Virgin Atlantic. After seeing the success of the no-frills operation offered by one American company, Haji-Ioannou decided that a distinct competitive advantage could be gained from drastically lower prices, so long as costs were kept to a minimum. The principal market would be that of the leisure traveller rather than the business-person. The owner's thinking was that low prices would attract more customers to air travel and help to create a larger market for this mode of travel. He appears to have been correct in this assumption, for his company has grown from two leased aircraft (Boeing 737s) on start-up in 1995 to six during 1997. Already easyJet is budgeting to carry more than £1.5 million passengers a year, and should be moving into reasonable profit during 1998. It presently flies six routes from Luton – four to Scotland and two overseas (Nice and Barcelona).

What are the consequences of basing a business on a strategy of low price in order to enter a new market? The principal answer is that operating costs must be kept to an absolute minimum, consistent with safety requirements. Haji-Ioannou decided that the following strategic decisions should enable costs to be managed and risks to be contained:

- Flights would be restricted to simple shuttle services between *short-haul* routes (such as Luton–Edinburgh, Luton–Barcelona).
- Licences would be sought only on these limited routes.
- A simplified booking system would be essential. In fact tickets are not required as, once booked, passengers merely have to identify themselves on arrival at the airport.
- Bookings would be made direct by telephone using a credit card to avoid using agents.
- Flights would only be made from Luton airport initially, since airport fees are lower, and landing slots easier to obtain, than at a major airport.
- There would only be one class on board – economy – thus freeing up more seats than on a typical competitor's aircraft.
- No meals or snacks would be provided, thus avoiding ordering, delivery and serving.
- The headquarters' offices would be modelled on the 'paperless office' by the comprehensive use of information technology.
- The offices would be adequate but basic.
- Staffing would be kept to a minimum, especially in terms of permanent staff.
- Tele-sales staff, paid on a commission-only basis, would be employed to deal with flight bookings.
- The organisation structure would be very flat.
- The build-up of future routes would proceed selectively, but only once initial routes were paying their way.

In effect easyJet is running an operation similar to a bus company, taking on passengers at a terminus and transporting them to a destination on a fixed route. As easyJet is not a charter company, but a scheduled airline, it does not have to wait for an aircraft to be chartered by travel agents, but offers a regular flight timetable and flies the passengers to their destination whether the aircraft is full or not. There is clearly a fair degree of risk involved here, with the possibility of aircraft flying half-empty and thus not paying their way. Nevertheless, any scheduled transport service has its peaks and troughs in terms of passengers carried, and has to find ways of optimising the number of seats that are filled. A scheduled service has the advantage that passengers have reasonable certainty that they will be able to travel at a time of their own choosing within the timetable.

The Debonair way

An even more recent newcomer to the low-fares operation in the UK is Debonair, a company founded by the American, Franco Marcassola, and also based at Luton. The company has a fleet of six BAe 146-200 aircraft operating to seven destinations – all overseas. In its first full year of operations the company carried 460,000 passengers. Like easyJet, the company operates only on a limited number of routes, and only on short-haul. Key routes from Luton include Barcelona, Madrid, Munich, Copenhagen and Rome. The company achieves its cost savings principally by:

- contracting out ground and baggage staff (who nevertheless wear Debonair uniforms)
- viewing the company as essentially a marketing operation to sell airline seats and deliver passengers safely to their destination
- offering a direct telephone booking service for customers (but unlike easyJet travel agents are used)
- employing flight crew direct, so as to ensure the safety and reliability of air operations
- employing cabin crew direct, so as to ensure customer care
- paying for maintenance by the flying hour, so as to reduce maintenance costs when business is slack
- using Luton airport (same reasons as for easyJet).

What future for the niche players?

Neither of the two companies is challenging the major airlines in their core business, but could pick off passengers on some of their marginal routes. They presently face competition on some of their routes from longer-established rivals, such as Air UK (based at Stansted). At present it does seem that the cheap-flight operators are able to attract sufficient numbers of new passengers to survive in the short-term. Luton, however, is not a particularly convenient location, and amongst the competition for internal short-haul flights are the newly-privatised railway operating companies. The latter are hardly likely to sit back idly and watch their passengers transfer to air travel for journeys to Scotland, for example. They in their turn will seek some new advantage for their travellers.

The availability of funds for expansion will be a major priority for the two airlines, especially if some of the larger companies decide to opt out of routes under 1000 miles, thus presenting a real opportunity for an expansion of services by short-haul operators. If the larger companies decided to use their power to restrict such opportunities to joint-venture operations, then the short-haul market might not be so attractive to operators such as easyJet and Debonair. The future of the two companies looks interesting rather than secure.

Questions

1. Given the current strategies of the two companies in the present market environment, how likely are they to survive, and what are their prospects for growth over the next 2–3 years? Give your reasons and note any differences in their respective fortunes, as you see them.

2. If you were asked to invest a major sum in either easyJet or Debonair, what sort of performance indicators would you look for in deciding whether or not to support it?

3. Consider the respective benefits of air travel and rail travel for passengers travelling from London to Scotland or London to Paris or Brussels. How might the short-haul airlines overcome the main benefits offered by the railways?

CS13: Mission to pensioners – the Universities Superannuation Scheme

Introduction

The Universities Superannuation Scheme Ltd (USS Ltd), the trustee company established for the universities in 1974, manages one of the largest private sector pensions funds in the UK – the Universities Superannuation Scheme (USS) – with assets now exceeding £12 billion, having grown from just over £6 million in 1992. The head office of the company is based in Liverpool, and the investment office is in London. At 31 March 1996 membership of the fund exceeded 125,000, of whom nearly 75,000 were active (i.e. contributing) members. The number of actual pensioners was over 24,000 and there were about 26,000 deferred pensioners. Total membership of the fund has increased by 26% over the past five years. Fund income during the year 1995/6 totalled £988 million derived mainly from contributions (£489 million) and investment income (£449 million). Benefits payable (pensions and lump sums) amounted to £355 million, and administration of the fund totalled £5.8 million.

The trustee company's total operating costs, recoverable from the USS, were £11.8 million for the year, up from £9.75 million the previous year. The increase in costs was due to three main factors: the headquarters move to a new office, staff restructuring costs (voluntary early retirements), and major enhancements to the company's computer systems. The company's concern for quality and efficiency led to the award of quality standard ISO9002 (formerly BS5750) in 1995 for both its administration of the pension scheme at Liverpool and the operation of its investment office in London.

Strategic aims and objectives

The corporate aim of USS Ltd is as follows:

'to carry out the duties of trusteeship and administration of the USS for the benefit of members, pensioners and participating institutions in an efficient and cost-effective manner in accordance with quality management principles.'

This aim is underpinned by a declaration of four strategic objectives, each containing a number of policy statements, which are followed by the detailed performance standards that the company's staff are expected to achieve in implementing the scheme.

The strategic objectives focus on the four key areas of *trusteeship*, *administration*, *investment* and *company management*. Each objective is supported by a number of policy statements indicating how, in general terms, the objective is to be achieved. The four objectives, with examples of their accompanying policy statements, are as follows:

❶ Trusteeship

'**Exercise the powers conferred by the USS trust deed and rules in a lawful and fair manner.**'

'We will make sure that there are resources to meet the benefits promised ....'

'We will ensure that the directors and staff are fully trained and are aware of their duties and obligations. We will control investment managers ... and receive full and regular reports from them.'

❷ Administration

'**Strive constantly for higher standards of scheme administration and service at an acceptable cost.**'

'We will demonstrate a high level of operational efficiency...'.

'We will publish regular reviews and where possible improve performance standards which are designed to meet the reasonable expectations of members.'

❸ Investement

'**Maximise the long-term investment return on assets consistent with the liabilities of the scheme.**'

'We will appoint custodians to hold the invested assets independently of the investment managers.'

'We will set demanding but realistic targets for all managers and monitor investment performance.'

❹ Company management

'**Strive constantly for improved management of the trustee company at an acceptable cost and in accordance with the company's Memorandum and Articles of Association and quality management principles.**'

'We will develop and maintain employment policies and practices consistent with being a fair and considerate employer.'

'We will adopt quality management principles, and ... will take account of best practice elsewhere and our own experience to improve our systems and procedures.'

In addition to the above strategic objectives and key policy statements, the USS Ltd also provides a detailed list of the *operational* performance standards to be achieved by its executive staff, thus adding credibility to the more generally-stated strategic intentions.

Operational performance standards

Typical examples of the performance standards are summarised below:

Retirements

- lump sum payments to be made to member on the first day of retirement or within five days of notification being received
- pension to be paid from the 21st of the month following retirement

Deaths

- pay surviving spouses their first instalment of pension within two working days of notification of a member's death
- pay the discretionary lump sum within 13 weeks in 90% of cases

Leavers

- issue a statement of options available within 20 working days in 80% of cases, and within 40 working days in all cases

Retirement Benefits

- supply a provisional statement of retirement benefits within 10 working days in 70% of cases, and within 30 working days in all cases

Correspondence

- reply to 60% of letters within 10 working days, 90% within 20 working days and all letters within 30 working days.

A key factor in the likely success of the executive staff in achieving these performance standards is the effectiveness of the company's computer systems. This is an issue which the company has faced in unequivocal terms by investing more than £500,000 in a brand-new, state-of-the-art electronic document management system. Already more than 5 million images, representing the personal records of active members and leavers, have been stored on optical disc, and all pensions staff work with computer screens instead of paper files.

The performance standards of staff are monitored regularly (quarterly) and whilst they have been met in the prompt payment of benefits to members, they have not been achieved in situations where pension transfers to and from other schemes are involved.

Another area where the company has been less than successful is in persuading newcomers to university institutions to take up membership of USS. The company estimates that about one quarter of eligible new employees are electing not to join, and comments that 'a significant number of university employees continue to take decisions about their pension arrangements which might not be in their best interests.' (Report and Accounts, 31 March 1996, p.12). As members are only required to contribute 6% of their salary per annum, whilst their employer contributes 18.55%, this omission is somewhat surprising. Few people in a personal pension scheme would be willing to invest nearly 25% of their salary each year, even if they were permitted to do so.

Questions

1. What view of strategy (see Chapter 1) do you see embedded in USS Ltd's approach to aims, objectives and key performance standards?

2. What evidence do you find in the above description for justifying the achievement of ISO9002 registration? What else would you be looking for in a quality review of the company?

3. The first strategic objective refers to training of directors and staff. What aspects of training would you see as important to the company in the light of the information given in the case-study?

CS14: Investing ethically: profits without pain?

Introduction

Investing in so-called 'ethical' funds is growing. In economically-developed nations such as the UK and the USA there is increasing investment in those businesses that are known not to abuse either people or the natural environment. It is estimated that the US ethical sector is growing by $50 billion a year, whilst in the UK ethical investment has quadrupled in the last six years alone to reach an estimated £1 billion in 1996. One of the main driving forces behind the development of separate ethical funds in the UK is that more than two out of every three major companies is reckoned to be involved in some 'unethical' activities. What is an 'unethical' activity? Clearly, this is a matter of opinion. What is ethical for one person (for example, armaments for 'defensive' purposes) may be anathema to another. However, enough people have indicated what is, and what is not, acceptable to them in a business, that a number of fund managers have taken the opportunity to draw up guidelines and portfolio lists for investors.

One such fund manager is Ethical Financial, one of the largest independent ethical specialists in the UK, which selects companies that it considers make a positive contribution to the environment and avoids those that may have a negative effect. Examples of activities it deems unsuitable include the following:

- manufacture of armaments and nuclear weapons
- activities which are environmentally damaging
- dealings with governments of oppressive regimes
- manufacture of tobacco products
- animal exploitation and experimentation
- pornography
- embryo research
- poor employment practices

By identifying companies with particular 'unethical' products or business dealings, a fund manager can enable investors to make a choice in accordance with their own values. By focusing on the *negative* aspects of a company's business, individual and corporate investors can be guided away from investments that they would find unacceptable or embarrassing.

The other side of ethical investment is to *positively* identify companies that actively pursue policies aimed at protecting the environment and controlling pollution, or who are engaged in the production of medical and healthcare products, and who show a concern for the sanctity of human life. Thus investors can make a decision on positive as well as on negative grounds. The thinking here is that ethical forms of investment can be viable and profitable alternatives to general investments where no consideration is given to posssibly dubious activities and practices. Ethical investment information enables investors to invest in a socially responsible way without contributing to any abuse of people, animals or natural resources.

Some negative business activities

Negative activities that have attracted media attention, as well as that of campaigning groups such as International Red Cross, Greenpeace and Friends of the Earth, include the following:

- the manufacture of certain kinds of riot control equipment (electric batons, CS gas and so on)
- the manufacture of anti-personnel mines
- indiscriminate destruction of rain forests in order to supply hardwoods
- pollution of the local environment by oil-producing companies
- the dumping of nuclear and other toxic forms of waste
- unauthorised use of human foetal tissue in bio-chemical experiments
- child labour employed for long hours in poor working conditions
- children and young persons exploited sexually in production of pornographic videos
- inflicting pain on animals in research into cosmetics.

Some of the above-mentioned activities are *illegal* in many countries (such as child labour, pornography), and some are certainly not encouraged even where they are permitted (for instance, unlicensed destruction of rain-forest by approved logging companies). Some of the activities are seen as necessary even though they may have negative consequences (for example, production of riot control equipment, or the dumping of nuclear waste). Others may be seen as unethical in one context or society but ethical in another. So, whereas most people might object to experiments on animals in cosmetics research, many would not object to the use of animals if the goal were that of saving human life (such as in immuno-deficiency cases or vaccine development). Similarly, whilst people in the developed world might feel strongly about the trapping or shooting of rare animals by rural natives in the tropics, it has to be recognised that many poor rural populations can only survive by following this dubious trade.

In the final analysis, what is, and what is not, seen as ethical is largely a matter of choice for both individuals and societies. Not surprisingly in this situation, it is almost inevitable that a majority of large well-known companies throughout the world will be engaged in some activity that many investors would find unacceptable. However, because of their overall reputation for social responsibility, they still have the capacity to attract investors who are prepared to compromise on certain issues. Investors who possess a strong social conscience, however, will have to rely heavily on those who give advice about 'ethical' investment.

A positive form of investment in the Third World

One way in which people in Britain can invest ethically is to buy shares in, or place deposits with, a co-operative lending society, such as the Shared Interest Society Ltd, which lends money to co-operatives and other producer groups of Third World farmers and artisans. Shared Interest is one of an international network of so-called 'fair trade' organisations, which work to off-set the often unjust terms of trade offered to primary producers in Third World countries, to enable such producers to gain access to world export markets. Shared Interest's loans are made direct to the producers, usually co-operatives, in areas of considerable disadvantage. The activity supported must be to the benefit of the local community and must respect the environment. The activity should be capable of self-sufficiency, including being able to repay the loan, which is made on generous terms. Wealthy entrepreneurs and middlemen are generally excluded from the arrangements.

UK depositors who invest in Shared Interest know that their money is being used to provide loans or credit to enable poor producers to sustain orders for their goods. Loans are typically spent on labour, materials and equipment. The transaction is often carried out via the *buyers* of the goods, including such fair trade buyers as Traidcraft, Oxfam Trading and Fairtrade Latin America. The fact that loans are usually tied to particular orders minimises the risk of non-payment. Such short-term loans are preferred by many producers, many of whom can only operate successfully on a seasonal basis. By spreading its support for projects over a range of categories in several different countries, Shared Interest is able to confine its bad debts to a minimum. Projects supported include coffee farming in Latin America, honey production in Tanzania, and the development of a tea plantation and factory in Southern India.

If ethical investment is to be encouraged, however, it must be attractive to investors. This means that consumers in the developed nations – the ultimate customers of many fair trade products – must find such products of acceptable quality and good value when they shop at their local store or supermarket. Only then will demand be sufficient to enable fair trade terms to be extended to more Third World producers. The signs are encouraging. In Europe alone it is currently estimated that some 12,000 tonnes of fair-trade coffee is purchased each year benefiting half a million farmers world wide.

What do investors get out of Shared Interest? First and foremost, the satisfaction of knowing that their money (anything from £100 to £20,000) is being used in a 'good cause' in the Third World. Secondly, that their investment is being dealt with on a professional footing with due regard to lending risks, with the allocation of funds between risk-bearing and non-risk bearing accounts (such as bad debt provision) in the Society. Thirdly, interest is paid annually on all loans, albeit at a low rate, and withdrawals may be made at any time, similar to a building society instant access account. Finally, every investor has one vote in the running of the company, can attend and vote at members' meetings, and can be elected to the non-executive Council, which has general oversight of the company and its executive Board. Both Council and Board members are subject to annual re-election.

The main risks for investors are that they may receive no interest on their investment, and indeed could lose all their funds if the Society made a large loss. Liability is limited to the amount invested. As a Society leaflet points out 'the fact that members accept the *possibility* of loss, which bank depositors do not...enables us to lend money where the banks cannot do so.' However, the Society assures potential investors that only if it miscalculated badly could a worst-case scenario arise. Individual investors appear to be reassured because, in the year ended 30 September 1996, Shared Interest's membership increased by over 1400, and gross receipts were up from £2.5 million in 1995 to £3.7 million. The company's total investments increased by 41% over the year. The signs are that such investment in the Third World by individuals in the developed world is likely to increase significantly as we move towards the millennium.

Questions

1. What arguments could an arms manufacturer put forward to convince potential investors that the company was not engaged in an unethical business? On what grounds might you refute some or all of these arguments?

2. Does it matter whether a product or activity is thought by some to be 'unethical', so long as there are people who benefit economically from it? Give your reasons.

3. You are a director of a European-based conglomerate organisation involved in open-cast mining, timber production and port operations. Your company has substantial interests in Third World countries, where most of the mining and timber operations are based. In a report to your fellow directors on the Executive Board of the company how would you justify the need for a strategy on company ethics?

CS15: Managing change at Legal & General

Introduction

The UK insurance industry is presently undergoing massive change: there is growing competition from newcomers, the establishment of direct-to-customer sales via the telephone or computer, the pervasive influence of computer-based systems that can standardise procedures and push decision-making down the line, changes in the legislation on pensions, the increasing globalisation of financial services, and last but not least the enhanced service expectations of customers.

Against this background Legal & General Group plc, one of Britain's largest insurance companies, is taking practical steps to devise and implement a strategy for change in its largest sector – Life and Pensions. The company's Annual Report for 1996 showed worldwide funds under management in excess of £48 billion, and an operating profit of over £290 million. The Group has operations in six countries – the UK, USA, Australia, France, Netherlands and Indonesia – and some 2.5 million policyholders served by 7,500 staff. The Group offers a broad range of financial services to both personal and corporate customers. The company's principal business lies in life assurance and pensions, which together produced £250 million of the total operating profit for the year. Over the year the company's broad strategy has been to increase the competitiveness of its products by achieving lower unit administration costs, more cost-effective sales distribution and maintaining an effective investment policy in a range of bonds, equities and property.

Life and Pensions services – managing change

The UK Life and Pensions sector of Legal & General provides an interesting case-study of the drive to reduce administration costs on the one hand, and to improve customer service on the other. Whilst the company's performance in 1996 was a steady improvement on the previous year, the competitive situation for the company is becoming increasingly difficult. In order to do more than stand still the company has to improve the efficiency of all its operations. Thus the Life and Pensions sector in the UK has drawn up a new Human Resource strategy aimed at changing both the way people work, and the culture (traditions) in which they work. In a key strategy statement to staff the company explains the rationale for the new approach:

> "It is a description of the changes we must all make to the ways we think, organise and work in order to ensure future success. It involves gaining widespread understanding of, and support for, these changes and creating a process for actually making them happen...While it is concerned to some degree with organisation, teams, skills and contracts of employment, it is actually much more about the 'psychological' contract we all have with the company – what is expected of me and what can I expect in return? The HR strategy is being implemented through a phased programme of change – led by the business."

HR – the vision for the future

The first element in the Legal & General 'Vision for the Future' is to change the way people work. From henceforth the majority of employees will deal direct with customers – by phone or by letter – to provide 'a polished and professional one-stop service'. Employees will work in teams of 10-15 people, where the team members themselves will take most of the responsibility for delivering a high-quality service to customers. Team roles, including that of team spokesperson, will be rotated within the team. Coaches and certain specialist roles will be provided to support individuals and teams in their development. Groups of teams, together with group coaches and specialists, will be under the general direction of a Customer Services Manager, who will report to a senior manager, reporting in turn to a director. The organisation will therefore be considerably flatter than in the past and will have a shorter chain of command.

Work routines will change as the company will be offering services to customers over a much longer period each day from early morning to late at night, and increasingly at the weekends. Teams will therefore have to work much more flexibly than previously, although the basic working week will remain at 35 hours. At peak times, when customer demand is high, employees will be expected to put in long hours, but when demand is slack, they will be able to leave early or take time off. The key point is that the operational situation is now being driven by customers, and the staff must respond appropriately. Pay will be related to local, not national, market rates, and will be made up of basic salary plus performance-related bonuses. Newcomers or less experienced staff will be paid according to starter or intermediate pay bands until they are equipped to enter teams as full members. Development prospects for staff range from gaining expertise in their principal role to becoming multi-skilled within their team and subsequently progressing to a coaching or specialist role or gaining promotion to a Customer Services Manager post.

The ultimate vision is of a competitive, flexible, team-based and customer-focused operation in which individuals have the chance to develop and savour success.

Implementing the HR strategy

In effecting the changes sought by the new strategy the company is aware of one important lesson from other companies, which is that 'changing long-established culture and working practices is not something that can be done successfully overnight.' Thus the changes are to be introduced over time in stages. The change programme is directed by a Strategy Steering group, which meets quarterly to review progress, plans, issues and priorities. Reporting to the steering group is a Programme Management Team, which meets weekly and is effectively in charge of the implementation of the programme. Local Transition Teams manage the introduction of the changes into their own areas, using key staff from the area together with support from a separate Programme Support Group comprised of business and HR representatives. The latter meet monthly to plan the development of the programme, ensure that team and organisational models remain valid, and provide training and other support to the Transition Teams. Thus, the whole change programme is moved forwards on a genuinely collaborative, not 'top-down', basis.

The Transition process

The core of the change programme is the Transition process, the outcomes of which at local level are based on an agreed 'Local Business Vision', which sets out the benefits to be delivered and the means by which they will be measured. The vision takes into account the risks and costs involved in attaining the target benefits, together with the staffing implications and the effects on other parts of the organisation. Each Local Business Vision has to be submitted to the programme Support Group for approval. Once approval has been given the local Transition Team undergoes a day-long preparation workshop prior to the drawing up of a Transition Project Plan timetabling who is going to do what and when. Progress against the plan is subsequently monitored weekly.

The next phase of the Transition Project Plan deals with two separate but related issues. The first is communication – staff and their union representatives are consulted about the proposed changes, their concerns are heard, and any problems addressed. The second issue is that of work design. New job and role definitions have to be drawn up, and appropriate staff skills and competencies identified. This phase continues with the task of matching people to jobs, where each person is assessed against their performance, or potential, in four key competencies:

1. **Customer focus**
2. **Results orientation**
3. **Team working**
4. **Ability to handle change**

As the changes are concerned primarily with new ways of working rather than with new forms of work, the core competencies do not refer to the technical content of individuals' work, which is taken as read. Over a period of several weeks all staff are given opportunities to demonstrate their abilities and discuss their career options in the light of the changes.

The conclusion to this phase is that suitable people will be allocated jobs in the new environment, others will be offered posts elsewhere in the company, some may be offered early retirement or voluntary redundancy, and a few may experience enforced redundancy. In the majority of cases where options are available, the staff are given three months in which to make their choice and sign new contracts. In agreeing the new working arrangements, the staff are committing themselves to flexible working in order to service the customer and to enable the business to become more adaptable to change in its external environment. The company has adopted a number of principles to support flexible working, including recognising that staff 'have personal commitments, responsibilities and interests which they have to balance with the demands of work' and stating that the company 'will not promote an excessive hours culture'.

For those who are selected there is a programme of training in team-working and other relevant development opportunities to facilitate the new culture and job structure. Transition Day ('T-Day') is marked by the formal launch of the new arrangements: 'not so much the end of the transition project as the beginning of new ways of working and thinking ... the day when we all recognise that something fundamental has changed in the area.' Further support is provided after 'T-Day' and a formal review is conducted about three months later. The feedback thus obtained enables the HR strategy to be maintained in a valid and relevant state in the light of the experience gained thus far. The cycle of strategic management is therefore maintained on a continually updated footing.

Questions

1. What are likely to be the key topics that will have to be addressed by HR and training staff in order to prepare people to work in teams in the way described in the case-study?

2. If you were assigned the duties of a team-support role (such as coach, trainer, etc.) what particular skills do you think you would require to be successful in enabling your assigned team to achieve a smooth transition to the new methods of working?

3. In the light of this case, what do you see as the principal steps that need to be taken to devise and implement a successful Human Resource strategy in a large company?

CS16: British Airports Authority – meeting the challenge of growth

Introduction

The steady increase in the demand for air travel both at home and overseas over the last decade has provided a growth market for BAA plc since its Stock Market float in 1987. The size of the demand has put severe pressure on the airports controlled by the former British Airports Authority. Despite the phenomenal growth in global communication systems over the same period, the number of people travelling on business has nevertheless soared, and about two thirds of all air travel is business-related. In the leisure market air holiday traffic has continued to expand, especially at peak seasons. The increased use of major airports as a means of travel has led to more flights over urban areas, more road traffic in the vicinity of the airports, and pressure on local authorities to allow runway extensions, motorway spur roads and other infrastructure developments, such as rail links. Such developments are not only costly but difficult to achieve in the short-term due to the public reaction of residents in the neighbourhood and the need for public enquiries and debate.

BAA owns and operates seven airports in the UK. These include the three principal airports for London – Heathrow, Gatwick and Stansted – together with the Scottish airports of Glasgow, Edinburgh and Aberdeen, and Southampton International Airport on the south coast. This makes BAA the largest commercial airport operator in the world. The scale of the services operated by Heathrow and Gatwick alone contribute massively to a situation where the company presently handles over 70% of all UK passenger traffic and over 80% of its air cargo. This near-monopoly status requires that BAA is subject to certain external checks, such as five-yearly reviews of its airport charges by the Monopolies and Mergers Commission in conjunction with the Civil Aviation Authority. The new levels of charges for the period 1997–2002 have already been set, but significantly they are still lower than the majority of other European airports, such as Frankfurt, Amsterdam and Brussels. Heathrow has been ranked sixteenth lowest out of eighteen, with Gatwick lowest of all, in an independent survey carried out in 1996.

Increase in air traffic at Heathrow, Gatwick and Stansted

Over the past decade BAA has seen the number of passengers carried rise from 63.7 million in 1987/8 to 98 million in 1996/7. The number of aircraft movements (slots) has increased several fold over the same period. Heathrow alone carried more than 56 million passengers in 1996/7. This is about equivalent to requiring one take-off or landing every two minutes. The completion of a fifth terminal at Heathrow will enable even more passengers to be catered for. Gatwick handled well over 24 million passengers in 1996/7, a rise of nearly 7 % over the previous year. Stansted is under less pressure at present, with almost 5 million passengers carried in 1996/7, but its growth over the previous year was a phenomenal 19%, making it the fastest-growing airport in Europe.

The major airports also handle air freight traffic. There have been major extensions to cargo handling and warehousing facilities at Heathrow, and even Stansted is now

Britain's third largest freight-handling airport. The demand for passenger and freight traffic has led to substantially increased on-site handling facilities, with all that this implies for employee numbers and road and rail traffic. The one benefit that can always be claimed for an airport (in addition, that is, to its air travel facilities) is that it provides large numbers of jobs of enormous variety for those living in its catchment area. The price to be paid is a more or less continuous flow of road and rail traffic in the area for the greater part of every twenty-four hours.

Services and facilities at BAA airports

BAA's central strategy is to concentrate on its core business of operating airports – safely, efficiently and profitably. Safety and security have the 'highest priority at all times', according to the company's annual report for 1996/7. The company has developed what it claims as the most advanced and effective hold baggage screening technology, and is well ahead with the implementation of 100% hold baggage screening at all its airports. Safety and security measures also include airport fire and crash emergency services, perimeter and aircraft parking security arrangements, and general workplace safety considerations.

Airport efficiency is one of the factors that most travellers rate as crucial when choosing air travel. BAA interviews some 150,000 passengers a year as part of its Quality of Service Monitoring survey. Passengers are asked for their views on a range of issues, including check-in procedures, baggage reclaim facilities, comfort, cleanliness and staff courtesy. The company has been investing in the region of £400 million a year since 1987 in order to expand and improve facilities for airlines, their customers and their cargoes. Typical outcomes of investment have been new terminal buildings, improved terminal layouts, more effective security screening for passengers and baggage, greatly improved shopping and refreshment facilities for passengers and crews, increased banking and bureau de change facilities, more accessible and comfortable departure lounges, additional parking and waiting areas for passengers, and last but not least, improved rail links.

The largest project under construction at present is the £440 million Heathrow Express rail link to Central London, which is due to commence operations in June 1998. BAA will be the sole operator of the service, working in conjunction with Railtrack, which owns the line between Paddington and the airport junction. The service will operate brand-new rolling stock to cut the time from Central London to Heathrow to some 15 minutes, and will include check-in facilities at Paddington. It is planned to offer an additional service from St Pancras station to Heathrow in 1999. It is estimated by BAA that the opening of the Heathrow Express service will remove around 1.1 million vehicle journeys a year to the airport. This will make a major contribution to the reduction of road traffic in the airport area, which attracts more than 16,000 train, bus and coach arrivals every day. The company aims to encourage 50% of its passengers to use public transport to travel to and from the airport. Gatwick and Stansted already have fast rail links to Central London.

Adding value in the future

One consequence of focusing on the core airport business is that eventually any airport reaches a peak in terms of its capacity to handle passengers, cargo and aircraft movements. Numbers will eventually level out. BAA has accordingly set itself further strategic aims in respect of fully developing the retail and property potential of its airports. The scale of present operations in retail and property can be judged from the contribution they make to total revenue. In 1996/7 *gross revenues* by function were as follows:

	£m	
Airport/traffic charges	467	
Retail operations	606	(£158m in 1986/7)
Property	252	
Other	48	

The company's pre-tax profits for the year amounted to £444 million, a 10% increase on the previous year. This growth in profits is greater than the underlying rate of increase in passenger traffic. Earnings per share and shareholder dividends also increased by 10% in the same period. These results are therefore very encouraging, especially given the high overall level of investment in the business. The terminal complexes alone had a net book value of £1.39 billion out of total operational assets of £2.56 billion in the year.

The importance of retail operations in the company's business is crucial. *Net income* in 1996/7 from retail operations (i.e. after deducting retail expenditure) was derived from the following sources:

	£m	
Duty/Tax Free shops	249	(sales of perfume, gifts, liquor, tobacco)
Car parking	64	
Bureaux de Change	28	
Bookshops	21	
Catering	21	
Car rental	18	
Advertising	12	
Other	13	

BAA's investment in terminal facilities is substantial, and so too are the operating costs involved. The retail side of the business is therefore expected to make a huge contribution to revenues. The company's strategy is to generate higher levels of sales per passenger by offering an attractive range of retail products, especially in the growth areas of perfume, gifts and liquor sales, and by ensuring a suitable range of other key facilities, such as money-changing, refreshment, reading material, car rental and car parking. In the duty-free areas, the company is currently establishing its own subsidiary companies to take over control of its general duty-free shops from previously contracted-out sources. This is estimated to achieve synergies in the form of procurement discounts and more cost-effective warehousing and distribution. In a contrary move, however, BAA is also developing specific single-brand outlets for whisky (for example, Glenfiddich and Johnnie Walker), which continues to be a growth product.

Prices for all goods offered at BAA airports are intended to represent good value, and there are guarantees of full refunds to anywhere in the world should a customer feel dissatisfied. In order to encourage repeat purchasing by customers a loyalty scheme – Bonus Points – was introduced in 1996 to reward customers with points for every retail transaction in any of BAA's airports. The scheme involves more than 150 retailers as well as the company's own outlets. As yet there are only 170,000 members, a tiny fraction of the number of passengers carried. The growth potential here therefore is quite enormous.

Questions

1. How are the retail purchasing requirements of airline travellers likely to differ from shoppers in a typical city centre shopping mall? Distinguish, where appropriate, between the separate needs of business and leisure travellers. What are the implications of your answer for the range of facilities that BAA should be providing for its airline customers?

2. It is likely in the near future that, due to European Union legislation on harmonisation, *duty-free transactions* for EU travellers will be restricted or removed. The rules will not affect international travellers from outside the EU. In what ways could BAA respond to this situation so as to minimise the effect on its retail sales?

3. How might BAA's present retail strategy at Heathrow be affected by a reduction of car journeys and a consequential increase in rail movements to and from the airport? Consider all aspects of retail operations at the airport, and indicate the potential advantages and disadvantages of such a change.

CS17: Formula One racing: cheques out for the chequered flag

Introduction

Despite the small scale of the Formula One industry – there are barely twelve championship constructors – it is nevertheless big business. It is currently estimated, for example, that every time a Formula One race takes place in the world there are in excess of one billion viewers watching the event. The advertising and promotional benefits that this fact brings for the sponsors of such events is enormous. Their products and services are on view in a truly global sense, and as described later they can pay handsomely for the privilege. Reputations as successful motorcar manufacturers can wax or wane according to success in the Formula One season. Implied in every purchase of a Renault or Honda saloon, for example, is the success of these two engine manufacturers in Grand Prix racing over the last decade. Their efforts in supplying winning engines to Formula One teams are rewarded by success in sales of vehicles to the ordinary motorist.

The top Formula One designers and their teams can command the best in money and facilities in their search for race-winning cars. British firms, in particular, have developed a world-class reputation for racing-car design with names such as Cooper, McLaren, Williams, Tyrrell and Lotus. The designers work in close collaboration with the suppliers of engines, and the constructors' championship entrants are usually identified by joint names, such as Cooper-Climax and Lotus-Ford in past times and Williams-Renault and McLaren-Honda more recently.

The drivers

As in many other sports, the key players are young men, usually aged about 25–30 years, at their peak of fitness and skill. They compete in races in very different climates and locations in Europe, Japan, Australia, Brazil and Canada. The introduction of a drivers' championship in 1950 provided a further element of competition in what was already a very competitive sport. British drivers have won the championship twelve times since 1950. There have been eight wins by Brazilian drivers, whilst Fangio alone won it five times for Argentina, and Prost four times for France. Other champions have come from Australia, Austria, Germany, Italy, USA, New Zealand, South Africa and Finland – exemplifying the worldwide appeal of this sport. However, one statistic that always reminds both viewers and participants of the potential dangers of this sport is the fact that 30 drivers have been killed during the 47 years in which the championship has been run. Given that straightline speeds nowadays can exceed 200 mph, it is clear that there is little margin for error.

Safety

There has always been a proper concern for driver safety both by the car designers and the race-track operators, but inevitably there will be serious accidents from time to time as the drivers push their vehicles and their competitors to the limits. The overall objective therefore is to limit the damage to drivers and members of the public in situations where an accident does occur. It is no surprise to learn that at a major Grand Prix event there may be around 300 race marshalls each responsible for a small section of track, pits or paddock. Vehicles can be signalled if there is danger ahead, race-course fires can be dealt with speedily, drivers can be cut free from wrecked vehicles, and damaged or obstructing vehicles can be moved quickly off the track. Safety is also a major consideration when refuelling cars in the pits, where the mechanics wear special flame-proof clothing and gloves, and are trained to deal in seconds with the massive sheets of flame that can envelope a car, if there is a spillage.

Sponsorship and promotion in Formula One

The sheer costs involved in promoting teams in Formula One nowadays require more than the personal fortunes of those who run the teams. The fact is that millions of pounds' worth of sponsorship and promotion are necessary to keep the sport in being. Of course, the size and scale of Grand Prix events were not always as huge as they are today. In the 1950s, when the drivers' championship first got under way, cars were raced only in their own colours and race number, all the advertising being located on the track-side. Today the cars (and the drivers themselves) are covered with sponsors' names or logos. Every body-shell, nose-cone, tail-fin, tyre-wall is marked; every helmet, visor, shoulder pad, sleeve and glove is identified with some sponsor or another. Such sponsors pay well for the privilege with a minimum contribution of £500,000 and more than £10 million for the leading sponsor – often a tobacco company. The engine manufacturers on their part may spend more than £20 million in developing and building the enormously powerful V10 engines that can provide speeds in excess of 200 mph. Last but not least are the fees paid to Formula One for the global television transmission rights, which amount to several million pounds each season.

The rewards

The rewards for those participating in the sport can be huge. Top drivers, such as Michael Schumacher, may receive more than £1 million *for a single race*, and even the least successful drivers can earn in excess of £300,000 a year. The leading team owners such as Williams, Benetton, Ferrari and McLaren operate companies, where their personal worth alone may be as much as £40–60 million. Even these figures pale into insignificance when compared with the fortune of the man who effectively runs the worldwide Formula One 'circus', Bernie Ecclestone, who was reputed to have drawn nearly £30 million in salary alone from his company in 1993.

Since the first world championship in 1950, when Guiseppe Farina won in an Alfa Romeo, the sport has been dominated by a few elite constructors and engine makers. The most frequent names that have appeared as world champion constructors – sometimes in combination - include Ferrari, Ford, Lotus, McLaren, Williams, Honda and Renault. Such is the prestige and glamour of Formula One that the manufacturers of vehicles for the mass market are keen to promote their family and fleet cars in the light of their involvement, and preferably success, in Grand Prix races. Other major firms such as Mercedes-Benz and Peugeot, which are substantial manufacturers of *commercial* vehicles as well as of passenger cars, are providing engines for the 1997 season, evidence of their interest in such high-profile entertainment. Other leading suppliers for the season are Ford, Renault, Honda and Ferrari. The engines for the top teams, it should be noted, are supplied free by the manufacturers.

The costs of running a Formula One team

The costs of running a Formula One team are substantial. Newcomers to the industry have to be backed by several million pounds just for one season (about 17 races). First there is the financing of the design and construction of a winning vehicle, which can easily surpass £1 million. Then there are the contracts for the two team drivers, which could amount to another million pounds even for second-rank drivers. The other major costs for a season are typically as follows:

Tyres	£1m
Spare parts	£5m
Engine servicing/modification	£4m
Transportation	£1m
Fuel/oil	£0.5m
Circuit fees	£5m

In addition to the above there are the labour costs of the various personnel who support the team: pit-teams; mechanics and engineers; software specialists, who ensure the reliability and accuracy of the sophisticated telemetric computer-systems that measure a car's performance on the track; public relations and marketing staff; secretaries, linguists and others. Taking all the various costs into account, a new team is likely to have to spend in the region of £20 million just for a single season, and will be looking for sponsorship to underwrite the bulk of this amount. For a well-known constructor sponsorship is likely to be forthcoming, even if, as in the case of the Tyrrell team, they have not won a race for a decade or more. The point is that every competition requires sufficient competitors to provide the spectacle that race-goers and television viewers want to see. Every race provides a worldwide stage for advertising. Therefore even 'unsuccessful' teams play a part in the overall Formula One circus. The chequered flag sport indeed requires a very large cheque book.

Questions

1. How would you assess the prospects of a new entrant to Formula One in terms of Porter's seven major barriers to market entry? Which barriers are the most crucial in this context?

2. If you were the owner of a new Formula One team, what key benefits could you sell to possible sponsors and advertisers in persuading them to support you?

3. Some critics have said that Formula One is no longer a sport, but rather a glorified advertising campaign for the sponsors. How far would you agree with the criticism that the sport has been overcome by the business interests behind it?

CS18: Water on tap; water down the drain – managing a vital resource

Introduction

Water is a commodity which affluent nations in the temperate climates have tended to take for granted. Recently, however, the combined effects of greatly increased demand for water and the generally drier climatic conditions have focused greater public attention on the water industry. In 1989 the water industry in England and Wales underwent a massive change from 'public utility' to management as a group of independent businesses, each potentially competing for markets in the economy, and each vying for investors' attention and funding.

How is the water industry in England and Wales now managed? In all there are nine major privatised water and sewerage companies with a combined total of 30,000 employees and a turnover of £5 billion per annum. The nine companies service the needs of a population of some 48 million people, operating nearly 1200 water treatment plants and a network of more than 244,000 kilometres of water mains. The companies are also responsible for over 6,000 sewage treatment works and some 280,000 kilometres of sewers.

Since 1989 the companies have invested £17 billion in what the Water Services Association describes as 'by far the biggest programme of modernisation since Victorian times .... [and] .... the biggest private environmental investment programme anywhere in Europe.' Most of this expenditure has been directed towards repairing and replacing water mains and sewers laid down in the last century. Like other former public sector businesses, the old public utility companies were considerably under-invested in terms of major capital funding. There has been a huge backlog of refurbishment and replacement of plant and pipelines, leading to the current emphasis on major infrastructure investment programmes. Examples of recent improvements include: (1) the laying of more than 220 km of new mains and the construction of 26 new water pumping stations in the Yorkshire Water company's area; (2) the development by the Severn Trent company of a strategic water 'grid' linking treatment plants in Wales with those of the East Midlands; and (3) the development of a new reservoir for Southampton by Southern Water.

Key objectives for the water companies

In their joint Vision Statement, the nine major water companies have set themselves eight key objectives for the coming years, which can be summarised as follows:

1 *Supply customers with the water they want when they want it, consistent with a duty to protect the environment.* This implies (a) reducing leakage from pipes, which, due to the age of much of the pipework, still constitutes a major challenge; (b) actively promoting the efficient use of water, both in terms of water delivery and avoidance of waste by customers; (c) obtaining new sources of water from deep underground water-bearing rocks, for example; (d) developing new resources for storing water, such as surface and underground reservoirs, consistent with their impact on the environment.

2 *Produce the best quality drinking water in the world* – where quality is measured in terms of the purity, taste and smell of the water, and is subject to independent inspection by the Water Inspectorate. Note: In 1995 this body took more than 3 million samples of water from reservoirs, water treatment works and customers' taps, and found that 99.5% met all UK and European standards.

3 *Manage waste water and sewage in an environmentally conscious way.* This implies (a) eliminating the discharge of untreated sewage into the sea and rivers, (b) ensuring that bathing waters and rivers meet the quality standards laid down by national and European environmental agencies, and (c) managing water resources so as to protect wetlands and slow-flowing rivers.

4 *Provide wildlife habitats and leisure and recreational facilities, as appropriate, at reservoirs and landholdings.* Inevitably this objective requires a balance to be struck between operational requirements (i.e. clean water provision) with environmental and leisure interests.

5 *Provide water services at the lowest possible cost to customers.* This implies (a) improving efficiency in the sourcing and supply of water, (b) developing better charging systems, and (c) limiting the demands of national regulators or European Directives in respect of capital investment in water projects and the regulation of competition between suppliers.

6 *Provide the highest standards of customer service of any British utility.* This implies communicating with customers, seeking their views and acting on the results.

7 *Strengthen commitment to local communities.* This is seen primarily in terms of consulting them about where and how new works should be sited, and establishing more visitor centres for the public at water company properties.

8 *Continue and develop leading edge research programmes in water technologies.* The main challenge here lies in the improved treatment of waste water (for example, by ultra-violet exposure of sewage, improved methods of sand filtration and other forms of cleaning technology), and the development of new sources of drinking water (such as by seawater desalination).

Current problems

The principal challenge of the moment is to replace and repair the thousands of kilometres of pipes that respectively pump drinking water to millions of customers' homes and carry sewage and waste water away from their homes. Since most water pipes are buried underground, sometimes in close proximity to other utilities' services, the necessary replacements or repairs are never easy to execute. Here, however, the researchers have come up with a novel device called a 'mole', which replaces existing decaying pipes *from the inside*, thus obviating the digging up of miles of road and pavements. Leakage from ageing or damaged pipes is a constant problem at present, and one which is not only obvious in its physical effects but which also brings adverse publicity for the companies concerned. The extent of the problem can be judged from the successes the companies have had with plugging leaks. Southern Water, for example, estimates it has saved 120 million litres of water a day as a result of efforts to find and remedy leaks from its network. North West Water has reduced its losses through leakage by more than 150 million litres a day.

Waste water dealt with in water treatment centres is usually of a very high standard, and causes no problems when discharged into rivers, canals or the sea. There is always the risk of pollution from other sources, such as farms, chemical works and other industrial processes, whose activities sometimes lead to accidental, or even wilful, spillage of noxious chemicals into streams, rivers and sewers. Water supply is not just dependent, therefore, on the effectiveness of the water companies, but also on the responsibility of persons using toxic chemicals and similar substances. The National Rivers Authority and the Environment Agency also have a key role in preventing accidents and reducing the incidence of bad practice among such users. Therefore, a partnership is required here. The principal concern of the *water companies* is to ensure the elimination of the discharge of untreated sewage into rivers, sea or other outlets.

Sewers represent a problem in their own right, partly because of their sheer scale and size in major cities and towns, but also due to the health threat posed by leaking sewage. Seaside towns, in particular, are conscious of the need to dispose of raw or semi-treated sewage well away from the beaches and shoreline. Earlier systems built during the Victorian age, when populations were much smaller than today, are often no longer suitable for the volume of sewage they have to carry. Investment by all the companies involved is substantial and includes the £900 million 'Clean Sweep' coastal waste water treatment programme in South West Water's area, and the construction by Southern Water of Europe's largest stormwater tunnel at Brighton.

Future issues

A major challenge is to develop and sustain longer-term sources of water. The reduced average rainfall in the British Isles over the last decade has led to an overall lowering of the water table in many areas, especially in the south, where the bulk of the population lives. Taking more water from rivers has to be agreed with the National Rivers Authority, who are increasingly refusing requests from the water companies because of the serious threats to the ecology of the rivers and their estuaries from excessive water extraction. Some areas in the north of Britain and in Wales do have more than adequate water supplies in their major reservoirs, but at present there is no pipeline system to connect these sources to those in the south to form a 'national grid' for water.

The development of new surface reservoirs, or the extension of existing ones, is usually a controversial process, since inevitably some people and their land will be displaced by the development. One recent development in this respect has been provided by Thames Water, which has started operating the largest single *underground* water source in Europe, capable of supplying 90 million litres of water a day. The challenge ahead is indeed substantial.

Questions

1. What do you see as the short-term risks that could be incurred by the water companies in diverting so much of their resources to capital investment programmes? In your response consider the cost-benefit perspectives of the following stakeholders: customers, employees (including management), and shareholders.

2. Once the present levels of investment to replace or refurbish the existing network of pipework and plant have been completed, where do you think the companies' priorities should lie in relation to the eight key objectives? Set out your reasons.

Index